T0330206

Dollar Hegemony

Dollar Hegemony

Past, Present, and Future

Edited by

Thomas Palley

Founding Editor, Review of Keynesian Economics *and Principal, Economics for Democratic and Open Societies, USA*

Esteban Pérez Caldentey

Editor, Review of Keynesian Economics *and Chief, Financing for Development Unit, Economic Commission for Latin America and the Caribbean (CEPAL), Chile*

Matías Vernengo

Founding Editor, Review of Keynesian Economics *and Professor, Bucknell University, USA*

A SPECIAL ISSUE OF THE REVIEW OF KEYNESIAN ECONOMICS

Edward Elgar

Cheltenham, UK • Northampton, MA, USA

Published by
Edward Elgar Publishing Limited
The Lypiatts
15 Lansdown Road
Cheltenham
Glos GL50 2JA
UK

Edward Elgar Publishing, Inc.
William Pratt House
9 Dewey Court
Northampton
Massachusetts 01060
USA

For further information on the *Review of Keynesian Economics* see
www.elgaronline/roke

A catalogue record for this book is available from the British Library

Library of Congress Control Number: 2023948392

This book is available electronically in the
Economics subject collection
http://dx.doi.org/10.4337/9781035320936

ISBN 978 1 0353 2092 9 (cased)
ISBN 978 1 0353 2093 6 (eBook)

Printed and bound by CPI Group (UK) Ltd, Croydon, CR0 4YY

Contents

Review of Keynesian Economics, Vol. 10 No. 4, Winter 2022, pp. 1–19

The international currency system revisited

Tabitha M. Benney*
The University of Utah, Salt Lake City, UT, USA

Benjamin J. Cohen**
The University of California, Santa Barbara, CA, USA

What does the international currency system really look like? Since World War II, the US dollar has prevailed as the international community's one truly global money. The currency system could loosely be described as unipolar, practically a monopoly. Is that still true? Opinions are sharply divided. Close to a decade ago the authors sought to resolve the issue with a detailed empirical analysis stretching back over a quarter of a century. Their conclusion was that loose talk of an increasingly multipolar currency system was at best premature. In reality, they could find few signs of significant change in the competitive structure of the system over the years under review. While acknowledging that a future of multipolarity could yet arrive, they saw no evidence that anything like that had happened yet. The aim of this paper is to extend the authors' previous analysis forward to encompass another decade. Their conclusion, overall, remains much the same as before. Despite some hints of minor erosion, the dollar remains as dominant as ever. A cluster of smaller currencies have begun to compete for attention, but multipolarity in any meaningful sense has still not arrived. The greenback still reigns supreme.

Keywords: *bipolarity, concentration ratios, dollar, Herfindahl–Hirschman Index, international currency system, multipolarity, unipolarity*

JEL codes: *F33, F59*

1 INTRODUCTION

What does the international currency system really look like? The question has long been debated. At issue is the degree of rivalry among major currencies. Since World War II, the US dollar has prevailed as the international community's one truly global money. The currency system could loosely be described as unipolar, practically a monopoly. Is that still true?

For some commentators, there is no doubt that the greenback's 'hegemony' is still alive and well and can be expected to continue. In the words of Anders Åslund, a senior fellow at the Washington-based Atlantic Institute, 'The U.S. dollar will dominate global transactions for the next half century' (Åslund 2020, p. 19). Mohamed El-Erian (2020, p. 26), a highly respected financial expert, echoes that the greenback 'will continue to retain its standing as the world's premier reserve currency.' For many others, however, the system has actually become more multipolar and is moving inexorably toward something more akin to oligopoly, with several popular currencies (poles) vying increasingly for market share. 'It's definitely conceivable,' Paul Krugman (2021) suggests, 'that one

*   Email: tabitha.benney@poli-sci.utah.edu.
**   Email: jcohen@ucsb.edu.

of these days something will displace the dollar from its current dominance.' Barry Eichengreen (2011, p. 150) is even more certain, declaring flatly that: 'A world of multiple international currencies is coming.' Opinions remain sharply divided.

The issue is by no means trivial. Currency dominance translates directly into geopolitical power. As one of us has written previously (Cohen 2015; 2019), global currency standing enhances an issuing polity's capabilities both directly and indirectly. On the one hand, the money *itself* may provide an effective instrument of state power, available for direct use as a means to achieve selected foreign-policy goals. In effect, the currency can be 'weaponized' (Drezner 2021; Oatley 2021). Political objectives can be promoted by putting the money to work variously as either carrot or stick – sometimes making it available as a form of reward or encouragement; at other times withholding access to it as a form of punishment or disapproval, as Washington demonstrated so effectively when it froze Russian dollar reserves after Moscow's invasion of Ukraine. On the other hand, the role of the currency may be more indirect, reinforcing power by enhancing the utility of *other* policy weapons. Widespread foreign acceptance of a currency enables the issuer to finance expenditures abroad with its own money, thus removing a payments constraint on government spending around the world. The nation can run 'deficits without tears' – what Charles De Gaulle many years ago referred to enviously as America's 'exorbitant privilege.'

De Gaulle had a point. For as long as it has reigned supreme in monetary affairs, the greenback has been counted as an important part of the foreign-policy arsenal of the US government. Washington decision-makers have not hesitated to exploit the country's currency power, both direct and indirect, when national security seemed at stake. Hence any loss of standing for the dollar equates with a substantial redistribution of capabilities at the international level. Much rests on the outcome.

Close to a decade ago the present authors sought to resolve the issue with a detailed empirical analysis (Cohen and Benney 2014). Our survey stretched back over a quarter of a century from the late 1980s (when comprehensive statistics on international currency use first became available on a regular basis) to 2010. Our conclusion was that loose talk of an increasingly multipolar currency system was at best premature. In reality, we could find few signs of significant change in the competitive structure of the system over the years under review. The dollar still reigned supreme. While acknowledging that a future of multipolarity could yet arrive, we saw no evidence that anything like that had happened *yet*.

But what about the years since? Much has happened since 2010 that might well augur a major transformation in currency relations. The euro has recovered notably from the debt troubles that hobbled Europe following the global financial crisis of 2008. The Chinese renminbi (RMB) has emerged as a potentially serious rival to America's greenback. The four years of Donald Trump's presidency gravely shook the hitherto rock-solid confidence of global investors and central banks in the security of their dollar claims. The disruptions of the COVID-19 pandemic have also revived the specter of global inflation. And most recently, Washington's sanctions against Russia during the Ukraine conflict have made many governments think twice about their own exposure to currency weaponization. The time seems right, therefore, to revisit the issue.

The aim of this paper is to extend our previous analysis forward to encompass an additional decade. Our conclusion, overall, remains much the same as before. Despite some hints of minor erosion (Arslanalp et al. 2022), the greenback remains as dominant as ever. A cluster of smaller currencies have begun to compete for attention, but multipolarity in any meaningful sense has still not arrived. The contribution of the dollar to US geopolitical capabilities has yet to be compromised to any great degree.

                    Journal compilation © 2022 Edward Elgar Publishing Ltd

2   CONCENTRATION

Following now-standard practice among monetary specialists, our earlier analysis parsed the several roles that a currency may play on the world stage, examining separately as many functions as the available data would allow. In each case, our aim was to trace any significant changes in the competitive structure of the currency system as indicated by variations in market share.

Ours was not the first such attempt, of course. Prior studies had also sought to delineate trends in the degree of rivalry among major currencies (Chinn and Frankel 2008; Subramanian 2011). Most researchers, however, have relied principally on the notion of polarity – unipolarity versus multipolarity – which is a notoriously crude measure of competition in any kind of system, economic or political. Using polarity alone implies that inequalities among the major players are basically unimportant. In effect, poles are assumed to be more or less structurally equivalent – not significantly different from one another in terms of capabilities or influence. That is an improbable notion at best. In reality, the competitiveness of key players is apt to be anything but uniform. If description of a system is to be at all accurate, it should consider not only the number of poles but also the inequalities among them – an alternative strategy encompassed by the concept of *concentration*. If we really want to know how competitive a system is, we need to think in terms of concentration, not just polarity. Concentration can integrate inequalities and polarity in a single measure of competitive structure. The novelty of our approach lay in our use of the concept of concentration, alongside polarity, to provide a more accurate picture of the competitive structure of the currency system.

The concept of concentration was first developed by economists for the study of industrial organization: the size of firms in an individual sector and the degree of competition among them. The greater the concentration of a market, the lower its level of competition. The idea is widely applied in competition law and anti-trust regulation and has also been used to analyse the commodity or geographic composition of international trade. Our argument in our previous paper was that the concept of concentration could also be usefully deployed to measure the structure of competition in the currency system. To our knowledge the concept had never previously been applied to the study of international monetary relations.

For purposes of empirical analysis, two tools have long been standard among economists to estimate market competition: concentration ratios (also known as N-firm ratios) and the so-called Herfindahl–Hirschman Index (HHI). Concentration ratios are relatively easy to calculate. First, the leading firms in the industry are identified, with the number N determined by sectoral characteristics. Where some industries (for example, large commercial aircraft or automobiles) have very few rival firms, warranting a small N, in other sectors (for example, textiles or hospitality) a larger number might be more realistic. Then the market shares of all the selected firms (expressed as fractions) are simply added up to give an overall percentage. But concentration ratios are also of limited analytical value, since they provide little insight into the distribution of firm size and also take no account of smaller firms below the selected threshold. All they measure is the aggregate market share of a given number of firms. Thus they too are a relatively crude indicator of market structure.

A more complete picture is provided by the HHI, named after the economists Orris Herfindahl and Albert Hirschman (Hirschman 1964). As equation (1) illustrates, the HHI is defined as the sum of the squares of the market shares of all the firms in an industry (again expressed as fractions) – not just the biggest firms, but all others as well, to ensure that the total of percentages adds up to 100 percent. Squaring market shares prior to summation gives added weight to larger firms, thus taking account of the distribution of firm size as well as the number of leading players. Results are proportional to the average of market share, weighted by market share.

$$HHI_t = \sum_{i=1}^{N_t} S^2 it \tag{1}$$

Formally, *HHI* is the Herfindahl–Hirschman Index at a given time, *S* is the market share of firm *i* at time *t*, and *N* is the number of firms at time *t*. Increases in the HHI indicate a decrease in competition and can range from 1/*N* (the equivalent of perfect competition) to 1.00 (monopoly). Anything above 0.25 (25 percent) is generally considered by US anti-trust regulators to be an excessively high level of concentration. The HHI is by no means a perfect measure for estimating market structure; reservations among economists are rife (Eeckhout 2021). But it is nonetheless useful and brings us closer to the mark than either polarity or concentration ratios for the purposes of an analysis like ours.

The HHI or some variant has been used on occasion by specialists in international relations (IR) to explore the nature of the global political system and the risk of international conflict (Mansfield 1992). In our analysis, we made use of both concentration ratios and the HHI, in addition to measures of polarity, to explore the evolution of the global currency system over time.

3   DATA

That currency internationalization involves a multiplicity of roles has long been acknowledged in the literature (Cohen 1971). Conventionally, studies distinguish between the three familiar functions of money – medium of exchange, unit of account, and store of value – at two levels of analysis: the private market and official policy, adding up to six roles in all. At the private level, sources speak of a currency's use as a *vehicle* for foreign-exchange trading (medium of exchange); as an instrument for trade *invoicing* (unit of account); and as a means to facilitate cross-border *investment* (store of value). At the official level, we speak of a money's use as an *intervention* currency (medium of exchange), an exchange-rate *anchor* (unit of account), and as a *reserve* asset for central banks (store of value). The taxonomy is summarized in Table 1, with each box of the matrix representing a different market segment or sector of activity. Market shares for individual currencies may vary widely, depending on which role we are talking about.

Unfortunately, because of data limitations, our earlier paper was able to address just three of these functions in detail: the vehicle, investment, and reserve roles. For the vehicle and investment roles, our source was the Bank for International Settlements (BIS). For the reserve currency role, the best available source was the International

Table 1   The roles of international money

Levels of analysis	Functions of money		
	Medium of exchange	Unit of account	Store of value
Private	Vehicle currency (foreign-exchange trading)	Trade invoicing	Investment currency
Official	Intervention currency	Exchange-rate anchor	Reserve currency

    Journal compilation © 2022 Edward Elgar Publishing Ltd

Monetary Fund (IMF). For many years, the IMF included information in its annual reports on the foreign-exchange holdings of central banks. Since 2005, the presentation has been formalized in a public database on the Currency Composition of Official Foreign Exchange Reserves (COFER), published quarterly. All three roles will be included in our analysis here as well.

Happily, in this paper we are able to expand the scope of our analysis to add a fourth function – the anchor role – thanks to the team of Ethan Ilzetzki, Carmen Reinhart, and Kenneth Rogoff, three US-based economists (Ilzetzki et al. 2021). A money functions as an anchor when other currencies are pegged to it in one way or another, formally or informally. In a Herculean effort, Ilzetzki and colleagues have produced a broad portrait of global exchange-rate patterns since World War II, highlighting the variety of formal and informal pegging arrangements in existence for nearly 200 countries and territories. We will make use of their data set in the discussion to follow.

The remaining two functions, the invoicing role and the intervention role, are still missing from our analysis. Recent years have seen a good deal of work on the invoicing role. Most notable is a massive empirical survey of invoicing practices in international trade by some eight economists affiliated with the IMF and the European Central Bank (Boz et al. 2020). Their study calculates the shares of exports and imports denominated in various currencies for more than 100 countries since 1990, accounting for about 75 percent of world trade. Despite its comprehensive coverage, however, the resulting data set lacks applicability for the purposes of our analysis since it is limited to percentages by individual country and estimates for many key players are missing for earlier years. Lacking numbers for the magnitude of each country's trade, the presentation does not allow for generalization about aggregate currency shares across the globe. Boz et al. (2020, pp. 3–4) claim that their data 'confirm previous findings on the US dollar's dominance and on the overall stability of invoicing currency patterns in global trade,' but provide no numbers to back up their assertion. However, their contention is consistent with other sources (for example, Gopinath 2015), which suggest that as many as half of all contracts in world trade are invoiced in greenbacks.

No estimates are available for the intervention role since, regrettably, most governments remain determined to keep their exchange-market operations confidential.

3.1   Private level

At the private level, data on the vehicle role of internationally traded currencies have been available since 1989, when the BIS began a systematic triennial survey of global exchange-market activity. At the level of wholesale foreign-exchange trading around the world, a small handful of currencies (led by the US dollar) have long dominated as intermediaries (vehicles) for trade between less widely used monies. A vehicle role is a direct consequence of high market turnover, which yields substantial economies of scale. Typically, it will be less expensive for a market agent to sell a local currency for a prominent vehicle currency (such as the greenback) and then use the vehicle currency to buy the needed foreign money than it would be to exchange one infrequently traded money directly for another.

Broad trends in the vehicle use of currencies can be seen in Table 2 and Figure 1. Further detail is provided in Appendix 1. Market shares in the foreign-exchange market are measured by the percentage of transactions in which each currency appears. Since every transaction involves two currencies, percentages add up to 200 percent. The BIS survey is always taken at the same time of year, once every three years, on or near 30 April. In Table 2 and Figure 1, as in all subsequent tables and figures,

          Journal compilation © 2022 Edward Elgar Publishing Ltd

Table 2   Vehicle currency role: key currency shares of the global foreign-exchange market (percentage of average daily turnover), 1989–2019

	1989	1992	1995	1998	2001	2004	2007	2010	2013	2016	2019
US dollar	90.0	82.0	83.3	87.3	89.9	88.0	85.6	84.9	87.0	87.6	88.3
Euro	33.0	55.2	59.7	52.5	37.9	37.4	37.0	39.1	33.4	31.4	32.3
Japanese yen	27.0	23.4	24.1	20.2	23.5	20.8	17.2	19.0	23.0	21.6	16.8
British pound	15.0	13.6	9.4	11.0	13.0	16.5	14.9	12.9	11.8	12.8	12.8
Swiss franc	10.0	8.4	7.3	7.1	6.0	6.0	6.8	6.4	5.2	4.8	5.0
Others	25.0	17.4	16.2	21.9	29.7	31.3	38.5	37.7	39.6	41.8	44.8

Note: Percentages add up to 200 percent.
Source: Bank for International Settlements.

the shares shown for the euro prior to its birth in 1999 are calculated as the sum of the shares of the old Deutsche mark, French franc, and other so-called euro 'legacy' currencies. The apparent sharp drop in the recorded share of the euro after 1998 can be attributed to the formal start of Europe's monetary union, which eliminated trading among the euro's constituent currencies. From 1999 onward, transactions among members of the eurozone became effectively 'domestic' and thus were no longer treated as part of the foreign-exchange market. Unfortunately, there is no easy way to strip out these 'domestic' transactions from the data prior to 1999.

Statistics on international banking and securities markets, vital for comparing the use of different currencies for investment purposes, have long been published by

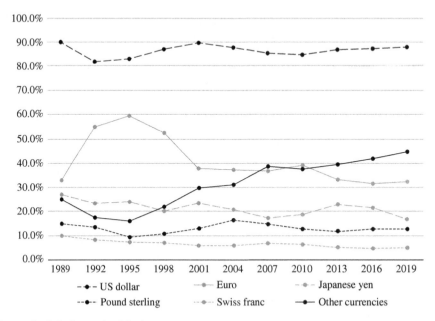

Source: Bank for International Settlements.

Figure 1   Vehicle currency role: key currency shares of the global foreign-exchange market (percentage of average daily turnover), 1989–2019

the BIS on a regular basis. Trends in the investment role of various currencies are shown in Tables 3 and 4 and Figures 2 and 3. Here, too, the data are presented at

Table 3   Investment currency role: percent currency shares of the international banking market (percentage of total cross-border bank claims), 1989–2016

	1989	1992	1995	1998	2001	2004	2007	2010	2013	2016
US dollar	58.9	52.6	45.9	48.8	48.6	43.3	42.2	43.2	44.1	48.7
Euro	17.3	22.9	28.0	26.3	31.7	39.1	39.6	39.4	36.4	33.7
Japanese yen	14.0	12.5	14.3	10.1	8.2	5.0	3.4	3.7	4.8	3.0
British pound	3.5	3.9	3.5	4.9	4.9	6.3	7.7	5.7	4.8	5.7
Swiss franc	3.9	4.3	4.0	3.0	2.3	1.8	1.6	1.5	1.6	1.6
Others	2.4	3.8	4.4	7.0	4.2	4.6	5.5	6.6	8.3	7.3

Source: Bank for International Settlements.

Table 4   Investment currency role: percent currency shares in the international securities market (percentage of total issues outstanding), 1992–2016

	1992	1995	1998	2001	2004	2007	2010	2013	2016
US dollar	42.4	38.5	48.0	51.4	40.4	36.0	37.8	36.6	42.7
Euro	24.7	26.8	24.2	30.0	43.0	47.3	46.0	44.0	38.8
Japanese yen	13.1	16.2	11.7	6.9	4.3	2.7	2.6	2.4	1.9
British pound	7.1	6.8	8.0	7.2	7.5	8.6	8.0	9.5	9.9
Swiss franc	7.3	6.8	3.8	2.0	1.8	1.5	1.4	1.7	1.4
Others	5.5	4.9	4.3	2.5	3.0	4.0	4.2	5.8	5.3

Note: Securities markets include international bonds, notes, and money-market instruments. No data are available for 1989 and 2019. The data in the first column are from September 1993.
Source: Bank for International Settlements.

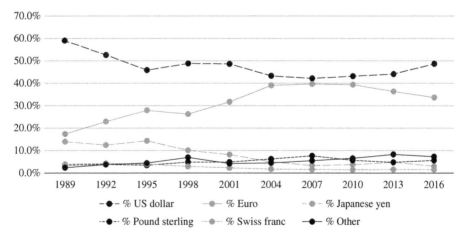

Source: Bank for International Settlements.

Figure 2   Investment currency role: currency shares of the international banking market (percentage of total cross-border bank claims), 1989–2016

                    Journal compilation © 2022 Edward Elgar Publishing Ltd

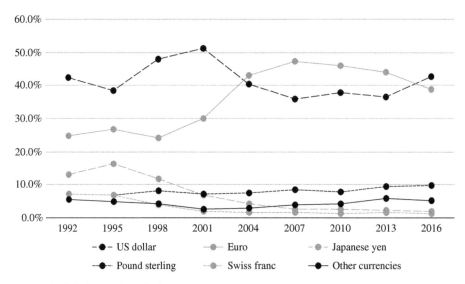

Source: Bank for International Settlements.

Figure 3   Investment currency role: currency shares in the international securities market (percentage of total issues outstanding), 1992–2016

three-year intervals to parallel the vehicle-currency data. Table 3 and Figure 2 trace trends in the currency composition of the international banking market, while Table 4 and Figure 3 show the currency composition of the international securities market, encompassing money-market instruments as well as notes and bonds.

Figures here depict amounts outstanding at the end of the first quarter of each year under review, with two exceptions. The first exception is to be found in Table 4 and Figure 3, due to the fact that comprehensive statistics for the international securities market are not available prior to September 1993. No entries are shown in Table 4 or Figure 3 for 1989, and the data for 1993 are treated as a proxy for 1992. The second exception, to be found in Tables 3 and 4 and Figures 2 and 3, is the exclusion of any numbers for 2019, due to a discontinuity in the data introduced when the BIS revised its reporting methodology in late 2015. No entries are shown for 2019, and data from 2015, the latest available under the Bank's older methodology, are treated as a proxy for 2016. The adjustments are regrettable, but the trends are still informative.

3.2   Official level

As indicated, we now have solid data on the anchor role of international currencies, thanks to the efforts of Ilzetzki et al. (2019). The picture is set out in Table 5 and Figure 4, showing the share of individual anchor currencies in the total population of moneys using a peg of some kind. Two currencies clearly stand out: the dollar and the euro. A few other currencies also play an anchor role (for example, Australia, India, South Africa), but only on a very minor scale for a handful of smaller neighbors.

As Ilzetzki et al. acknowledge, measurement of the anchor role is somewhat problematic. A money functions as an anchor when other 'dependent' currencies are pegged to it in one way or another. But it is not always easy to know when such an exchange-rate

Table 5   Exchange-rate anchor role: percent key currencies by year and country of anchor currency, 1989–2019

	1989	1992	1995	1998	2001	2004	2007	2010	2013	2016	2019
US dollar	47.4	55.3	57.6	60.0	58.7	57.4	57.0	57.7	57.0	56.3	54.2
Euro	11.6	12.6	12.1	11.7	28.3	28.9	28.5	27.8	28.5	28.6	28.9
Others	41.0	32.1	30.3	28.3	13.0	13.7	14.5	14.4	14.5	15.1	16.8

Source: Ilzetzki et al. (2019).

relationship exists. The link is obvious when a formal (*de jure*) peg is announced, but more difficult to specify when pegs are informal (*de facto*) or are maintained in relation to a 'basket' of currencies. The authors address the issue by classifying dependent currencies on a sort of 'winner takes all' basis, assigning each money entirely to a single anchor according to minimum variance in exchange-rate relationships. The approach is not perfect. Arguably, it might be more accurate to decompose exchange-rate movements into those associated with each anchor separately and assigning each currency accordingly – a kind of 'proportional representation' approach, as advocated *inter alia* by Ito and McCauley (2019). But no such analysis has yet appeared in the literature.

There is also a challenge in estimating the relative importance of diverse exchange-rate links. Simply adding up the total of currency pegs, formal or informal, could be misleading. As many as 40 countries currently align their currencies to some extent with the euro (as compared with some 60 countries that align more or less closely with the dollar). But of those 40, four are European mini-states (Andorra, Monaco, San Marino, and the Vatican) and another 16 include the 14 members of the *Communauté Financière Africaine* (CFA; African Financial Community) franc zone in Africa together with two affiliated economies (Cape Verde and Comoros), all small and poor nations. How do we compare these anchor relationships with links to the dollar maintained by much larger economic powers like China, Hong Kong, and Saudi Arabia? Differences like these must be kept in mind in any comparative analysis of currency pegs.

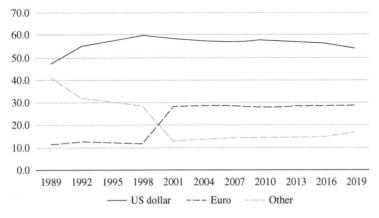

Source: Ilzetzki et al. (2019).

Figure 4   Exchange-rate anchor role: key currencies by year and country of anchor currency, 1989–2019

                    Journal compilation © 2022 Edward Elgar Publishing Ltd

Table 6 Reserve currency role: currency percent shares of foreign-exchange reserves (percentage of total 'allocated' reserves), 1989–2019

	1989	1992	1995	1998	2001	2004	2007	2010	2013	2016	2019
US dollar	52.4	55.1	56.8	65.7	72.3	67.1	65.1	62.2	62.0	65.5	61.8
Euro	34.8	26.0	22.9	14.5	17.7	23.4	25.1	27.1	23.4	19.6	20.3
Japanese yen	7.4	7.5	6.8	5.3	5.5	4.5	3.1	3.0	3.9	3.7	5.3
British pound	2.6	3.0	3.1	3.8	2.8	2.8	4.6	4.3	3.9	4.7	4.6
Swiss franc	1.6	1.0	0.8	0.7	0.3	0.2	0.2	0.1	0.3	0.2	0.1
Other	1.2	7.4	9.6	10.0	1.4	2.0	2.0	3.4	6.6	6.5	7.9

Source: International Monetary Fund.

Finally, we come to the reserve role, which is by far the most frequently studied of all the functions of an international currency. As indicated, the best available source for this role is the IMF. Regrettably, the Fund's COFER data have always been less than complete, owing to the fact that not all countries report the distribution of their reserve holdings. *Faute de mieux*, however, the numbers for so-called 'allocated' reserves are the best we have and are generally assumed to be sufficiently representative to be useful for analytical purposes. Fortunately, COFER's coverage has grown substantially over time, especially since the mid 1990s. Whereas previously no more than 55 percent of global reserves were included, today that figure has grown to more than 90 percent. A summary of market shares for the principal reserve currencies is provided in Table 6, with changes over time charted in Figure 5. Shares are calculated as a percentage of allocated reserves only. Again, as with the investment data in Tables 3 and 4 and Figures 3 and 4, the reserve data are presented at three-year intervals and depict amounts outstanding at the end of the first quarter of each year shown.

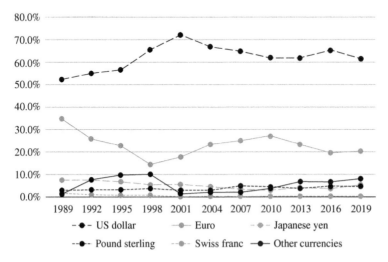

Source: International Monetary Fund.

Figure 5 Reserve currency role: currency shares of foreign-exchange reserves (percentage of total foreign-exchange reserves)

4   POLARITY

Tables 2–6 and Figures 1–5 update the data analysed in our earlier paper to encompass the decade of the 2010s. What do the updated data tell us?

4.1   Unipolarity?

Most obvious is the sustained predominance of the dollar, which still plays an outsized role in all categories just as it did a decade earlier. In the global foreign-exchange market, the greenback appears on one side or the other of nearly half of all transactions. The dollar also leads in the international banking and securities markets, functions as an anchor for some 54 countries, and accounts for close to 60 percent of global reserves. Obvious too is the failure of other currencies to make any significant inroads on the dollar's dominance. For most roles, the distance between the greenback's market share and that of other currencies remains as wide as ever or even wider.

The only seeming exception is to be found in the currency composition of central-bank reserves, where the greenback's market share appears to have drifted down noticeably since the turn of the century. Prominent experts make much of the fact that the dollar share of reserves most recently has been some 12 percentage points lower than it was at the start of the new millennium (Arslanalp et al. 2022). In reality, however, the change is far less dramatic than suggested. As noted earlier, currency statistics at the turn of the century were distorted by the formal start of Europe's monetary union, which caused an apparent sharp dip in the recorded share of the euro. Correspondingly, the dollar's recorded share was artificially elevated for a time, spiking to above 70 percent in 2001 before dropping down again in subsequent years. Over the most recent decade, the greenback's share seems to have stabilized in the neighborhood of 60 percent, about where it was back in the 1990s.

Predominance, however, is not the same thing as unipolarity. As mighty as the greenback appears to be, it is not without rivals with significant market shares of their own – especially in global investments, where the dollar has been regularly challenged by the euro. Also notable is a modest decline in the number of countries pegging to the dollar. Once upon a time, it may have been accurate to think of America's currency as a Gulliver among the Lilliputians, enjoying something close to monopoly in the monetary system. But that, clearly, is no longer true.

4.2   Multipolarity?

Is it true, then, that the system is indeed becoming multipolar, as many have asserted? Not if the data for the last decade are to be believed. In fact, predictions of a new normal of multipolarity appear to be, at best, premature – and at worst, a gross caricature. Even a quick glance confirms that in reality the global system is dominated in varying degrees by just two currencies: the US dollar and the euro. This is a pattern that has persisted consistently for more than two decades. Routinely, the dollar and euro together predominate across the board.

Admittedly, a few other currencies are also used widely enough to warrant separate mention. In what has been called the global currency pyramid (Cohen 1998), two tiers may be distinguished below the pair of leaders: the first tier down consisting of the traditional secondary currencies, including the British pound, the Japanese yen, and the Swiss franc; and the next tier below consisting of newer emerging currencies

          Journal compilation © 2022 Edward Elgar Publishing Ltd

such as the Australian and Canadian dollars, the Swedish krona, and the South Korean won. None of these secondary monies, however, is in the same class as the dollar or the euro. They are clearly no more than 'also rans' in the international currency race. For no role is their market share more than a few percentage points – certainly not great enough to qualify for description as a distinct pole. Significantly, most of the gains among the smaller currencies over the last decade have come at the expense of the euro rather than the dollar.

Even further back is the RMB, which is barely visible in any sector, owing in particular to China's extensive exchange restrictions and capital controls. Overall, the RMB remains a dwarf among international currencies, despite manifold efforts by the authorities in Beijing to promote its global standing. It poses little threat to the greenback at present.

4.3   Bipolarity?

What about bipolarity? As noted, the dollar and the euro together clearly dominate the data. Accordingly, some have suggested that the system could therefore be described as a duopoly (Auboin 2012). But as we argued in our earlier paper, that too would be, at best, premature. The euro hardly qualifies as a polar power co-equal with the dollar. The disparities between the two currencies are simply too great. Indeed, the gaps between them appear to be growing, not shrinking.

Their inequalities can be clearly seen in Table 7, which summarizes the shares for the dollar and the euro in the vehicle, investment (banking and securities shown separately), and reserve segments in 2010 and 2019. For illustrative purposes, a simple arithmetic average of the four ratios for the two years is also shown, though without any pretense that this can be considered as anything other than a very crude indicator of the overall competitive structure of the system. The table does not appear to depict a genuine duopoly. Quite the opposite, in fact. In all four categories, the distance between the two currencies has actually widened since our earlier analysis.

Moreover, it is well known that while the dollar continues to be used virtually everywhere, the euro's domain has remained confined to a limited number of economies with close geographical and/or institutional links to the European Union. Arguably it would be more accurate to describe the broader system as falling somewhere between bipolar and unipolar – perhaps more favorable to the euro than Cohen's (2011) characterization of a 'one-and-a-half currency system,' but certainly not a relationship of equals. Considerations like these highlight why it is essential to think about not only the number of poles in the system but also the inequalities between them.

Table 7   Summary of currency capacities: US dollar and euro, 2010 and 2019

	Vehicle	Banking	Securities	Reserves	Average
2010					
US dollar	42.4%	43.2%	37.8%	62.2%	46.4%
Euro	19.5%	39.6%	46.0%	27.1%	33.0%
2019					
US dollar	44.2%	48.7%	42.7%	61.8%	49.4%
Euro	16.2%	18.2%	38.8%	20.3%	23.4%

Table 8   Concentration ratios (CR2), top two currencies, 1989–2019

Sector	1989	1992	1995	1998	2001	2004	2007	2010	2013	2016	2019
Vehicle ($N = 2$)	61.5	68.6	71.5	69.9	63.9	62.7	61.3	62	60.2	59.5	60.3
Banking ($N = 2$)	76.2	75.5	73.8	75.1	80.4	82.4	81.8	82.5	80.5	82.4	n.a.
Securities ($N = 2$)	n.a.	67.0	65.3	72.2	81.4	83.4	83.3	83.8	80.6	81.5	n.a.
Anchor ($N = 2$)	59.0	68.0	70.0	72.0	87.0	86.0	85.0	86.0	85.0	85.0	83.0
Reserve ($N = 2$)	87.2	81.1	79.7	80.2	90.0	90.5	90.1	89.2	85.4	85.0	82.1
Average ($N = 2$)	71.0	72.0	72.1	73.9	80.5	81.0	80.3	80.7	78.3	78.7	75.1

Note: n.a. = not available.

Table 9   Concentration ratios (CR5), top five currencies, 1989–2019

Sector	1989	1992	1995	1998	2001	2004	2007	2010	2013	2016	2019
Vehicle ($N = 5$)	87.5	91.5	92.4	89.1	85.2	84.4	80.8	81.2	80.1	79.1	77.6
Banking ($N = 5$)	97.6	96.2	95.6	93.0	95.8	95.4	94.5	93.4	91.7	92.7	n.a.
Securities ($N = 5$)	n.a.	94.5	95.1	95.7	97.5	97.0	96.0	95.8	94.2	94.7	n.a.
Anchor ($N = 5$)	61.0	70.0	72.0	74.0	89.0	88.0	87.0	89.0	88.0	88.0	86.0
Reserve ($N = 5$)	98.8	92.6	90.4	90.0	98.6	98.0	98.0	96.7	93.5	93.5	92.1
Average ($N = 5$)	86.2	89.0	89.1	88.4	93.2	92.6	91.3	91.2	89.5	89.6	85.2

Note: n.a. = not available.

5   CONCENTRATION RATIOS

Moving, therefore, beyond polarity to concentration, we begin with some simple concentration ratios as shown in Tables 8 and 9 and Figures 6 and 7. Even admitting their limited analytical value on their own, concentration ratios represent an improvement over simple notions of polarity.

As in our earlier paper, two ratios are shown for each market segment to assure representative coverage. One is for the dollar and euro alone ($N = 2$), the two most prominent international currencies. The second also includes the three other traditional

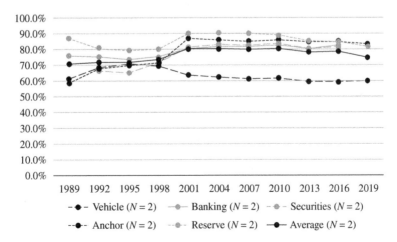

Figure 6   Concentration ratios (CR2), top two currencies, 1989–2019

          Journal compilation © 2022 Edward Elgar Publishing Ltd

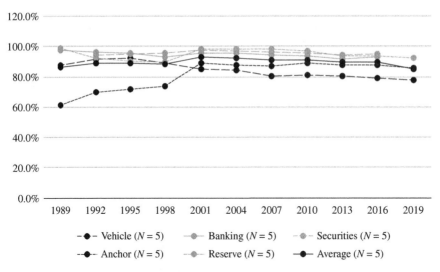

Figure 7   Concentration ratios (CR5), top five currencies, 1989–2019

but now second-tier currencies – the yen, the pound, and the Swiss franc ($N = 5$). For illustrative purposes, a simple arithmetic average of all five ratios for each year is also shown, though without any pretense that this can be considered anything other than a very crude indicator of the overall competitive structure of the system.

Our previous paper showed virtually no net change in the level of concentration in the system through the first decade of the new century. Extending the data forward for another decade clearly reaffirms our earlier results. As before, there have been some fluctuations up and down in individual measures. But for the most part we find a relatively stable horizontal trend. Whether calculated for $N = 2$ or $N = 5$, most of the ratios have barely budged from where they were in 2010.

In the foreign-exchange market and in central-bank reserves there are some signs of increased competition, with modest gains recorded by smaller currencies like the Australian and Canadian dollars and Swedish krona (Appendix 1). Most of the shift, however, has been at the expense of the euro and other traditional but now second-tier currencies (the pound, the yen, and the Swiss franc) rather than the dollar. China's RMB has also begun to stake out a role, but, with a market share of foreign-exchange transactions or central-bank reserves of little more than 2 percent, remains a very minor player. In the banking and securities sectors, by contrast, concentration has actually risen a bit because of notable increases in foreign use of Europe's money. Once the euro was born, outside borrowers were attracted by the opportunity to tap into the much broader pool of savings created by the promised consolidation of European financial markets. Both bank lending and securities issues denominated in euros increased substantially. Overall, however, the average level of competition in the global system, as shown by concentration ratios, seems to indicate little net change from the late 1980s to 2019.

6   HERFINDAHL–HIRSCHMAN INDICES

Even more telling is the picture drawn by extending our calculations of Herfindahl–Hirschman Indices forward to include the second decade of the twenty-first century,

Table 10   Herfindahl–Hirschman Indices, 1989–2019

	1989	1992	1995	1998	2001	2004	2007	2010	2013	2016	2019
Vehicle HHI	0.272	0.272	0.287	0.286	0.279	0.272	0.269	0.268	0.274	0.277	0.283
Banking HHI	0.400	0.350	0.314	0.326	0.348	0.349	0.345	0.351	0.339	0.360	n.a.
Securities HHI	n.a.	0.271	0.258	0.312	0.365	0.357	0.363	0.364	0.341	0.346	n.a.
Anchor HHI	0.406	0.425	0.438	0.454	0.442	0.432	0.427	0.431	0.427	0.422	0.406
Reserve HHI	0.402	0.383	0.390	0.457	0.558	0.508	0.490	0.464	0.447	0.475	0.434
Average system HHI	0.370	0.340	0.338	0.367	0.398	0.384	0.379	0.376	0.365	0.376	0.374

Note: n.a. = not available.

as shown in Table 10 and Figure 8. Where concentration ratios simply add up the market shares of top players, the HHI gives us a more complete sense of competitive structure by taking explicit account of structural inequalities. Here, too, extending the data forward mostly reaffirms our earlier results.

Our previous paper showed a remarkable stability, rather than a decline, in the overall level of concentration in the system, despite some fluctuations in individual sectors. Adding another decade does not change the picture significantly. There does appear to have been some increase of competition in central-bank reserves from 2010 to 2019, where gains were recorded by several smaller currencies. But, as noted earlier, most of those gains have been at the expense of the euro and other traditional secondary moneys rather than the dollar. In some cases, gains observed in the third-tier currencies are purely presentational, resulting from increased disaggregation of published data. In contrast to earlier years, these currencies are now listed by name and are no longer lumped together in the category of 'other currencies.' Real changes in their overall standing, however, are minimal. Indeed, if we start back at 1989 or the early 1990s, we actually see a rise of concentration in the currency composition of reserves over time. And that seems true as well of most other market segments, where the trend of the HHI over the full length of the last quarter-century has been level or even modestly upward, indicating greater concentration.

Our previous paper also demonstrated that concentration and polarity do not always move in tandem. This observation too is unaffected by adding another decade. In both

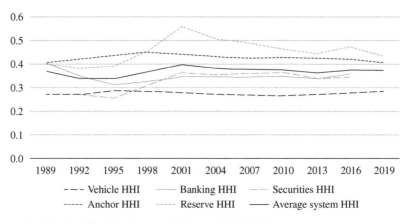

Figure 8   Herfindahl–Hirschman Indices, 1989–2019

the foreign-exchange market and official reserves, as we noted in our earlier analysis, the dollar share has long been more than twice that of the euro. Yet the levels of concentration, as measured by the HHI in the two segments, remain vastly different – strikingly low in the foreign-exchange market but much higher in reserves. Inequalities have always differed significantly for the two currency roles, suggesting yet again why reliance on the notion of polarity alone can be quite misleading.

7   CONCLUSION

The general conclusion is unmistakable. Contrary to the popular impression of an emerging multipolarity in the monetary system, our earlier paper found little evidence of significant growth in the degree of competition among international currencies. Extending the analysis forward another decade does little to change the story. To the present day, there appears to be just one true pole in the system – namely, the US dollar. The euro, number two globally, lags well behind the greenback; other secondary currencies appear to be little more than niche players; and the RMB is so far back in the race that it still barely even registers. More to the point, levels of concentration show no sign of significant decline. Taking account of inequalities as well as the number of poles, it appears that the most striking feature of the overall competitive structure is its relative stability, rather than any dramatic change. For another decade the dollar has remained the only truly global currency, still dominant for most purposes. The system still cannot be described as anything like a true oligopoly.

Change has not been entirely absent, of course. But where change has occurred in the currency pyramid over the last decade, it has been mostly *below* the dominant dollar, in the relative standing of a handful of secondary currencies. While the greenback continues to reign supreme, competition in the tiers immediately below appears, if anything, to have accelerated modestly. Most striking is the fading popularity of some of the system's more traditional second-tier currencies as well as of the euro itself, which has fallen further behind the greenback in every market segment since Europe's debt troubles of the early 2010s (Table 7). Both the yen and the Swiss franc have also lost market share. In the second tier, only the British pound has managed to hold its own in most roles. Increasingly, the traditional secondary currencies are being challenged by newer emerging currencies in the third tier. Most of the gains of emerging currencies have come at the expense of the euro, yen, and Swiss franc rather than the greenback.

In practice, it is difficult to say when the competition among traditional and emerging secondary currencies first began to accelerate. The new emerging currencies were not separately listed in most data sources until quite recently. But a hint is provided in Appendix 1, which disaggregates the vehicle currency role as far back as 1998. It is evident that while some smaller currencies, like the Australian and Canadian dollars, had already established themselves as players by the turn of the century, others were still scarcely visible. That was the case, for example, with the Swedish krona and South Korean won. And it was certainly true of China's RMB, which did not begin to move up until six years ago.

Admittedly even a span of three decades, as covered in this paper, constitutes a relatively short period in historical terms. Over a longer period of time, more change at the systemic level might reasonably be expected. But three decades is surely enough to establish our basic point, which addresses the stability of the system *today*. Nothing in our discussion rules out the possibility of greater change in the future. Assuming

                    Journal compilation © 2022 Edward Elgar Publishing Ltd

that Europe can sustain the recovery from its recent debt troubles, the euro might yet mount an effective challenge to the dollar; the RMB might eventually take a place commensurate with the size of the Chinese economy; and one or more of the other secondary currencies might begin to attract really extensive international use. Our message is simply that none of that has happened *yet*. Loose talk about the shape of the currency system as it presently exists is misleading and a deterrent to serious analysis. Just as we concluded a decade ago, multipolarity is still not the new normal.

REFERENCES

Arslanalp, S., B. Eichengreen, and C. Simpson-Bell (2022), 'The stealth erosion of dollar dominance: active diversifiers and the rise of nontraditional reserve currencies,' Working Paper WP/22/58, Washington, DC: International Monetary Fund.

Åslund, A. (2020), 'The greatest threat to the supremacy of the dollar is loose monetary policy,' *The International Economy*, 34(1), 19–20.

Auboin, M. (2012), 'Use of currencies in international trade: any changes in the picture?,' Staff Working Paper ERSD-2012-10, Geneva: World Trade Organization.

Boz, E., C. Casas, G. Georgiadis, G. Gopinath, H. Le Mezo, A. Mehl, and T. Nguyen (2020), 'Patterns in invoicing currency in global trade,' Working Paper WP/20/126, Washington, DC: International Monetary Fund.

Chinn, M. and J. Frankel (2008), 'Why the euro will rival the dollar,' *International Finance*, 11(1), 49–73.

Cohen, B. (1971), *The Future of Sterling as an International Currency*, London: Macmillan.

Cohen, B. (1998), *The Geography of Money*, Ithaca, NY: Cornell University Press.

Cohen, B. (2011), *The Future of Global Currency: The Euro Versus the Dollar*, London: Routledge.

Cohen, B. (2015), *Currency Power: Understanding Monetary Rivalry*, Princeton, NJ: Princeton University Press.

Cohen, B. (2019), *Currency Statecraft: Monetary Rivalry and Geopolitical Ambition*, Chicago: University of Chicago Press.

Cohen, B. and T. Benney (2014), 'What does the international currency system really look like?,' *Review of International Political Economy*, 21(5), 1017–1041.

Drezner, D. (2021), 'The United States of sanctions: the use and abuse of economic coercion,' *Foreign Affairs*, 100(5), 142–154.

Eeckhout, J. (2021), 'Book review: *The Great Reversal* by Thomas Philippon,' *Review of Economic Literature*, 59(4), 1340–1360.

Eichengreen, B. (2011), *Exorbitant Privilege: The Rise and Fall of the Dollar and the Future of the International Monetary System*, New York: Oxford University Press.

El-Erian, M. (2020), 'It is extremely challenging to replace something with nothing,' *The International Economy*, 34(4), 26–27.

Gopinath, G. (2015), 'The international price system,' Working Paper 21646, Cambridge, MA: National Bureau of Economic Research.

Hirschman, A. (1964), 'The paternity of an index,' *American Economic Review*, 54(5), 761–762.

Ilzetzki, E., C. Reinhart, and K. Rogoff (2019), 'Exchange arrangements entering the twenty-first century: which anchor will hold?,' *Quarterly Journal of Economics*, 134(2), 599–646.

Ilzetzki, E., C. Reinhart, and K. Rogoff (2021), 'Rethinking exchange rate regimes,' Working Paper 29347, Cambridge, MA: National Bureau of Economic Research.

Ito, H. and R. McCauley (2019), 'A key currency view of global imbalances,' *Journal of International Money and Finance*, 94, 97–115.

Krugman, P. (2021), 'Krugman wonks out: the greenback rules. So what?,' *The New York Times*, 28 May.

Mansfield, E. (1992), 'The concentration of capabilities and the onset of war,' *Journal of Conflict Resolution*, 36(3), 3–24.

Oatley, T. (2021), 'Weaponizing international financial interdependence,' in D. Drezner, H. Farrell, and A. Newman (eds), *The Uses and Abuses of Weaponized Interdependence*, Washington, DC: Brookings Institution, pp. 115–129.

Subramanian, A. (2011), *Eclipse: Living in the Shadow of China's Economic Dominance*, Washington, DC: Peterson Institute of International Economics.

APPENDIX 1

Table A1   Percent currency shares of the global foreign-exchange market (percentage of average daily turnover) for the top 15 currencies, 1998–2019

	1998	2001	2004	2007	2010	2013	2016	2019
US dollar	87.30	89.90	88.00	85.60	84.90	87.00	87.60	88.30
Euro	52.50	37.90	37.40	37.00	39.00	33.40	31.40	32.30
Japanese yen	21.70	23.50	20.80	17.20	19.00	23.00	21.60	16.80
British pound	11.00	13.00	16.50	14.90	12.90	11.80	12.80	12.80
Swiss franc	7.10	6.00	6.00	6.80	6.30	5.20	4.80	5.00
Australian dollar	3.00	4.30	6.00	6.60	7.60	8.60	6.90	6.80
Canadian dollar	3.50	4.50	4.20	4.30	5.30	4.60	5.10	5.00
Chinese renminbi	0.00	0.00	0.10	0.50	0.90	2.20	4.00	4.30
Hong Kong dollar	1.00	2.20	1.80	2.70	2.40	1.40	1.70	3.50
New Zealand dollar	0.20	0.60	1.10	1.90	1.60	2.00	2.10	2.10
Swedish krona	0.30	2.50	2.20	2.70	2.20	1.80	2.20	2.00
South Korean won	0.20	0.80	1.10	1.20	1.50	1.20	1.70	2.00
Singapore dollar	1.10	1.10	0.90	1.20	1.40	1.40	1.80	1.80
Norwegian Krone	0.20	1.50	1.40	2.10	1.30	1.40	1.70	1.80
Mexican peso	0.50	0.80	1.10	1.30	1.30	2.50	1.90	1.70
Indian rupee	0.10	0.20	0.30	0.70	0.90	1.00	1.10	1.70
Others	10.30	11.20	11.10	13.30	11.50	11.50	11.60	12.10

Note: Since every transaction involves two currencies, percentages add up to 200 percent.
Source: Bank for International Settlements.

Review of Keynesian Economics, Vol. 10 No. 4, Winter 2022, pp. 20–56

Theorizing dollar hegemony: the political economic foundations of exorbitant privilege

Thomas Palley*
Principal, Economics for Democratic and Open Societies, Washington, DC, USA

This paper explores dollar hegemony, emphasizing that it is a fundamentally political economic phenomenon. Dollar hegemony rests on the economic, military, and international political power of the US and is manifested through market forces. The paper argues that there have been two eras of dollar hegemony which were marked by different models. Dollar hegemony 1.0 corresponded to the Bretton Woods era (1946–1971). Dollar hegemony 2.0 corresponds to the Neoliberal era (1980–today). The 1970s were an in-between decade of dollar distress during which dollar hegemony was reseeded. The deep foundation of both models is US power, but the two models have completely different economic operating systems. Dollar hegemony 1.0 rested on the trade and manufacturing dominance of the US after World War II. Dollar hegemony 2.0 rests on the Neoliberal reconstruction of the US and global economies which have made the US the center of global capitalism and the most attractive place to hold capital. It is a financial model and intrinsically connected to Neoliberalism. Consideration of dollar hegemony leads to two further questions. One is whether there is a better way of organizing the world monetary order, which is associated with a debate about the possibility of a new Bretton Woods. The other is: what is the future of dollar hegemony?

Keywords: *dollar hegemony, Neoliberalism, power, currency competition, capital mobility, Bretton Woods*

JEL codes: *F00, F02, F30, F33*

1 INTRODUCTION: REVISITING DOLLAR HEGEMONY

The US dollar is the world's dominant currency measured by the value of trade invoiced in dollars, the denomination of international lending, and the share of central bank foreign exchange reserves held in dollars. As such, the dollar constitutes the world's hegemonic currency. That standing increases US power and yields significant economic benefits, which former French Finance Minister Valéry Giscard d'Estaing referred to in the 1960s as 'exorbitant privilege' (cited in Eichengreen 2011, p. 4). This paper revisits the theory of dollar hegemony and examines the past and present of dollar hegemony.

To the extent that currency hegemony is even addressed in mainstream economics, the theoretical approach can be described as 'functionalist' with the hegemonic currency being largely explained in terms of delivering better on the functions of money. This paper seeks to expand that frame by adding a 'structuralist' dimension whereby currency

---

* Email: mail@thomaspalley.com.

hegemony is explained as the product of political economic structure. That approach joins economics with the political science sub-discipline of International Political Economy (IPE), which has long emphasized the significance of structural factors.

The principal novel analytical contributions of the paper are fourfold. First, the paper provides a simple political economic framework showing how political and economic power interact to support dollar hegemony, and how dollar hegemony feeds back to support political and economic power. A political economic frame emphasizes the role of state power. It contrasts with economists' thinking which looks to explain dollar hegemony as a market equilibrium outcome produced by agents' competitive pursuit of their self-interest. The economist's market equilibrium narrative suppresses politics and state power. It is both always right and always misleading. It is always right as in the moment market forces determine private sector behaviors and asset demands. It is misleading because private sector behaviors and choices take place within an economic structure established by state power, and states also have their own demands for foreign exchange (FX) reserves. The political is therefore intrinsic to understanding the economic outcomes generated by the international monetary system (IMS), as emphasized by IPE.

Second, the paper re-examines the history of dollar hegemony and shows how it has had a changing operational basis. The phenomenon of dollar hegemony has endured for 75 years, but its operational basis has changed. Power (in its various forms) is always the foundation of currency hegemony, but the way that currency hegemony operates varies with economic structure. The economic functioning of dollar hegemony in 2022 is very different from the economic functioning of dollar hegemony in the 1952. Recognizing that role of structure surfaces new theoretical explanations of how dollar hegemony operates.

Third, the paper emphasizes the relational role of hegemony. Hegemonic standing is a relational construct. The implication is that dollar hegemony is not made by just the US. Other countries contribute to it by policy choices and policy failures. It is easy to overlook that contribution by focusing excessively on US power. Dollar hegemony prevails in part because of choices foisted on the global economy by the US, which is the system hegemon, but it also prevails because of choices made by other participants.

Fourth, the paper introduces a new characterization of currency hierarchy in terms of an inverted cone. The cone contrasts with the existing currency pyramid representation. It shows how currency hegemony is associated with the size and quality of asset markets, which is captured by the cone's three-dimensionality.

The structure of the remainder of the paper is as follows. Section 2 provides some descriptive data on dollar hegemony. Section 3 introduces the concept of the currency cone and elaborates a political economic model of dollar hegemony. Section 4 discusses some analytical implications of the model. Section 5 explores the role of market forces in manifesting dollar hegemony. Section 6 applies the theoretical model to analyse the history of dollar hegemony. Section 7 further excavates why foreign interests have embraced the dollar. Section 8 concludes the paper.

2   SOME DATA ON DOLLAR HEGEMONY

By way of beginning, this section presents some data supportive of the notion of dollar hegemony. Table 1 provides a range of financial indicators for the period 2000–2020. Row 1 shows the US share of global GDP which provides a benchmark for assessing the relative extent of dollar hegemony. There is a declining trend through to 2010, but

Table 1   Financial data assessing dollar hegemony

	2000	2005	2010	2015	2020
1. US share of global GDP (current dollars)	31.00%	28.00%	23.00%	24.00%	25.00%
2. US dollar share of global reserves	71.10%	66.50%	62.20%	65.70%	58.90%
3. Ratio of dollar reserve share to US GDP share[a]	2.29	2.38	2.70	2.74	2.40
4. Share of cross-border banking claims denominated in dollars	57.20%	55.80%	56.40%	62.10%	60.80%
5. Ratio banking claims to US GDP share[a]	1.85	1.99	2.45	2.59	2.43
6. Share of cross-border banking liabilities denominated in dollars	53.90%	53.00%	54.20%	63.90%	57.00%
7. Ratio banking liabilities to US GDP share[a]	1.74	1.89	2.40	2.66	2.28
8. Dollar share of foreign currency debt issuance	72.70%	73.40%	66.00%	65.80%	64.70%
9. Ratio of debt issuance share to US GDP share[a]	2.35	2.62	2.87	2.74	2.59

Source: Federal Reserve Board, The International Role of the U.S. dollar, Accessible Data, 6 October 2021, https://www.federalreserve.gov/econres/notes/feds-notes/the-international-role-of-the-u-s-dollar-accessible-20211006.htm#fig1 https://www.forbes.com/sites/mikepatton/2016/02/29/u-s-role-in-global-economy-declines-nearly-50/?sh=ad057d45e9e7. a. Author's calculation.

the share has been flat since then. Row 2 shows the dollar share of country foreign exchange reserves, which is the classic metric of dollar hegemony. There is a declining trend, which is suggestive of diminishing dollar hegemony. Row 3 shows the ratio of the dollar FX reserve share relative to the US share of world GDP. The ratio far exceeds one (by over a factor of two) which would be the measure if the US share were equal to its share of world GDP. Furthermore, the ratio is flat, so that dollar hegemony is unchanged according to that metric.

Rows 4–7 show the extent of dollar dominance in cross-border banking. The dollar share of cross-border banking claims and liabilities has increased slightly, as has the ratio relative to GDP share. That points to increased dollar hegemony in cross-border banking activity. Lastly, rows 8 and 9 show dollar hegemony in foreign currency debt issuance. Row 8 shows a decline in the dollar share, but row 9 shows the debt issuance share has increased relative to the US share of global GDP.

Table 2 shows the extent of dollar dominance in over-the-counter currency transactions. The dollar share of such transactions has remained stable, but has increased relative to the US share of global GDP. Table 3 shows the share of US dollar banknotes held by foreigners, which has increased steadily. This metric is indicative of the dollar's merits as a classic medium of exchange and store of value. It is also positively impacted by the size of the black economy outside the US, and negatively impacted by the decline in use of cash within the US. Table 3 shows an increase in the foreign share of dollar banknote holdings, showing that dollar notes continue to have standing with foreigners as a medium of exchange and store of value.

Lastly, Table 4 shows the average annual use of the dollar for export invoicing over the period 1999–2019 in four regions of the globe. No trend can be determined as this is an average annual statistic. However, the dollar is totally dominant in all regions except Europe. The dominance is also huge relative to the US share of global GDP which averaged approximately 26 percent over the period. Thus, in all regions except Europe, the dollar export invoicing was close to three times the US share of global GDP.

Table 2   Share of over-the-counter foreign exchange transactions

	2001	2007	2013	2019
Dollar share of FX transactions	90%	86%	87%	88%
US share of global GDP (current dollars)	32%	25%	22%	24%
Ratio of dollar FX transactions to 2 × US GDP share	1.41	1.72	1.98	1.83

Note: Transactions sum to 200 percent as every FX transaction involves two currencies.
Source: Federal Reserve Board, The International Role of the U.S. dollar, Accessible Data, 6 October 2021, https://www.federalreserve.gov/econres/notes/feds-notes/the-international-role-of-the-u-s-dollar-accessible-20211006.htm#fig1 https://www.forbes.com/sites/mikepatton/2016/02/29/u-s-role-in-global-economy-declines-nearly-50/?sh=ad057d45e9e7.

Table 3   Share of foreign holdings of US dollar banknotes

	2002	2005	2010	2015	2020
Share of foreign holdings of US dollar banknotes (at year end)	36.4%	35.4%	34.8%	42.3%	45.5%
Total currency in issue ($ billions)	6829	760	984	1424	2081

Source: Federal Reserve Board, The International Role of the U.S. dollar, Accessible Data, 6 October 2021, https://www.federalreserve.gov/econres/notes/feds-notes/the-international-role-of-the-u-s-dollar-accessible-20211006.htm#fig1 and https://www.federalreserve.gov/paymentsystems/coin_currcircvolume.htm.

Table 4   Average annual share of export invoicing, 1999–2019

Currency	Americas	Asia–Pacific	Europe	Rest of world
US dollar	96.3%	74.0%	23.1%	79.1%
Euro	1.6%	5.0%	66.1%	14.2%
Other	2.0%	21.0%	10.8%	6.7%

Source: Federal Reserve Board, The International Role of the U.S. dollar, Accessible Data, 6 October 2021, https://www.federalreserve.gov/econres/notes/feds-notes/the-international-role-of-the-u-s-dollar-accessible-20211006.htm#fig1.

In sum, the evidence shows dollar hegemony is alive and well, measured by multiple different metrics. The only metric showing meaningful decline is the dollar's share of FX reserves, and even there the share has held up when measured relative to the US share of global GDP.

3   A POLITICAL ECONOMIC MODEL OF DOLLAR HEGEMONY

The next step is a theoretical model for understanding dollar hegemony. The model is termed a political economic model because political considerations and interests are inextricably present. That contrasts with the standard economic perspective which neglects those factors and focuses exclusively on market forces. The model is presented in Figure 1 and consists of four blocks: dollar hegemony, US economic power, US military power, and US international political power. The blocks echo Strange's (1989) seminal construction of power in terms of productive power, military

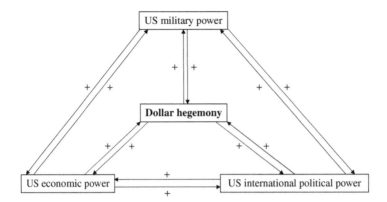

Note: + = sign of impact effect.

Figure 1   A political economic model of US power and dollar hegemony

power, knowledge power, and financial power which provided the foundation for her conception of the US as a transnational empire.

The four blocks are characterized by bidirectional interaction, with all affecting each other. Moreover, every interaction is characterized by positive feedback as represented by the plus signs, which generates a reinforcing feedback loop. An increase in the scale of the components of US power increases the extent of dollar hegemony and vice versa.[1]

3.1   Dollar hegemony

Dollar hegemony refers to the US being the world's dominant financial force, and it produces the pattern of empirical outcomes shown in Section 2. The dollar dominates central bank holdings of foreign exchange reserves, dominates international banking and international debt markets, dominates international trade invoicing, and is widely held as cash by foreigners. In extreme cases it may even entirely displace other currencies in their own home country, an outcome referred to as 'dollarization.'

Dollar hegemony is essentially a relational phenomenon that can be represented in terms of a currency hierarchy. Cohen (1998, pp. 116–118) describes that hierarchy as a 'currency pyramid' which he identifies as having seven layers. Working from top to bottom, the layers are: top currency, patrician currency, elite currency, plebeian currency, permeated currency, quasi currency, and pseudo currency.

Figure 2 presents a simpler, more mundane pyramid consisting of hegemonic currency, major strong currency, minor strong currency, weak currency, and junk

1.   In terms of a mathematical model of the process, the plus signs correspond to the signs of partial derivatives. The system in Figure 1 might be mathematically represented as a four-equation simultaneous model with the endogenous variables being dollar hegemony, US economic power, US military power, and US international political power. If the system is stable, it would exhibit strong multiplier effects because of the positive feedback loops. Increases in any one source of power unleash developments that positively influence other sources of power, triggering feedbacks (multiplier effects) that further amplify the initial change.

                    Journal compilation © 2022 Edward Elgar Publishing Ltd

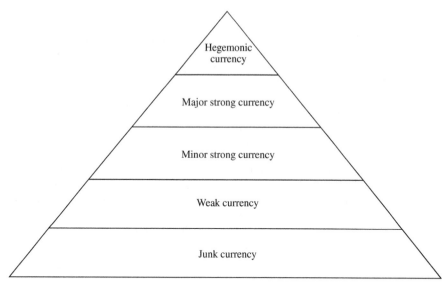

Figure 2   A suggested five category currency pyramid

currency. The hegemonic currency is the equivalent of Cohen's top currency; the major strong currency corresponds to the patrician and elite currencies; the minor strong currency corresponds to the plebeian currency; the weak currency corresponds to the permeated currency; and the junk currency corresponds to the quasi currency and the pseudo currency. From a functional perspective, major strong currencies play a role in the international economy and may be held as FX reserves by central banks. Examples are the euro and Japanese yen. Minor strong currencies perform all the standard functions of money (unit of account, medium of exchange, store of value) in the domestic economy but have no international role. An example is the Swedish krone. The Chinese renminbi is a minor strong currency that is transitioning to major strong currency status. The Mexican peso is a minor strong currency that was a weak currency two decades ago, but it lives permanently in the threatening shadow of the dollar owing to Mexico's proximity to and economic dependence on the US.

Weak currencies have lost some of their ability to deliver on the functions of money, with the store of value function being the one that tends to go first. Thus, a currency may initially lose its ability to be a store of value, but it is still used on a daily basis and serves as a medium of exchange. It may also cease to be used in certain types of asset-related transactions. The Argentine peso exemplifies a weak currency. High inflation undercuts its store of value function, and it is not used in real estate purchases which are conducted in dollars. Junk currencies are those in which the currency has substantially lost its capacity to deliver on the functions of money. They remain legal tender, but another currency (for example, the dollar) circulates widely in parallel. Parallel prices are quoted in dollars and dollars are commonly used as the medium of exchange. Of course, the currency hierarchy is a continuum so there may be judgement calls at the borders regarding which category a currency fits in. Currencies may also change categories as economic conditions and beliefs (that is, credibility) about the currency change. Thus, a currency's standing is endogenous.

3.1.1 A currency cone rather than a currency pyramid?

Currency hierarchy ordering is influenced by the forces of currency competition. Cohen (1998, pp. 109–113) identifies those forces as currency internationalization (CI) and currency substitution (CS). The former promotes the use of a currency in the international economic sphere, while the latter has a foreign currency supplanting domestic currency. Those forces emphasize the relative ability of currencies to perform the classic functions of medium of exchange and store of value.

The argument developed in this paper is that contemporary dollar hegemony represents a form of systemic financial domination. Economic agents look to hold assets denominated in dollars, and not just use and hold dollars as money. They are drawn to the dollar owing to the US having deep liquid financial markets that offer an extensive asset menu. Those markets are part of a larger economic system which is structured to favor financial interests, and that economic system is advantaged and privileged by the network of power described in Figure 1.

A systems perspective suggests an alternative representation of currency hierarchy in terms of an inverted cone, as shown in Figure 3. The base end of the cone is at the top and the point is at the bottom. The categories remain the same: hegemonic currency, major strong currency, minor strong currency, weak currency, and junk currency. The area of each segment represents the depth, liquidity, and array of assets available in each

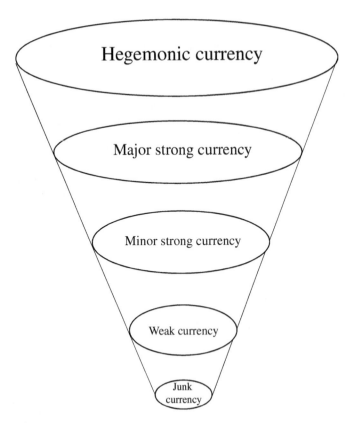

Figure 3 The currency cone

     Journal compilation © 2022 Edward Elgar Publishing Ltd

currency denomination. Thus, at the top comes the dollar which dominates asset and liability denomination in global financial markets. At the bottom come junk currencies whose asset market representation is negligible, both in volume and quality.

The cone representation captures the economic logic of currency substitution and currency internationalization. The hegemonic currency is advantaged by the quality of its financial markets measured in terms of market size, market liquidity, and the asset menu. Networking effects lower transaction costs, there are economies of scale from spreading fixed costs over larger volumes, and the portfolio possibility span is larger. The structural financial advantage of the hegemonic currency can be thought of in terms of the ratio of cone slice surface areas. Junk and weak currencies are relatively more structurally disadvantaged against the hegemonic currency than are major and minor strong currencies, which is symbolized by their smaller cone slices.

The three-dimensionality of the cone is suggestive of the multi-dimensionality of dollar hegemony, directing attention to the systemic aspect. Anticipating the rest of the paper, it is essential to realize that the US financial system is embedded in an economy that favors financial interests and the economy is advantaged by the underlying power of the US. Those deeper structural features work to further advantage the US financial system and can be considered the true foundation of dollar hegemony.

3.2 Economic power

Economic power rests on a vector of factors including the size of a country's economy, the country's productivity and state of technological advance, its engagement in international trade and foreign direct investment, its accumulated net wealth, and the standing of its financial markets. That standing rests on the size of financial markets, their liquidity, the array of available assets, and the quality of governance. Moreover, everything is relative to the economic factors characterizing rivals. That relativity is intrinsic to the issue of power, about which more below.

It is the vector of factors that matters. Economic power is associated with size, but size alone does not make a hegemon, which is why the renminbi is not hegemonic despite China being the world's largest economy. Likewise, economic productivity matters but high productivity alone does not make a hegemon, which is why the Swiss franc is not hegemonic.

Nor are size and productivity sufficient. In the inter-war years (1919–1939) the US was the world's largest and most productive economy and had a high level of productivity and technological advance, yet the dollar was not hegemonic. At that time, the US still lacked the appetite for hegemony and sufficient engagement with the international economy. The lack of appetite reflected US international political withdrawal owing to the triumph of Republican foreign policy isolationism following the experience of World War I. Lack of international economic engagement reflected the continental size of the US, which meant its economy could prosper without foreign economic engagement. There were plenty of internal investment opportunities as capital was still scarce, a plentiful supply of natural resources and primary products reduced the need for supply from international sources, and the domestic market was sufficiently large to support the economies of scale required by modern industry. After World War II, all the elements for dollar hegemony were in place. The US was the global economic hegemon, it was politically ready to step up for a hegemonic role, and an opening (almost a vacuum) had been created by the bankrupting of the UK and the disintegration of the British Empire caused by the two world wars.

 Journal compilation © 2022 Edward Elgar Publishing Ltd

3.3 Military power

The third block is military power, which refers to the size and capability of a country's armed forces. Here, one might distinguish between 'defensive' and 'offensive' military capability. Offensive capability would seem the critical characteristic, being needed to project military force outside the hegemon's country in the service of the hegemon's interests. In the pre-1914 era of sterling hegemony, Britannia 'ruled the waves' and it was the era of gunboat diplomacy. Since 1945 the US has been the unchallenged Western military hegemon, and since the end of the Cold War in 1990 it has been the unchallenged global military hegemon. China's military has only local defensive capability. A debated issue is whether China aspires to have global offensive military capability.

3.4 International political power

The fourth block is international political power which can be identified with diplomatic and 'soft' power. It too consists of a vector of factors that includes economic, political, and military alliances; cultural leadership, which includes global standing of a country's institutions of higher education; and multinational business relationships that serve to link and ally countries.

The US is the undisputed international political hegemon, having been the leader of the liberal international order since its establishment after World War II. It has leadership in all the institutions of the liberal order. These include the North Atlantic Treaty Organization (NATO) military alliance; the United Nations (UN) system; the multilateral financial institutions (MFIs), which include the International Monetary Fund (IMF), the World Bank, and the Inter-American Development Bank; and the Organisation for Economic Co-operation and Development (OECD). The US leads the global trading system, being the hegemonic voice in the World Trade Organization (WTO), and it was the hegemonic voice in the General Agreement on Tariffs and Trade (GATT) system before that. It is the lead country in the Bank for International Settlements (BIS), the leader of the Organization of American States (OAS), and it has other bilateral and multilateral defense and economic cooperation agreements with multiple countries that are too numerous to list.

The US higher education system is regarded as the best in the world, drawing students from around the globe. Most of those students return to their countries to exercise power and influence, inculcated with US thinking and points of view. Multinational corporations (MNCs) are also a powerful source of international political power, having influence in foreign countries and employing millions of foreign workers and executives. These corporations have linkages into both foreign governments and the US government, with government affairs departments and trade associations being connected to the US government at the highest level. Just as MNCs can access the US government, the US government can access them. That source of soft power is symbolized by President Fox of Mexico (2000–2006) who was President of Coca-Cola Mexico at one stage in his career.[2]

---

2.   In some respects, the US domination of the international political economic system is now so total that the construct of a liberal international order has become unsustainable. That construct was always open to realist questioning on grounds that such a system requires a benevolent hegemon to make it work, and a benevolent hegemon is ontologically impossible in a world of self-interested nation states. Now, given the scale of US dominance, the global order might be

                    Journal compilation © 2022 Edward Elgar Publishing Ltd

3.5   Linkages between US economic power, military power, and international political power

The outer linkages in Figure 1 are well established and accepted, but for purposes of analytical completeness they are briefly recapitulated below. US economic power positively impacts US military power, with a large technologically advanced economy capable of supporting a large technologically sophisticated military. Economic power provides the US with the resources to ring the globe with military bases and deployments, and the US spends more on defense (as of 2021) than the combined defense budgets of the next nine biggest spending countries according to the Stockholm International Peace Research institute (Siddique 2022).[3]

Likewise, the US's large and sophisticated military has positive impacts on the economy. Cypher (1987) argues that the US military has played a role as a form of surrogate industrial policy, helping the private sector develop and commercialize new technologies. Mazzucato (2015) details many of the technologies produced by that military–industrial policy.[4]

US economic power also positively impacts US international political power. First, it provides the resources to support US soft power initiatives. That includes directly financing foreign aid, educational and cultural initiatives, and diplomatic service-related initiatives. It also includes financing and justifying the dominant US presence in the IMF, the World Bank, the Inter-American Development Bank (IDB), and other multilateral financial institutions. Second, the opportunities within the US economy provide an incentive for foreign countries to ally and do business with the US, with countries wanting trade and investment access to the US market.

Conversely, US international political power is good for US economic power. Thus, domination of the institutions of global governance enables the US to work them to the benefit of the US economy. Schwartz (2019) argues that this has been particularly so with the new rules of global trade established under the WTO regime which have expanded intellectual property right (IPR) protections to the benefit of corporate profitability, with the US benefitting the most as it is the global leader in IP production (Soskice 2022).

Similarly, soft power connections are a form of indirect investment in the US. US institutions of higher education attract foreign talent. Scientists and high-tech engineers often remain and add to US human capital. Meanwhile, economists and Masters of Business Administration (MBAs) are inculcated with a US-friendly intellectual perspective and return home to become business and policy leaders. Business opportunities are significantly relational so that the relationships formed generate economically beneficial opportunities. Such relationships are also fostered by diplomatic service activity and by the MNC–US government–foreign government network.

---

better described as a US international order. Before, it was a multilateral negotiated order that had the appearance of a liberal order because such an arrangement benefitted the US interest, especially in the Cold War era when the US faced challenges from the Soviet Union.
3.   See 'List of United States Military bases' at https://en.wikipedia.org/wiki/List_of_United_States_military_bases.
4.   That said, there is also a dissident counter-view which sees military spending as intrinsically unproductive, and such spending would generate greater returns and well-being if directed to other uses. That is the critique of military–industrial Keynesianism, but it can be accused of overlooking the global power dividend the US receives. The two views can be reconciled by arguing that the US overspends (perhaps massively) on military might. By reducing and redirecting military spending, the US could have both: it would still retain the power and industrial innovation dividends, but it would gain the benefits gleaned from redirected spending.

                        Journal compilation © 2022 Edward Elgar Publishing Ltd

Lastly, there is a positive feedback loop between military power and international political power. Cypher (2016) examines how US military power enhances US diplomatic clout. Countries may seek protection under the US military umbrella, and the presence of US military bases may even send a subtle message of threat if countries do not conform. The line between occupying force and ally can be thin. Those influences show up in extensive alliances consisting of acquiescent allies. The size of the US military means it has pre-eminence within NATO, thereby creating a huge network of relationships between national militaries, defense contractors, and politicians. There is a revolving door between all three components of that network which further reinforces the network. The impacts of the network also ricochet back into the economy as the military–international political power network may then generate large orders for weaponry produced by the US aerospace and defense sector, which is a critical dynamic sector of the US economy.

3.6   Linkages between dollar hegemony and the components of US power

The political economic approach to dollar hegemony has been developed in the political science sub-discipline of IPE. That IPE literature is reviewed in a symposium in *International Studies Perspectives* (Norrlof and Poast 2020, pp. 109–153). The model described in Figure 1 can be used to frame and organize that literature. The inner linkages within Figure 1 are the core. They show how US power augments dollar hegemony and dollar hegemony augments US power.

3.6.1   *Economic power and dollar hegemony*

The most obvious linkage is the impact of dollar hegemony on economic power. That impact is captured by Giscard d'Estaing's comment in the 1960s about the US enjoying an 'exorbitant privilege' owing to dollar hegemony generating asymmetric operation of the financial system. The notion of exorbitant privilege captures the idea that the US gets to enjoy the benefits of the international economy without sacrificing domestic macroeconomic policy capability. The US is substantially freed of an external balance of payments constraint, unlike other countries whose macroeconomic policy possibilities collide with the external constraint. That exorbitant privilege has only grown with the suspension of the Bretton Woods system in 1971 (about which more below).

There are multiple economic benefits from dollar hegemony. The most commented on is seignorage, resulting from the fact that dollars are near costless to issue but foreigners must give over real resources to acquire them. As of 2020, foreigners held approximately $950 billion in dollar notes, which is a very nice gift. However, even larger benefits come from other financial stocks. In 2020 the dollar constituted 58.9 percent of foreign country FX reserves, 33.8 percent of marketable US Treasury debt was held by foreigners, and 60.8 percent of international foreign currency banking claims and liabilities were dollar denominated.[5]

Those financial stocks have a magnitude in trillions. On some (for example, Treasury debt) the US must pay interest, albeit at a favorable rate for reasons discussed below. However, US banks receive interest on banking claims that they generate, and the

5.   *Source:* Federal Reserve Board, The International Role of the U.S. dollar, Accessible Data, 6 October 2021.

resource cost of such claims is essentially zero in a world of endogenous fiat money. That constitutes a significant perpetual 'golden crumb' which the US enjoys by having the dollar be the money of the international economy. Those benefits are behind Desai and Hudson's (2021) construct of the US as a 'creditocracy.'

On top of the direct seignorage benefit, the US receives major financial market and economic policy benefits. Being the dominant currency and having the world's dominant financial markets increases the attractiveness of US financial assets. That attractiveness is enhanced by the dollar having 'safe haven' status. First, since the US has more macroeconomic policy space owing to its exorbitant privilege, it is better able to stabilize the macroeconomy against shocks. Second, loans to the US are dollar denominated (that is, the US borrows in its own currency) which means there is no risk of default as the Federal Reserve can issue dollars to repay those debts. Third, the lion's share of international lending is dollar denominated, as shown in Table 1. US banks have access to the financial backstop of the Federal Reserve, which can support them in the event of a financial crisis, thereby inoculating the US against financial crisis risk. The same is not true for foreign banks that make dollar denominated loans, which means foreign financial systems are more at risk.[6]

Fourth, dollar hegemony confers a privileged standing on dollar denominated assets. That standing increases demand for US financial assets, which lowers interest rates and increases US asset prices and wealth. That is good for aggregate demand and growth. US MNCs also have access to cheaper credit and can use their higher valued equity capital to buy foreign assets, effectively on the cheap.

Hausmann and Sturzenegger (2005) invoke the playful notion of 'dark matter' to explain the superior US return on FDI compared to other countries, but it may just be a product of dollar hegemony and the cost of capital/rate of return profile it creates. US corporate purchases of foreign assets result in a change of ownership which dollarizes those assets, causing an upward revaluation. The reverse holds for foreign purchases of US assets, which result in dedollarization and a downward revaluation.

Caballero (2006) argues that the world is short of safe assets and the US produces safe assets, which he claims explains the US trade deficit that is the result of the rest of the world seeking to acquire safe assets. That too may simply reflect dollar hegemony. The US produces safe assets because US financial markets are under the umbrella of dollar hegemony, and not because the US financial system is intrinsically better.[7]

Fifth, US firms benefit from lower transactions costs as they transact in their own currency, and they also avoid the cost of hedging exchange rate risk. On the downside, dollar hegemony appreciates the exchange rate by increasing demand for dollars. That is bad for manufacturing, though it also lowers import costs, which benefits consumers and helps tamp down inflation.

In sum, dollar hegemony confers major economic benefits that enhance US economic power. Enhanced economic power then feeds back to enhance dollar hegemony through the mechanisms discussed earlier, such as increased US economic size; deeper, more liquid, more stable financial markets; and engagement of foreign nationals in dollar denominated financial activity.

---

6.   That risk effect was evident in the 2008 global financial crisis when the Federal Reserve initiated emergency currency swap arrangements with major currency central banks as a way of channeling dollar liquidity to those banks which they could then lend to their commercial banks. Those provisions continue in the form of now *de facto* permanent currency swap arrangements.
7.   Palley (2012, pp. 112–114) offers multiple other critiques of the safe asset shortage explanation of the US trade deficit.

3.6.2   Military power, international political power, and dollar hegemony

Dollar hegemony also positively impacts military and international political power, and those impacts are examined concurrently as they involve similar mechanisms. Dollar hegemony creates the 'exorbitant privilege' of fiscal space and freedom from an external economic constraint, which helps provide the US with resources for its expansive international military and soft power operations (Oatley 2015).

The other side of the loop has military and international political power supporting dollar hegemony. Perhaps the clearest example of military support is the 1974 petro-dollar accord with Saudi Arabia (Gwertzman 1974). The House of Saud committed to price oil in dollars and recycle its petrodollar trade surplus via Wall Street in return for US military protection. The agreement ensured the global oil market would be priced in dollars, thereby cementing one of the pillars of dollar hegemony. The *quid pro quo* was security guarantees which the US could provide because of its military power. That episode and its antecedents are examined by Croteau and Poast (2020).

The literature on the security (military and international political) foundations of dollar hegemony is assessed in Norrlof (2020). Zimmerman (2002) provides details of the Cold War era tacit agreement between Germany and the US, whereby Germany held dollars and helped manage the dollar exchange rate in return for the US stationing troops in Germany that protected against the Warsaw Pact threat. US international political power also positively impacts the willingness of countries to hold dollar reserves by fostering alliances and political affinities with them. Liao and McDowell (2015) show that countries which are politically distant from the US and close to China tend to hold more renminbi reserves.

The above political and economic benefits of dollar hegemony are not the musings of academics. They are clearly understood within the US government. Thus, Christopher Smart, former Special Assistant to the President at the National Economic Council and National Security Council and former Deputy Assistant Secretary of the Treasury, writes:

> Currency dominance has also been a linchpin in America's efforts to shape a global order around free markets and democracy while serving as a foundation for the sustained growth of a more integrated global economy … . Issuing the world's reserve currency offers the prospect to literally print money everyone accepts to buy guns without giving up butter. The dollar's dominance also allows the United States to delay or shift any costs of global adjustment to other countries. (Smart 2018)

4   REFLECTIONS ON THE THEORETICAL MODEL

The theoretical model in Figure 1 explaining the basis of dollar hegemony contains several insights and implications.

1. Power. The system is about power, and power is at the heart of dollar hegemony. There is simply no way of understanding dollar hegemony without reference to the role of power – economic power, military power, and international political power. A narrowly economic market forces approach to dollar hegemony misses those foundational elements.

2. Power is both an input and an output. The elements of the system are simultaneously both inputs and outputs. The system relies on power as an input, and it produces power as an output. Economic power and military power can be viewed as goals in themselves, enhancing national well-being and national pride. They are also inputs

                    Journal compilation © 2022 Edward Elgar Publishing Ltd

in the pursuit of those goals, which makes them both inputs and goal outputs. Dollar hegemony is an input that is useful in the pursuit of those goals, and it is produced by the triptych of power elements. However, it is not a goal in of itself (which is likely also true of international political power).

3. The state and currency hegemony. The system that produces dollar hegemony intrinsically involves the state. First, state power in its different forms is at the core of the system. Second, the dollar is a state money and its use and standing in the international financial system depend on the actions and standing of the state. There is simply no understanding dollar hegemony without recognition of the role of the state. Attempts to theorize currency hegemony (for example, the currency cone) by reference to market forces alone are inevitably flawed.

4. Power and relative power. Currency hegemony is about power, and power is intrinsically a relative concept because the increased power of one party is implicitly a diminution of the power of rivals. Figure 1 focused on dollar hegemony and US power, the flipside of which is the power of other countries. That flipside is illustrated in Figure 4, which shows how dollar hegemony impacts the power of the rest of the world (RoW). The structure of the figure is the same as Figure 1, and the outer linkages have the same positive feedback loops. However, the interior feedback loops are different and are negatively signed. Thus, an increase in dollar hegemony decreases the power of the RoW, and an increase in the power of the RoW decreases dollar hegemony.[8]

The relationship between the RoW's power and dollar hegemony has received insufficient attention. One immediate question is: why do countries participate in the dollar hegemony system if it diminishes their power? One reason is that there

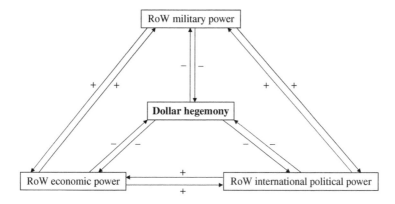

Note: + and − = sign of impact effect.

Figure 4   The relationship of the rest of the world's (RoW) power with dollar hegemony

8.   Just as the model in Figure 1 can be represented by a system of simultaneous equations, so too can the model in Figure 4. The difference is dollar hegemony would enter the RoW economic, military, and international political power equations with a negative sign, and the power variables would also enter the dollar hegemony equation with a negative sign. The two systems can be combined to yield a seven-equation general equilibrium system in which the dollar hegemony equation includes both the US and the RoW power variables.

                              Journal compilation © 2022 Edward Elgar Publishing Ltd

may still be significant other benefits. For instance, there may be significant economic gains from acquiring dollar denominated US financial assets, and invoicing in dollars may increase exports. Moreover, if countries are allied with the US, the cost of lost power will be greatly diminished. A second reason is that there may be no alternative to the dollar system. In effect, the international monetary system is characterized by a form of transactions network natural monopoly. The issue of foreign participation is discussed further in Section 7 below.

The issues raised in Figure 4 also implicate the future of dollar hegemony and the international relations frictions that may arise. At its outset, many anticipated the euro would challenge dollar hegemony, yet the euro has punched persistently below its weight. That disappointing performance should be understood by reference to both the success of the US in developing its power base and the failure of eurozone governments to develop theirs. Consequently, the eurozone has suffered a relative power decline. That decline is the result of a trio of failures: failure to develop a sound monetary–fiscal framework for the eurozone (see Herr et al. 2017; Palley 2011; 2017), failure to develop an independent and coherent pan-European military strategy, and failure to develop an independent and coherent pan-European geopolitical strategy.

Geopolitical incoherence has now become especially significant. In the first years of the euro's existence (1999–2012) the dominant problem was the flawed monetary–fiscal framework. That was substantially patched in 2012 by the European Central Bank's (ECB) declaration of willingness to buy weak member country bonds and to push the ECB lending rate to zero. However, since then, the geopolitical incoherence of eurozone governments has become increasingly important. Thus, it can be argued that the euro (and the European Union) suffers from overexpansion that has incorporated Central and Eastern European countries that are politically alien and have divergent political interests. Additionally, Europe has chosen to play camp follower to the US as regards geopolitics and conflict.[9] In accordance with the signing pattern in Figure 4, relative decline of European power across the spectrum has increased dollar hegemony.

Lastly, a relative power perspective is relevant for understanding the international relations frictions that may develop in response to challenges to dollar hegemony from Russia and China. Wang (2020) explores the impact of China on the international financial system and introduces a distinction between threats to the liberal order and threats to US domination of the liberal order. The purpose is to provide a richer understanding regarding China's actions and to question charges that it is a threat to the liberal order. However, from the hegemon's perspective (that is, the US perspective), the distinction is substantively moot as the US will be resistant to China's financial rise regardless of whether it challenges the liberal order or not. Power is relative, so the US has an incentive to block China's financial rise. Furthermore, it also has an incentive to portray challenges to its dominance as challenges to the liberal order as a way of marshalling allied support against China.

---

9.   That has been visibly on display in the Ukraine conflict from which Europe has suffered enormously, whereas the US has been a net geopolitical beneficiary. Europe has suffered huge economic costs in the form of energy supply disruption, inflation, and loss of the huge Russian export market for luxury and capital goods. Contrastingly, the US has gained new energy markets in Europe, ensnared Europe in even greater subservience to the US military, and created permanently heightened tensions with Russia that benefit the US geopolitically. Those factors are reflected in the 2022 surge in the value of the dollar and fall in the value of the euro.

The inherently relative power dimension of currency hegemony means dollar hegemony has latent rivalrous tendencies. Those rivalrous tendencies are most pronounced with countries that are politically distant from the US, but they are also present with US allies. Allies (for example, Western Europe) may want to secure some of the economic benefits of currency hegemony for themselves and they may have their own geopolitical identity and projects. They may also chafe under US hegemonic power, especially if it is abused.

5   MARKET FORCES AND CURRENCY HIERARCHY

Market and state are both relevant for understanding currency hegemony, and they play off each other interactively. The framework in Figure 1 is static and identifies the role of state power in its various dimensions. This section introduces the role of market forces in the dollar hegemony process, which brings in traditional economic analysis.

Market forces are critical in sorting currencies and establishing the currency hierarchy. Those forces work within the international monetary system (IMS). Metaphorically, the IMS is the international economy's financial plumbing, with the 'dollar' pipes and liquidity reservoirs being far larger than the pipes and reservoirs of other currencies. Furthermore, the more the dollar pipes are used, the greater the incentive for others to use them, as there are beneficial network externalities from currency usage.

The IMS has evolved over time in response to both changing market forces and state interventions, and the two interact. That interaction is illustrated in Figure 5, which consists of three concentric loops. The outer loop concerns the deep structural forces of relative economic, military, and international political power which were discussed in the previous section. That power configuration changes slowly and is the bedrock of dollar hegemony, and it is influenced by state policies. The configuration of power impacts market forces that feed back to impact the configuration of power. The middle loop has states' policies impacting the IMS, with states responding to

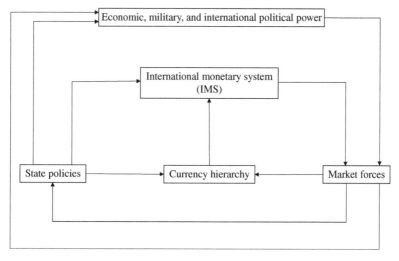

Figure 5   The interaction between market forces and state policy

market forces that may generate instability or persistent disequilibrium outcomes. The interior loop concerns the determination of the currency hierarchy.

The currency hierarchy is determined by both state policy and market forces. State policy manifests itself directly in the choice of composition of FX reserve holdings, and indirectly via the influence of policies on the IMS and the international matrix of power. Market forces influence the currency hierarchy via the forces of currency competition. Those forces are analysed by Cohen (1998, ch. 5, pp. 92–118), who singles out the forces of currency internationalization and currency substitution. The former refers to the use of a currency in the international sphere, including trade invoicing and provision of international credit. The latter refers to the displacement of a currency in the domestic sphere. Market forces are therefore both international and domestic.

The notion of the IMS being the plumbing fits with the issues raised by Khanna and Winecoff (2020) and McDowell (2020), who emphasize the power that comes with providing the transactions payments infrastructure. It is as if the US owns the plumbing through which global business is financed and transactions settled, and owning the plumbing makes the US (that is, the dollar) indispensable and a source of power. The plumbing constitutes a form of network, and owning it confers network power on the US, as the US has the power to deny access to the plumbing.[10] With that power comes the political risk of abusing power via overpenalizing foreign banks that fall foul of US policy, which can induce a backlash to develop an alternative clearing mechanism that is outside of US jurisdiction (McDowell 2020).

6   APPLYING THE MODEL: THE HISTORY OF DOLLAR HEGEMONY

This section applies the above theoretical framework to analyse the history of dollar hegemony. That history reveals two types of changes. The first is the change of hegemon. The second is the changing economic operation of hegemony. As the global economy and the IMS have evolved, the economic operation of dollar hegemony has changed. Those changes in the global economy and the IMS are the joint product of market forces and state policy.

Figure 6 provides a stylized history of currency hegemony in the modern era, from 1873 through to today. That history is divided into two overlapping eras, consisting of the gold standard era (1873–1971) and the dollar hegemony era (1946–today). The eras overlap because the post-war Bretton Woods regime was a modified gold standard in which the dollar was the hegemonic currency.

Each era is divided into three sub-periods. The gold standard era consists of a golden age period of sterling hegemony (1873–1914), a transitional period of sterling decline (1914–1946), and the Bretton Woods period (1946–1971) which saw the arrival of dollar hegemony. The dollar hegemony era consists of the Bretton Woods period, which was the first period of dollar hegemony, a decade of dollar distress (1971–1980) in which dollar hegemony was in doubt, and a second period of restored dollar hegemony associated with financial globalization that is ongoing (1980–today). Each sub-period

---

10.   The key institution is the Clearing House Interbank Payments System (CHIPS) through which dollar transactions are cleared. That system is owned by private banks operating under US jurisdiction in the form of the Federal Reserve. The Society for Worldwide Interbank Financial Transactions (SWIFT) is based in Belgium, and it wires money transfer instructions to banks, but dollar transactions between banks clear through CHIPS.

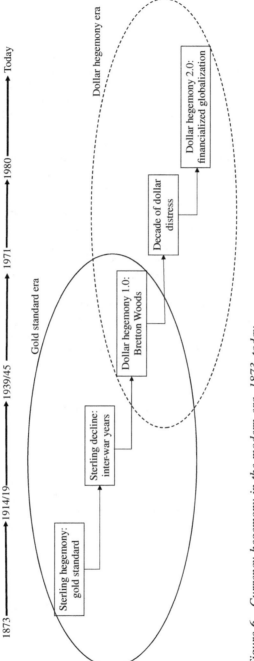

Figure 6   Currency hegemony in the modern era, 1873–today

has its own particularities which shed light on the workings and basis of dollar hegemony.

6.1   Sterling hegemony (1873–1914)

The starting point is the period of sterling hegemony under the classic gold standard in which sterling was convertible into gold by both governments and individuals. Including the era of sterling hegemony helps us to understand dollar hegemony within the broader theory of currency hegemony by showing how hegemony regimes have different economic operating systems. The transition era also highlights the role of relative power.

Though Britain had been on the gold standard before 1873, the modern era is dated as beginning then with the German empire's abandonment of its silver standard and adoption of a gold standard. Within the system, sterling was the hegemonic currency, and its hegemony is easily understandable in terms of the theoretical framework described in Figure 1.

As regards economic hegemony, Table 5 shows that in 1870 the UK was the world's largest economy, producing 9.1 percent of world GDP. Moreover, shares of world output are somewhat misleading, as China was not integrated into the world economy, so the UK's effective weight was larger. As shown in Table 6, if the analysis is restricted to Western Europe and Western offshoots, the UK's share of total output rises to 20.8 percent.

Output shares also understate the UK's economic hegemony, which may be better reflected in export share. Table 7 shows the UK's share of world exports in 1870 was 24.3 percent. Furthermore, as shown in Table 8, its exports were a relatively far larger share of its GDP at 12.2 percent. Since UK exports were manufacturing goods, that implies that the UK dominated global manufacturing, which was the technologically

Table 5   Shares of world GDP (percent of world total)

	1820	1870	1913	1950	1973	1998
UK	5.2	9.1	8.3	6.5	4.2	3.3
US	1.8	8.9	19.1	27.3	22.0	21.9
Western Europe & Western offshoots[a]	25.5	43.8	55.2	56.9	51.0	45.7
World	100.0	100.0	100.0	100.0	100.0	100.0

Note: Western offshoots = US, Canada, Australia, and New Zealand.
Source: Author's calculations based on Maddison (2001, p. 263, table B-20). a. Author's calculation.

Table 6   UK and US shares of GDP of Western Europe and Western offshoots (percent of total)

	1820	1870	1913	1950	1973	1998
UK[a]	20.3	20.8	15.0	11.4	8.2	7.2
US[a]	7.1	20.3	34.6	48.0	43.1	47.9
Western Europe & Western offshoots	100.0	100.0	100.0	100.0	100.0	100.0

Note: Western offshoots = US, Canada, Australia, and New Zealand.
Source: Author's calculations based on Maddison (2001, p. 263, table B-20). a. Author's calculation.

Table 7   Percent share of world exports

	1870	1913	1950	1973	1998
UK	24.3	18.5	13.3	5.6	4.8
US	5.0	9.0	14.6	10.3	12.8
World	100.0	100.0	100.0	100.0	100.0

Source: Author's calculations based on Maddison (2001, pp. 361–362, tables F-2 and F-3).

Table 8   Merchandise exports as percent of GDP in 1990 prices

	1870	1913	1929	1950	1973	1998
UK	12.2	17.5	13.3	11.3	14.0	25.0
US	2.5	3.7	3.6	3.0	4.9	10.1
World	4.6	7.9	9.0	5.5	10.5	17.2

Source: Maddison (2001, p. 363, table F-5).

dynamic sector of the time. In contrast, US exports were one-fifth of UK exports, despite the two economies being similar in total size. Moreover, US exports were significantly primary products, particularly cotton.

As regards military and diplomatic hegemony, this was the era of the *Pax Britannica* in which Britannia 'ruled the waves' and the Royal Navy was globally supreme. Lastly, as regards international political hegemony, the era corresponded to the apogee of the British Empire which circled the globe, included 23 percent of the global population in 1913, and covered 24 percent of the Earth's total land area.[11] In sum, all the pieces making for currency hegemony were in place.

Reflection on the gold standard era of sterling hegemony is instructive. First, sterling hegemony rested on economic hegemony, but that was not simply a matter of economic size. It also reflected the UK's dominant position in global trade as reflected by export volumes and composition of exports (that is, manufactured goods). Export dominance entailed sterling invoicing, which created demand for sterling. Second, during the gold standard era, London was the world's dominant financial center, and by 1913 the UK accounted for approximately 50 percent of cumulative global capital investments (Darwin 2013, p. 185). As the largest global creditor, debts were sterling denominated which created a demand for sterling to service those debts. Additionally, the depth of Britain's capital markets and the *Pax Britannica* fostered confidence in sterling, giving London an advantage in attracting gold which was necessary to back the system. That confidence also advantaged Britain regarding the deposit interest rate settings needed to support its fiduciary issue (that is, money created in excess of gold reserves) by diminishing fears of a run from sterling to gold.

In sum, trade and finance interacted to jointly support sterling hegemony. Sterling hegemony was initially built on the UK's manufacturing and export dominance, which made Britain a global creditor and supported the growth of London as a financial center. Britain's creditor position and financial dominance then reinforced sterling hegemony. Among economists there is an inclination to explain currency hegemony in terms of real factors (for example, manufacturing and export dominance). Those factors were key to sterling hegemony, but Britain's financial dominance was also key.

11.   *British Empire*, see https://en.wikipedia.org/wiki/British_Empiredom.

                                    Journal compilation © 2022 Edward Elgar Publishing Ltd

6.2   Sterling decline (1919–1939)

The inter-war years correspond to the period of sterling's decline. The gold standard had been suspended with the onset of World War I in 1914, but the US returned to the gold standard in 1919 and the UK returned in 1925. That timing sequence speaks to the changed political economic conditions wrought by World War I.

In terms of the currency hegemony theoretical framework in Figure 1, the UK was a diminished power in multiple ways. Economically, the war had reduced the UK's net wealth via borrowing from the US and the Soviet Union's default on UK loans to Tsarist Russia. That decline in wealth is shown in Table 9. The UK had also lost export markets during the war, and both the US and Japan had increased their manufacturing and export capabilities (Crafts 2018, p. 120). Moreover, on the disastrous instruction of Chancellor of the Exchequer Winston Churchill, the UK returned to the gold standard at the pre-war gold exchange rate parity despite there having been significant price inflation since suspension of convertibility in 1914. That made UK exports less competitive, so that in the mid 1920s they were just 75 percent of their 1913 level (ibid., p. 120).

Regarding international political power, the UK was confronted by a 'Crisis of empire' (Tooze 2014, ch. 20). It was confronted by crisis in Ireland, Egypt, and India, with British imperial governance being challenged. Britain's military weakness was also exposed by Turkey in the 1922 conflict with Greece which Britain supported.

In short, the foundations of sterling's hegemonic standing had been substantially weakened. Furthermore, side by side with those adverse developments, the US had transformed from a debtor into a creditor, enhancing its relative power, which is critical in understanding currency hegemony. As shown by Eichengreen (2011, pp. 30–37), the US dollar was already in position to challenge sterling, having become the dominant form of FX reserves by 1925.

Despite those unfavorable conditions, sterling continued to be the hegemonic currency, albeit a limping hegemon. One reason was that the US was far less engaged in international trade, as shown earlier in Tables 7 and 8. Consequently, sterling export invoicing still dominated dollar invoicing, maintaining the demand for sterling. A second reason was that sterling still benefitted from the support of Britain's colonial governments and the Dominion countries (for example, Australia, New Zealand, and South Africa), which kept their FX reserves in sterling out of loyalty to Britain (Eichengreen 2011, p. 37). A third reason was US domestic politics, which were marked by isolationism. The US polity was not ready for international prime time, which meant the dollar was not ready for hegemony.

Moreover, the window of opportunity was short-lived, and closed with the Wall Street crash of 1929 and the onset of the Great Depression which triggered a global turn to trade

Table 9   UK overseas assets and liabilities, 1913–1951 (billion pounds at current value at year end)

	Assets (billions of pounds)	Liabilities (billions of pounds)	Net assets (billions of pounds)	Ratio of net assets to GDP
1913	4.6	0.4	4.2	1.8
1924	6.8	1.6	5.2	1.3
1937	5.3	1.3	4.0	0.9
1951	6.9	7.6	−0.7	−0.5

Source: Matthews et al. (1982, p. 128, table 5.2) cited in Chick (2020, p. 308).

protectionism. In 1931 the UK went off the gold standard and suspended the right to convert, and the US followed suit in 1933. The analytical point is that the inter-war years show how currency hegemony has both economic and political foundations.

6.3   Dollar hegemony 1.0: the Bretton Woods era (1946–1971)

The next sub-period was the Bretton Woods era, which is widely regarded as inaugurating the contemporary era. However, it was much more transitional, being a mix of old and new. The old was the continuation of an official monetary role for gold: the new was the inauguration of dollar hegemony.

As regards gold, central banks committed to convert government official balances into gold, but private sector agents had no such right. The official gold price was set at $35 per ounce, reflecting that the dollar was now the standard. Differentiated convertibility rights immediately created a dual gold market in which the private market price slightly exceeded the official price.

Institutionally, the new features of Bretton Woods were: provision of balance of payments adjustment assistance, the right to adjust exchange rates in response to persistent unsustainable deficits, and retention of financial capital controls. Those arrangements differentiated the Bretton Woods gold standard from the classical gold standard's *laissez-faire* position. Deficit countries were given adjustment assistance, the semi-fixed exchange rate system gave some flexibility but guarded against competitive devaluation, and capital movement was restricted.

Reflecting the transfer of power and the new political economic order of dollar hegemony, the Bretton Woods arrangements represented the US policy position and stopped short of Keynes's (UK position) bancor proposal which sought to create an international clearing union in which surplus countries would have to help the adjustment process by importing more.[12]

6.3.1   Foundations of the new hegemony

In terms of the theoretical framework in Figure 1, after World War II everything was in place for the dollar to become hegemonic. Among Western countries, the US was the undisputed economic, military, and international political hegemon. In effect, it occupied the equivalent place Britain had occupied in 1873.

As regards economic power, the US had the largest and most productive economy. It already had the advantages of natural resource bounty, scale of domestic markets, and more modern factories owing to its more recent industrialization. To this were added the advantages of no war destruction and the free transfer of a huge amount of European scientific capital.[13] Consequently, the US was the globally dominant manufacturing power and had a robust current account position. Those features were key to

12.   *Bancor:* see https://en.wikipedia.org/wiki/Bancor.
13.   Part of that transfer was the pre-war flight of scientists from continental Europe, which was symbolized by the Manhattan Project that built the atom bomb using that acquired expertise. Another part of the transfer was the extraordinary (and little known) September 1940 Tizzard transfer. Fearing that Britain would be overrun by Germany and its scientific knowledge captured, Winston Churchill authorized Sir Henry Tizzard to freely transfer to the US all the UK's top-secret novel military technology which included radar, sonar, the jet engine, the rocket engine, plastic explosives, gyroscopic gunsights, and self-sealing fuel tanks. After the war, the

   Journal compilation © 2022 Edward Elgar Publishing Ltd

the establishment of dollar hegemony 1.0, just as they were to the establishment of sterling hegemony. They are necessary conditions for hegemony under a gold standard regime. However, as argued below in Section 6.5, they are not necessary in a non-gold standard regime. Part of economists' misunderstanding of contemporary dollar hegemony stems from continuing to think they are.

As regards finance, the US was the recipient of large amounts of continental European emigree gold. Most importantly, it was the recipient of the UK's accumulated imperial treasure. In World War I, the US profited by supplying the British and French militaries and became a net creditor, but Britain also remained a large international creditor. World War II changed that, and Britain became a net debtor as shown in Table 9. Most importantly, the debt to the US was dollar denominated, placing the boot on the US foot as Britain now needed dollars to service its debts.[14]

As regards military power, the US ended World War II with a large modern military, a huge modern defense industry, and was in possession of all the latest military technology, some of which Britain had freely transferred in 1940 as part of the Tizzard transfer (see footnote 13). In effect, the *Pax Americana* replaced the *Pax Britannica*. After the Spanish–American War of 1898 the US had begun the process of developing overseas military bases. World War II and the Cold War catapulted that process, with the US acquiring permanent massive military and naval garrisons in Japan, South Korea, and Western Europe, and the number of permanent foreign deployments has only grown with time. That expansion symbolizes the US polity's rejection of isolationism which inhibited dollar hegemony in the inter-war years.

As regards international political power, here too World War II catapulted the US into global leadership. In 1947 the United Nations was headquartered in New York. The International Monetary Fund and World Bank – the multilateral financial institutions (MFIs) – were formed in 1944 and established in Washington, DC, with the US being given a dominant say and having veto power over amendments. The Inter-American Development Bank (IDB) was established in Washington, DC in 1959, again with US veto power. The North Atlantic Treaty Organization (NATO) was established in 1949, with the US the undisputed helmsman. US higher education institutions (for example, Harvard, Yale) became go-to destinations for foreign elites and powerful means for instilling US ideologies and loyalties to the US. Scholarships were provided under the Fulbright Program established in 1946, but the universities had sufficient charisma to attract student elites with or without assistance.

The MFIs were (and continue to be) important as most of their lending was done in dollars, thereby tying countries into the dollar network centered on Wall Street and requiring them to acquire dollars for repayment. The MFIs could also engage in politically motivated strategic lending to US political clients, turning on the loan spigot for friendly governments and turning it off for governments tagged as critical of the US. The multilateral organizations also won the loyalties of foreign elites by providing generously paid employment, with the IDB earning a special reputation as a revolving door placeholder for friendly Latin American politicians and elites.

US continued to drain German scientific human capital and willingly forgave Nazi scientists, as exemplified by the rocket scientist Werner von Braun who was instrumental in NASA's 1960s space program.

14.   The US profited in World War I and it profited again in World War II in the period September 1939–December 1941. The Roosevelt administration's famous Lend–Lease program charged top dollar prices for military supplies, hoovered up Britain's gold reserves, and saddled Britain with dollar denominated debts.

                    Journal compilation © 2022 Edward Elgar Publishing Ltd

In sum, all these organizations became powerful and enduring ways through which US international political influence could be disseminated and expanded. Lastly, the flipside of rising US international political power was declining British power caused by the two World Wars nearly bankrupting Great Britain, and the accelerated disintegration of the British Empire. The power and standing of others are always part of the theory of currency hegemony.

6.3.2   From bliss to distress (1960–1971)

Explaining the history of the Bretton Woods era is not the purpose of this paper, but some explanation is needed. That is because the problems experienced generated US responses that became the novel basis of restored dollar hegemony. Parenthetically, those responses were all taken in the US interest, speaking to the strength of realist international relations theory.

The late 1940s and 1950s were a period of international bliss for the US economy. The US was the world's dominant manufacturing power and the world needed dollars – to purchase commodities, to purchase US capital goods to rebuild, and to service dollar debts. The problem was limited supply of dollars and dollar credit. The shortage was filled by Marshall Plan assistance and foreign aid, US overseas military spending, US multinational corporation foreign direct investment (FDI), and growing US imports.[15] In effect, the US was operating without an external financial constraint.

That slowly changed. On the financial side, the emergence of the eurodollar market solved the problem of shortage of dollar credit. On the real side, Western Europe and Japan rebuilt, with significant focus on exporting aimed at solving their FX shortage problem. That challenged US manufacturing, increased exports to the US, moderated imports from the US, shifted the US into trade deficit, and shifted Europe and Japan into trade surplus. Additionally, the US adopted Keynesian policies that generated full employment, and by the mid 1960s it was also fighting a resource-consuming war in Vietnam. Those conditions caused inflation and aggravated the trade deficit problem.

That matrix of conditions undermined confidence in the long-term value of the dollar, encouraging governments (particularly France) to convert dollars into gold, thereby threatening to deplete US gold holdings and raising further confidence concerns. As currency hegemon, the US could not devalue the dollar as that would encourage further gold conversions. The only solution was retreat from full employment and empire (cut foreign 'aid' and foreign military spending) which the US was politically unwilling to do. Instead, in August 1971 the US suspended governments' right to convert dollars into gold and floated the dollar.

Three closing points should be made. First, the Bretton Woods system was a gold standard, and the gold standard always imposes the discipline of convertibility on the hegemon which the US was unwilling to live by. Second, the US response was motivated by national self-interest. That is summed up in US Treasury Secretary John Connally's famous comment upon suspension of convertibility: 'The dollar is our currency but it's your problem.' Third, the eurodollar market contributed to undermining dollar hegemony 1.0 by solving the shortage of dollar credit. That reduced the need for dollars supplied via US FDI, US government overseas spending, and the US current account. However, from a longer-term perspective, the eurodollar market can be

15.   This was the era of massive FDI in Europe by US multinationals like GM, Ford, Chrysler, IBM, and Eastman Kodak. Greenfield investments stimulated European recovery and provided the dollars with which to buy US capital goods.

viewed as the beginning of dollar hegemony 2.0, as it established dollar denominated international lending in foreign financial markets. That has made foreign banks susceptible to bank runs that their national central banks cannot solve. Consequently, those central banks have become dependent on the Federal Reserve's willingness to supply emergency liquidity as happened in the 2008 global financial crisis via the provision of central bank currency swaps, an arrangement which continues.

6.4   The decade of dollar distress (1971–1980)

The Bretton Woods system was the US's first engagement with dollar hegemony. It worked well until the US became a deficit country and subject to the disciplines of gold standard convertibility, at which stage it was abandoned.

The ensuing decade of the 1970s was a decade of dollar distress in which hegemony was in doubt. Ultimately, dollar hegemony was salvaged and reconstructed, with the new system of hegemony that emerged in the 1980s being significantly different regarding the way it operates and the outcomes it permits. Moreover, as also argued by Vernengo (2021), dollar hegemony 2.0 has proven even more dominant than dollar hegemony 1.0. Hudson (1972 [2021]) brilliantly intuited and anticipated the shape of the new system with his construct of 'super-imperialism' which was informed by a Marxist finance capital perspective, awareness of the tacit imperial nature of the US international project, and awareness of the fact that Treasury bonds are promises to pay fiat money.

6.4.1   A sneak peak ahead

The differences in structure and outcome between dollar hegemony 1.0 and 2.0 are easily visible in the data. Table 10 shows that US GDP was 40 percent of global GDP in 1960, but only 22 percent in 2014. Figure 7 shows the US trade balance as a share of GDP for the period 1800–2018. Until the very end of the Bretton Woods period, the US ran a trade surplus. Since then, it has run persistent large deficits that peaked at 6 per cent of GDP in 2006. That shows trade surplus is no longer a requirement for dollar hegemony. Figure 8 shows the US current account as a share of GDP for the period 1960–2022. Until near the very end of the Bretton Woods period, the US ran a current account surplus. Thereafter, it shifted into growing deficits, which peaked at 6 percent of GDP in 2006. That shows current account surpluses are no longer necessary for dollar hegemony.[16]

Table 10   US GDP as percent of global GDP

1960	1970	1980	1990	2000	2010	2014
40%	36%	26%	27%	31%	23%	22%

Source: Patton (2016).

16.   One of the surprising features to contemporary eyes is how small external deficits were as a percentage of GDP, yet they were still able to destabilize the system. That reflects two features. First, the era was pre-Neoliberal globalization, so that trade was a much smaller share of GDP (see Palley 2018). Second, the gold standard was unaccommodating of imbalances owing to the discipline of convertibility.

                    Journal compilation © 2022 Edward Elgar Publishing Ltd

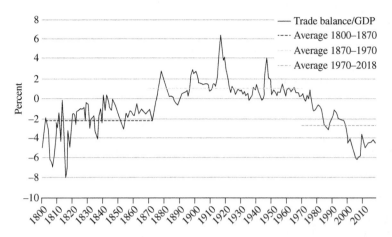

Source: Reinbold and Wen (2019).

Figure 7   US goods trade balance as a percentage of GDP, 1800–2018

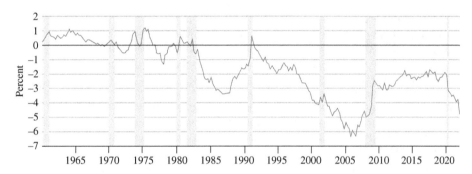

Note: Gray bars are periods of recession.
Source: FRED, St. Louis Federal Reserve Bank, https://fred.stlouisfed.org/series/USAB6BLTT02STSAQ.

Figure 8   US total current account balance as a percentage of GDP, 1960–2022

The above data show the diminished significance of relative size of GDP and the external balance (trade and current account) for currency hegemony. That distinguishes dollar hegemony 2.0 from both dollar hegemony 1.0 and sterling hegemony. Previously impossible trade and current account deficits have become the norm. That became apparent almost immediately after the 1971 suspension of convertibility. There was an immediate dollar depreciation that briefly improved US external balance position, and thereafter the shift to persistent large external deficits set in.

The key to the new pattern is absence of convertibility combined with increased demand for US assets. Bretton Woods dollar hegemony was built on US industrial might and the ability to run trade surpluses. Neoliberal dollar hegemony is built on the standing of the US as the center of global capitalism. The failure of mainstream economists to appreciate this tectonic shift is why they have persistently misinterpreted the US trade deficit as a harbinger of dollar collapse (Bergsten 1987; 2009a; 2009b; Roubini and Setser 2005).

Dollar hegemony has been restored and strengthened despite the decline in conventional measures of US economic power, indicating conventional economic power has become less significant. Instead, dollar hegemony 2.0 rests on the elevation of financial market power, combined with military and international political power which continued to accumulate in the Bretton Woods era.

As argued below, dollar hegemony 2.0 should be understood as part of Neoliberalism, which is a political economic ideology that has been adopted by national elites globally and has informed the design of the global economic system. Viewed in that light, dollar hegemony 2.0 is the capstone of the Neoliberal system, an integral component of the system rather than a separate phenomenon.

6.4.2   The remaking of dollar hegemony

The 1970s saw implementation of piecemeal changes that eventually aggregated into dollar hegemony 2.0. The first decisive change was suspension of dollar convertibility which forced foreign central banks into holding US Treasury bonds, creating a dollar Treasury bill standard in place of gold (Hudson 1972 [2021]). In that fashion, foreign surplus economies implicitly financed US overseas imperial activity. Meanwhile, US Treasury bills were simply promises to repay dollars which are issued by the Federal Reserve Bank.

That is the key feature of dollar hegemony 2.0. The US issues debt in its own currency on which it cannot default unless it chooses to.[17] However, that left unresolved willingness to hold those bonds and the exchange rate. Unwillingness to hold bonds would adversely affect interest rates, while unwillingness to hold dollars would depreciate the dollar and lower the dollar's overseas purchasing power. Dollar hegemony 2.0 has closed those holes by locking the world economy into the dollar.

A second critical development was the US–Saudi accord of 1974 (see Gwertzman 1974) whereby Saudi Arabia agreed to sell oil only in dollars in exchange for US military protection. That agreement reflected the role of US military and international political power, and it sent a global message. In the immediate moment, it plugged the financial consequences of OPEC's 1970s oil price increases. Longer term, it rendered the huge global energy and commodity sector a dollarized sector, thereby locking both producers and consumers of energy and commodities into the dollar financial network.[18]

A third related development was the petrodollar recycling system that developed on the back of the US–Saudi accord. That system had petrodollars deposited in New York, and then lent to other countries (particularly in Latin America) which needed dollar financing to cover the higher cost of oil. Though there were subsequent Latin American defaults (about which more below), the recycling system created dollar debts that required dollar income to service and deepened engagement in the dollar financial network.

A fourth critical development concerns European foreign exchange controls, which were progressively abolished beginning in the late 1970s. The process began with the

---

17.   Britain failed to do that. The gold standard bound it to convertibility, and the US lent in dollars in World War II.

18.   Henry Kissinger, the architect of the agreement, described it as 'a milestone in our relations with Saudi Arabia and the Arab countries in general (*New York Times*, June 9, 1974).' The only two Arab leaders who have threatened this status quo are Iraq's President Saddam Hussein and Libya's President Muammar Gaddafi. Both were deposed and executed, with the US being instrumental. As of 2022, Russia's President Putin has now challenged the status quo by demanding payment in rubles for Russian oil and gas.

                                    Journal compilation © 2022 Edward Elgar Publishing Ltd

UK's Thatcher government abolishing controls in June 1979. France and Italy dismantled their exchange controls in the second half of the 1980s. The importance of that abolition is it created a huge demand for US financial assets among private sector agents who had been substantially restricted from accumulating foreign currency denominated assets for a generation.[19] That flags two important points. First, it shows how dollar hegemony also depends on the actions of other countries, and not just the actions and policies of the US. Second, Thatcher's and Europe's embrace of unrestricted financial capital mobility was an ideological turn driven by the triumph of Neoliberal thinking, with its mantra of 'market forces.' The Neoliberal revolution in economic policy was substantially spawned in the US, led by the Chicago School of economics. That speaks to the importance of the international political hegemony of the US.[20]

6.5   Dollar hegemony 2.0: the dollar restored (1980–today)

At the end of the 1970s the dollar was still distressed. The 1980s and 1990s saw the restoration of dollar hegemony, with Treasury Secretary Rubin's (1995–1999) 'strong dollar' policy marking the completion of that process.

The first step was the high interest rate policy of Federal Reserve Chairman Paul Volker (actually begun in late 1979). High interest rates constitute classic monetary policy for strengthening a currency by increasing the return to holding the currency, but now they were applied to transform the economy. The goal was to squeeze inflation out of the economy and intimidate organized labor via high unemployment. Moreover, the message was that zero tolerance of inflation was here to stay.

The second step, which is intimately related to the first, was the remaking of the US economy in a Neoliberal image. That remaking and image are reflected in the phenomenon of financialization, which is a formulation of Neoliberalism that favors finance capital (Hudson 2021; Palley 2007; 2021). The key feature of Neoliberal financialization has been redistribution of income from labor to capital, plus a shift in the composition of capital income toward finance capital.

Dollar hegemony requires that the US be the center of global capitalism. Neoliberal financialization contributed to that by hugely increasing the attractiveness of US capital in terms of profit rate, low taxation, business friendly corporate governance, and labor unfriendly economic policy. Asset price inflation supported by monetary policy is another component of the US Neoliberal financialization model and it has helped draw financial capital to the US, thereby bolstering dollar hegemony.[21]

19.   Helleiner (1994) also emphasizes the importance of the elimination of capital controls in the making of financial globalization, explaining it in terms of cross-country competitive deregulation. The focus and argument are slightly different here, being the making of dollar hegemony. There is also the separate additional question of the impacts of abolishing capital controls on the UK and Europe.

20.   Leading figures at Chicago were Milton Friedman and George Stigler. Friedman had an especially strong influence on Thatcher via the Institute for Economic Affairs (IEA), which is the British analog of the American Enterprise Institute. The specific influence of Friedman was visible in Thatcher's embrace of Monetarism. The influence of Neoliberalism was visible in her embrace of privatization, small government, and anti-trade-unionism.

21.   The above argument regarding financialization contrasts with Vernengo (2021) who argues that capital interests brought down Bretton Woods to bring down Keynesianism. The view in this paper is different. Bretton Woods collapsed owing to the unacceptable restraint on US

The above domestic US agenda was complemented by a Neoliberal international economic agenda. At the center of the international agenda has been globalization which is marked by increased trade, increased FDI, and the creation of a new disarticulated global production network. Globalization has complemented the domestic Neoliberal agenda, helping shift the distribution of income by reducing the wage share. It has done this by putting manufacturing in the crosshairs of global labor competition, and in doing so it has also destroyed unions which were a political opponent of Neoliberalism (Palley 2018).

That globalization effect was enhanced by Treasury Secretary Rubin's 'strong dollar' policy which appreciated the exchange rate and put additional downward pressure on manufacturing wages. The strong dollar policy also benefitted various capital interests. Wall Street benefitted as the strong dollar increased its capacity to buy foreign assets and increased the need for US trade deficit financing which was recycled back into US financial markets. US MNCs benefitted because it lowered the dollar cost of foreign sourcing, thereby increasing margins on their US sales of foreign sourced production. And Big Box retailers like Walmart benefitted because it lowered the costs of manufactured imports which those retailers sell.

In addition to increasing the profitability of US capital, globalization has increased the need for and standing of the dollar. With global economic activity substantially executed in dollars, globalization has increased the need for dollar financing for trade and FDI. That has increased seignorage and the 'golden crumb' from dollar denominated commercial lending. It has also increased US geopolitical power by increasing the necessity of access to the US controlled global financial system plumbing.

Furthermore, global Neoliberalism has increased inequality in countries across the board. Increased inequality tends to increase the demand for wealth as the rich save more. That has been good for US assets, and by extension the dollar, as the US has been re-engineered to be the place to hold capital. For wealthy foreigners, the US has security of property rights and US citizens are strongly pro-property rights; taxation is friendly toward capital; and, as shown by the Pandora Papers, the US is friendly to inflows of ill-gotten assets with state law (for example, Delaware) permitting shell companies that provide ownership annonymity.

The globalization agenda has been pushed using the US's international political power, exercised through the multilateral institutions. As noted earlier, Latin American countries incurred large dollar debts in the 1970s, but Mexico defaulted in 1982, triggering a shutdown of private lending to the region. The US organized a bail-out and the IMF stepped in to provide credit, but the condition was that Latin America accept the Neoliberal program widely referred to as the 'Washington Consensus.' That program opened Latin American economies to US investors while removing capital controls, thereby further integrating Latin America into the dollar sphere. The episode showcases US hegemony. It also shows the role of local elites which, in Latin America, embraced the program as a way of looking after their interests. That underscores

---

(footnote 21 continued)

hegemony posed by gold convertibility. Ironically, Bretton Woods inhibited the US's ability to pursue Keynesian policy. Capital controls persisted long after the 1971 collapse of Bretton Woods and were only abolished with the triumph of Neoliberalism. That said, the bringing down of Keynesianism (writ large as social democratic macroeconomic policy) was necessary for the restoration of dollar hegemony because post-war Keynesianism tended to put labor interests ahead of those of capital.

how dollar hegemony is a product of both US power and the choices of other countries.[22]

Throughout the 1980s and 1990s the IMF was a critical institutional force driving globalization and integration into dollar dominated finance. This was done via 'conditionality' of its balance of payments assistance which required countries adopt the 'Washington Consensus' economic policy program, and through its dominance of regional policy discourse. The IMF has acted as a mix of bail-out provider, credit enforcement agency, loan pusher, and promoter of export-led growth that makes countries dependent on the US market (about which more below).[23]

Another soft-power-driven aspect of the international agenda was regional and international trade agreements: the North American Free Trade Agreement (NAFTA) and the GATT Uruguay round that established the World Trade Organization (WTO). Those agreements enabled the new international production system of offshore outsourcing and global supply chains. They also established a global regime of international property rights (IPR). Both have greatly increased US multinational corporation profits, which has increased the value and attractiveness of US capital (Schwartz 2019). Enhanced IPR have especially benefitted the US as it is the world's leader in ownership and production of intellectual property (Soskice 2022). Additionally, the new global production arrangements have increased dollar engagement to the extent that the global supply chain is invoiced in dollars.

Lastly, in contrast to the Bretton woods era, the phenomenon of emerging market export-led growth has been transformed to support dollar hegemony. In the Bretton Woods era, German export-led growth threatened the dollar by creating trade deficits. In the 1970s, Japanese export-led growth created trade deficits and threatened US manufacturing. In the Neoliberal era, those adverse effects have been sidestepped by abandonment of convertibility and abandonment of domestic manufacturing in favor of global sourcing.

Palley (2006) describes the new relationship between export-led growth and dollar hegemony as constituting a Keynesian 'buyer of last resort' theory of currency hegemony.[24] The logic is as follows. Export-led growth economies are short of demand and rely on the US market to provide demand. They also rely on an undervalued real exchange rate to ensure competitiveness. Consequently, they must hold their trade surpluses in dollars or else their currency will appreciate (and the dollar depreciate), which increases demand for dollars. That situation is exemplified by China, and the logic also applies to Germany and Japan which have been unable to abandon their export-led growth models.

The net result is that export-led growth has been transformed into a system that is supportive of dollar hegemony. It provides the US with real resources (that is, imports); it increases the demand for dollars to conduct international trade; it strengthens the demand for US assets; it bolsters Wall Street financial interests by promoting a

22.   The US and the IMF also sought to implement a similar program in East Asia after the East Asian financial crisis of 1997, but that attempt was significantly rebuffed by East Asian countries.
23.   A recent egregious example of such behavior was the 2018 record-sized loan to the center-right Macri government of Argentina, made prior to the election at the pushing of the US government which sought to help President Macri win the election.
24.   Schwartz (2019, pp. 499–503) has independently made a similar argument, also emphasizing how export-led growth integrates the financial sectors of foreign countries into the US financial sector.

strong dollar; and it integrates the financial sectors of foreign countries into the US financial sector via the process of recycling trade surpluses.

In sum, the abandonment of dollar convertibility, the petrodollar/commodity pricing system, the foreign country abandonment of capital controls, the remaking of the US economy in a Neoliberal image, and the inauguration of Neoliberal globalization combined to create a new economic matrix that has supported dollar hegemony 2.0. The deep foundations of dollar hegemony 2.0 remain the same as those of dollar hegemony 1.0 (and sterling hegemony before that): economic power, military power, and international political power. However, the way the two systems look and operate is completely different as they rest on entirely different economic models.

6.6   Dollar hegemony 2.0: ideologically coordinated but not planned

It is tempting to view dollar hegemony 2.0 as a planned system, but it is not. Instead, it is the outcome of an evolving US response to challenges and constraints, with that response being guided by the political economic ideology of Neoliberalism. That ideology has guided and coordinated the interests of capital, making it look as if dollar hegemony 2.0 were planned.

Neoliberalism stands behind dollar hegemony 2.0, and class interest stands behind Neoliberalism. That means class interest stands behind dollar hegemony 2.0. This aspect of dollar hegemony is strangely absent in the IPE literature. The US establishment claims dollar hegemony is in the national interest (see Smart 2018), but the above argument suggests it is in capital's interest.[25]

The significance of Neoliberal ideology points to the critical role of mainstream economics. As argued in Palley (2012, ch. 11), Neoliberalism is deeply informed by mainstream economics, which provides the basis for its core claims about the efficiency of market economies. Beyond that, economics has provided the policy specifics of Neoliberalism. Capital interests have been guided in their thinking by economics. Economics has informed, helped coordinate, and rationalized capital's choices. Those choices have then been politically sold using the libertarian rhetoric of Neoliberalism.

Though dollar hegemony 2.0 has ended up being the destination, it was not foreseen. That is illustrated by the fact that mainstream economists have continued to perceive the dollar through the lens of manufacturing and trade, which was the lens of the gold standard and dollar hegemony 1.0. Consequently, many have persistently thought large US trade and current account deficits would trigger a crisis. That view is exemplified by Bergsten (1987; 2009a; 2009b), who was an influential advocate and promoter of the Neoliberal globalization policies that have enabled dollar hegemony 2.0, yet who also worried about a dollar collapse for 35 years. Nouriel Roubini (Roubini and Setser 2005) famously predicted a dollar crash would trigger a global financial crisis. The dollar crash never happened, but the global financial crisis (2008) did. The notion of dollar collapse has also been embraced by progressives who argued that the hollowing out of manufacturing created trade deficits that posed a financial threat (Faux 2002).

---

25.   National interest is a substantially empty construct absent reference to who defines national interest. Elites always have an incentive to claim their policy actions are in the national interest as that provides a cloak which works to their advantage.

                    Journal compilation © 2022 Edward Elgar Publishing Ltd

7   THE GLOBAL EMBRACE OF DOLLAR HEGEMONY

Contemporary dollar hegemony is a global financial system organized on the US dollar, the fulcrum of which is US financial markets operating within the context of a US and global economy shaped by Neoliberalism. The previous section traced the sequence of major developments that have contributed to making dollar hegemony.

In telling that story there is a danger of overemphasizing the will of the US and overlooking the role of other countries. Dollar hegemony rests on US hegemony, which includes military might. Undoubtedly, the US has used that might, especially in Latin America – occasionally directly (as in Chile in 1973) and often indirectly by putting its heavy thumb on the democratic scale in favor of friendly governments. However, dollar hegemony has not been imposed by force. Instead, it has been embraced willingly through the interactive combination of market forces and support of foreign elites.

7.1   Foreign elites and the voluntary embrace of dollar hegemony

In 1979 the UK abolished capital controls, and France and Italy abandoned them in the 1980s. As noted earlier, that abolition was an important step in the making of dollar hegemony, but it was done voluntarily by foreign governments. Understanding that abolition begins with recognition that the Thatcher government was ultra-Neoliberal. That points to how foreign embrace of dollar hegemony was driven by elites who viewed the Neoliberal model as advancing their class interests.

One benefit was the ability to invest in US financial assets. A second benefit was that the removal of capital controls enables financial markets to pressure policy via the threat of exit, thereby enabling a cross-country competitive dynamic for deregulation and pro-business policies. Much attention has been paid to how globalization has promoted a race to the bottom in labor standards, with emerging market economies pressuring wages in industrialized economies. However, there is also a less talked about symmetric capital-based race to bottom that operates via financial markets. The ability to exit is key, which gives elites an incentive to implement capital mobility.[26] Just as the US capitalist class has benefitted from the adoption of Neoliberalism, so too have foreign country capitalist classes. Though Neoliberalism has entailed dollar hegemony, foreign elites have still gained from it.

The embrace of dollar hegemony was a political process, and that process was facilitated by ideological developments. That leads back to the multiple channels of US soft power. Particularly important is the capture of economics. As noted earlier (see footnote 20), Mrs Thatcher was an early believer in Milton Friedman's Chicago School of economics. That view is now widely adopted by the European and global economics profession, albeit caveated by varying degrees of market failure. The Chicago view promotes free trade and capital movement which are necessary building blocks of dollar hegemony. Consequently, economists have both inculcated and rationalized foreign elite support, putting the idea there if it was not already there, and strongly justifying it if it was.

26.   Regarding taxation, there is some evidence that the US has led the race to the bottom, acting as a Stackelberg leader which has cut its own corporate tax rates and led other countries down that path (Kumar and Quinn 2012).

   Journal compilation © 2022 Edward Elgar Publishing Ltd

The IMF was especially influential in pushing the embrace of dollar hegemony in Latin America, both via simple advocacy and by conditioning balance of payments assistance on the adoption of the Washington Consensus program. Belief in the merits of financial capital mobility is an enduring tenet of the IMF, though it is now verbally hedged to inoculate versus the political backlash against Neoliberal globalization. The creed is captured in a 1997 official speech by IMF Managing Director Stanley Fischer, who was the US appointee and a liberal former professor of macroeconomics at MIT. The policy goal was to amend the IMF's Articles of Association to make unrestricted financial capital mobility the IMF's baseline and a condition of membership. To that end, Fischer (1997, para. 11) argues:

> Put abstractly, free capital movements facilitate a more efficient allocation of global savings, and help channel resources into their most productive uses, thus increasing growth and welfare. From the individual country's perspective, the benefits take the form of increases in both the potential pool of investible funds, and the access of domestic residents to foreign capital markets. From the viewpoint of the international economy, open capital accounts support the multilateral trading system by broadening the channels through which developed and developing countries alike can finance trade and investment and attain higher levels of income. International capital flows have expanded the opportunities for portfolio diversification, and thereby provided investors with the potential to achieve higher risk-adjusted rates of return. And just as current account (trade) liberalization promotes growth by increasing access to sophisticated technology, and export competition has improved domestic technology, so too capital account liberalization can increase the efficiency of the domestic financial system.

Though the attempt to change the IMF's Articles failed, it speaks to economists' and the IMF's thinking.

7.2   Currency competition and the voluntary embrace of dollar hegemony

A second driver of foreign embrace of dollar hegemony is market forces associated with currency competition. The forces of currency competition can be divided into push and pull factors, though to an extent they are mirrors of each other. Push factors are domestic, and they push foreign elites to engage with the dollar. Pull factors are external and pull foreign elites to engage with the dollar.

Push and pull factors operate in every economy, but they are most easily illustrated by reference to developing economies. The classic push factor is domestic monetary failure associated with high inflation. Under such conditions, domestic money loses its store of value and invoicing capability. In the extreme there can be dollarization whereby the domestic currency is abandoned for the dollar. Another reason for shifting to the dollar and dollar denominated assets is domestic tax evasion. That can encourage invoicing in dollars, with payment into foreign bank accounts and only partial repatriation. Additionally, developing countries often have high income inequality and are subject to political instability. That can implicate the security of property rights and give reason to park wealth outside a country.

As regards pull factors, developing countries have thin asset markets with few assets for saving and holding wealth, so elites are incentivized to seek offshore stores of wealth. That practice is also often motivated by tax evasion, which is a push factor. Broadly speaking, the US has a superior macroeconomic environment measured by inflation, exchange rate volatility, and growth rate volatility. It also has thick liquid financial markets that offer a wide array of assets with varying risk-return properties, and it is favorably disposed to property. Those characteristics make it attractive for foreign elites to hold US financial assets, which pulls money into the US.

The US is also a major tax haven and facilitates hiding and laundering wealth, as revealed by the Pandora Papers (Vittori 2021). Delaware, Nevada, and South Dakota all have corporate secrecy provisions that shelter money, which pulls wealth out of other countries.[27]

The set of push and pull factors connect with the economic logic embedded in the currency cone which was discussed earlier. First, the greater depth and the favorable political economic characteristics (that is, favorable to capital) of US financial markets explains the logic of the pull of the dollar versus weak and junk currencies. Moreover, migration from weak and junk currencies further strengthens the advantage of the dollar, creating a form of cumulative causation.

Second, attention has focused on the pull out of weak and junk currencies, but the pull also applies to strong and minor major currencies. That is evident in shrinking small country stock markets as companies transfer listings to larger markets. The process is exacerbated by the financial advantage conferred on US companies by dollar hegemony. Thus, US corporations receive superior valuations and have easier access to credit, enabling them to buy foreign rivals. Those rivals are then de-listed from stock markets and their headquarters transferred.

Third, the above cumulative causation logic of dollar hegemony suggests it should be of policy concern to other countries. A national currency and national financial markets confer major economic benefits. A national currency yields seignorage for public finances and enables government to manage economic activity. National financial markets may facilitate entrepreneurship, capital accumulation, and households' ability to provision for the future. Those features are good for macroeconomic stability, growth, and societal well-being. The cumulative causation logic of dollar hegemony puts those benefits at risk by undermining the national currency and national financial markets, which may warrant a protective policy response. Financial competition may be like cultural competition, endogenously producing an increasingly tilted playing field by systematically increasing the advantages of the advantaged.

8   CONCLUSION

This paper has revisited dollar hegemony, emphasizing that it is a fundamentally political economic phenomenon. Dollar hegemony rests on the economic, military, and international political power of the US and is manifested through market forces. The paper argued that there have been two eras of dollar hegemony which were marked by different models. Dollar hegemony 1.0 corresponded to the Bretton Woods era (1946–1971). Dollar hegemony 2.0 corresponds to the Neoliberal era (1980–today). The 1970s were an in-between decade of dollar distress during which dollar hegemony was reseeded. The deep foundation of both versions is US power, but the two versions have completely different economic operating systems. Dollar hegemony 1.0 rested on the trade and manufacturing dominance of the US after World War II. Dollar hegemony 2.0 rests on the Neoliberal reconstruction of the US and global economies which have made the US the center of global capitalism

---

27.   Worse yet, it facilitates illegal economic activity, tax evasion, and anti-social elite financial behavior in the global economy.

and the most attractive place to hold capital. It is a financial model and intrinsically connected to Neoliberalism.

Consideration of dollar hegemony leads to two further questions. One is whether there is a better way of organizing the world monetary order, which is associated with debate about the possibility of a new Bretton Woods (see Bibow 2022; Priewe 2022). The other is: what is the future of dollar hegemony?

REFERENCES

Bergsten, C. (1987), 'Economic imbalances and world politics,' *Foreign Affairs*, 65(4), 907–923.

Bergsten, C. (2009a), 'The dollar and the deficits: how Washington can prevent the next crisis,' *Foreign Affairs*, 88(6), 20–38.

Bergsten, C. (2009b), 'The dollar and the deficit,' VoxEU/CEPR, 27 November.

Bibow, J. (2022), '"King dollar" forever? Prospects for a New Bretton Woods,' *Review of Keynesian Economics*, 10(4), 559–579.

Caballero, R.J. (2006), 'On the macroeconomics of asset shortages,' NBER Working Paper No 12753, December.

Chick, M. (2020), *Changing Times: Economics, Policies, and Resource Allocation in Britain Since 1951*, Oxford: Oxford University Press.

Cohen, B. (1998), *The Geography of Money*, Ithaca, NY: Cornell University Press.

Crafts, N. (2018), 'Walking wounded: the British economy in the aftermath of World War I,' in S. Broadberry and M. Harrison (eds), *The Economics of the Great War: A Centennial Perspective*, London: CEPR Press, pp. 119–126.

Croteau, S. and P. Poast (2020), 'Dollars for oil,' *International Studies Perspectives*, 21, 132–137.

Cypher, J.M. (1987), 'Military spending, technical change, and economic growth: a disguised form of industrial policy?,' *Journal of Economic Issues*, 21(1), 33–59.

Cypher, J.M. (2016), 'Hegemony, military power projection and US structural economic interests in the periphery,' *Third World Quarterly*, 37(5), 800–817.

Darwin, J. (2013), *Unfinished Empire: The Global Expansion of Britain*, London: Bloomsbury Press.

Dessai, R. and M. Hudson (2021), 'Beyond dollar creditocracy: a geopolitical economy,' *Real World Economic Review*, 97(September), 20–39.

Eichengreen, B. (2011), *Exorbitant Privilege: The Rise and Fall of the Dollar and the Future of the International Monetary System*, Oxford: Oxford University Press.

Faux, J. (2002), 'Falling dollar, rising debt,' Viewpoints, Economic Policy Institute, Washington, DC, 26 September.

Fischer, S. (1997), 'Capital account liberalization and the role of the IMF,' Presented at the seminar 'Asia and the IMF,' Hong Kong, China, 19 September, available at: http://www.imf.org/external/np/apd/asia/FISCHER.HTM.

Gwertzman, B. (1974), 'Milestone pact is signed by US and Saudi Arabia,' *New York Times*, 9 June.

Hausmann, R. and F. Sturzenegger (2005), 'Dark matter makes the US deficit disappear,' *Financial Times*, 7 December.

Helleiner, E. (1994), *States and the Re-Emergence of Global Finance: From Bretton Woods to the 1990s*, Ithaca, NY: Cornell University Press.

Herr, H., J. Priewe, and A. Watt (2017), *Saving the Euro: Redesigning Euro Area Economic Governance*, Lexington, KY: SE Publishing.

Hudson, M. (1972 [2021]), *Super-Imperialism: The Origin and Fundamentals of US Domination*, 3rd edn, London: Pluto Press.

Hudson, M. (2021), 'Rent-seeking and asset price inflation: a total-returns profile of economic polarization in America,' *Review of Keynesian Economics*, 9(4), 435–460.

Khanna, A. and W.K. Winecoff (2020), 'The money shapes the order,' *International Studies Perspectives*, 21, 113–119.

Kumar, M.S. and D.P. Quinn (2012), 'Globalization and corporate taxation,' IMF Working Paper 12/252, Fiscal Affairs and Finance Department, International Monetary Fund, Washington, DC.

Liao, S. and D. McDowell (2015), 'Redback rising: China's bilateral swap arrangements and renminbi internationalization,' *International Studies Quarterly*, 59, 401–422.

Maddison, A. (2001), *The World Economy: A Millennial Perspective*, Development Centre Studies, Paris: OECD.

Matthews, R.C.O., C.H. Feinstein, and J.C. Odling-Smee (1982), *British Economic Growth, 1856–1973*, Stanford, CA: Stanford University Press.

Mazzucato, M. (2015), *The Entrepreneurial State: Debunking Public vs. Private Sector Myths*, London: Anthem Press.

McDowell, D. (2020), 'Payments power: the overlooked role of the dollar as the top international payments currency,' *International Studies Perspectives*, 21, 120–125.

Norrlof, C. (2020), 'The security foundations of dollar primacy,' *International Studies Perspectives*, 21, 126–132.

Norrlof, C. and P. Poast (2020), *Global Monetary Order and the Liberal Order Debate*, Symposium in *International Studies Perspectives*, 21, 109–153.

Oatley, T. (2015), *A Political Economy of American Hegemony: Buildups, Booms, and Busts*, New York: Cambridge University Press.

Palley, T.I. (2006), 'Why dollar hegemony is unhealthy,' *YaleGlobal*, 20 June, available at: https://archive-yaleglobal.yale.edu/content/why-dollar-hegemony-unhealthy.

Palley, T.I. (2007), 'Financialization: what it is and why it matters,' Levy Economics Institute of Bard College Working Paper No 525, Bard College, NY. (Published in E. Hein, T. Niechoj, P. Spahn, and A. Truger (eds) (2008), *Finance-Led Capitalism? Macroeconomic Effects of Changes in the Financial Sector*, Marburg: Metropolis-Verlag, pp. 29–60.)

Palley, T.I. (2011), 'The European Union needs a government banker,' *Challenge*, 54(July–August), 5–21.

Palley, T.I. (2012), *From Financial Crisis to Stagnation: The Destruction of Shared Prosperity and the Role of Economics*, Cambridge, UK: Cambridge University Press.

Palley, T.I. (2017), 'Fixing the euro's original sins: the monetary–fiscal architecture and monetary policy conduct,' *Real World Economics Review*, 81(September), 15–26.

Palley, T.I. (2018), 'Three globalizations, not two: rethinking the history and economics of trade and globalization,' *European Journal of Economics and Economic Policy*, 15(2), 174–192.

Palley, T.I. (2021), 'Financialization revisited: the economics and political economy of the vampire squid economy,' *Review of Keynesian Economics*, 9(4), 461–492.

Patton, M. (2016), 'US share in the global economy declines almost fifty percent,' Forbes.com, available at: https://www.forbes.com/sites/mikepatton/2016/02/29/u-s-role-in-global-economy-declines-nearly-50/?sh=158d5da15e9e.

Priewe, J. (2022), 'Old and new proposals for global monetary reform,' *Review of Keynesian Economics*, 10(4), 533–558.

Reinbold, B. and Y. Wen (2019), 'Historical US trade deficits,' *Economic Synopses*, No 13, Federal Reserve Bank of St. Louis, available at: https://research.stlouisfed.org/publications/economic-synopses/2019/05/17/historical-u-s-trade-deficits.

Roubini, N. and B. Setser (2005), 'Will the Bretton Woods 2 regime unravel soon? The risk of a hard landing in 2005–2006,' Paper Prepared for a Conference Organized by the Federal Reserve Bank of San Francisco, February, p. 5, available at: http://www.frbsf.org/economics/conferences/0502/Roubini.pdf.

Schwartz, H.M. (2019), 'American hegemony: intellectual property rights, dollar centrality, and infrastructure power,' *Review of International Political Economy*, 26(3), 490–519.

Siddique, A. (2022), 'US still spends more on military than next nine countries combined,' Blog, National Policy Priorities Project, 22 June.

Smart, C. (2018), 'The future of the dollar – and its role in financial diplomacy,' *National Interest*, 16 December.

Soskice, D. (2022), 'Rethinking varieties of capitalism and growth theory in the ICT era,' *Review of Keynesian Economics*, 10(2), 222–241.

Strange, S. (1989), 'Towards a theory of transnational empire,' in E. Czempial and J. Rosenau (eds), *Global Changes and Theoretical Challenges*, Lexington, KY: Rowman and Littlefield, pp. 161–176.

Tooze, A. (2014), *The Deluge: The Great War and the Remaking of Global Order*, London: Allen Lane.

Vernengo, M. (2021), 'The consolidation of dollar hegemony after the collapse of Bretton Woods: bringing power back in,' *Review of Political Economy*, 33(4), 529–551.

Vittori, J. (2021), 'Five things the United States can do to stop being a haven for dirty money,' Commentary, Carnegie Endowment for International Peace, 7 October.

Wang, H. (2020), 'China and the international financial system: challenging the United States or the liberal order?,' *International Studies Perspectives*, 21, 137–143.

Zimmerman, H. (2002), *Money and Security: Troops, Monetary Policy, and West Germany's Relation with the United States and Britain, 1950–1971*, New York: Cambridge University Press.

Review of Keynesian Economics, Vol. 10 No. 4, Winter 2022, pp. 57–70

Will the Chinese renminbi replace the US dollar?

Michael Pettis*
Peking University, Beijing, People's Republic of China

This article makes three related points. First, for China to upend the dominance of the US dollar and replace it, even partially, with the renminbi would require major – and probably disruptive – changes in China's financial markets and monetary policies. Second, the end of US-dollar dominance would probably come about only after specific actions were taken by US policymakers to limit the ability of foreigners to use US financial markets as the absorber of last resort of global savings imbalances. And third, the US economy and financial system absorbs nearly half of the world's savings imbalances (with much of the rest absorbed by the other major Anglophone economies, for many of the same reasons). A global economy without the US dollar as the dominant currency would also likely be one without large, persistent trade and savings imbalances. This would force substantial and potentially disruptive structural changes on economies whose growth depends partly on their ability to externalize the costs associated with their international 'competitiveness,' which in turn depends on distortions in the distribution of income between households and businesses.

Keywords: *reserve currency, China, dollar dominance, renminbi*

JEL codes: *F02, F30, F33*

1 INTRODUCTION

This article makes three related points. First, for China to upend the dominance of the US dollar and replace it, even partially, with the renminbi would require major – and probably disruptive – changes in China's financial markets and monetary policies. These would include Beijing giving up control of China's current and capital accounts, abandoning the moral hazard that underpins the Chinese growth model, and accepting a governance system in which the decisions of a wide range of authorities would be subject to a transparent and predictable legal process. While Beijing and the People's Bank of China (PBoC) often say they would like to see rising global use of the renminbi, they have also made clear that they are not willing to take any of these steps except in very limited and constrained ways.

Second, the end of US-dollar dominance would come about only after specific actions were taken by US policymakers to limit the ability of foreigners to use US financial markets as the absorber of last resort of global savings imbalances. It would require, in other words, a decision by Washington to undermine US-dollar dominance. That's because the world doesn't use the dollar because of American political pressure. The world uses the dollar because of the depth and flexibility of American financial

*   Email: michaelxpettis@gmail.com.

markets, their superior governance, and, above all, the willingness and ability of the US to accommodate and absorb the savings imbalances of the rest of the world, or, which is the same thing, its willingness and ability to run large trade deficits. Unless Washington were to intervene to limit these conditions, the rest of the world would be extremely unlikely to want to give up these benefits.

This leads directly to the third point. The US economy and financial system absorbs nearly half of the world's savings imbalances (with much of the rest absorbed by the other major Anglophone economies, for many of the same reasons). A global economy without the US dollar as the dominant currency would also likely be one without large, persistent trade and savings imbalances. This would force substantial and potentially disruptive structural changes on economies whose growth depends partly on their ability to externalize the costs associated with their international 'competitiveness,' which in turn depends on distortions in the distribution of income between households and businesses.

It is not just a coincidence that in economies that run large, persistent trade surpluses, whether high-income (Germany, Japan, the Netherlands, South Korea) or low-income (China, Malaysia, Vietnam), direct and indirect wages are lower relative to productivity than among their trading partners. This is because the various subsidies to manufacturing that underlie their international competitiveness must be paid for by the household sector, whether in the form of low wages, weak social safety nets, financial repression, depreciated currencies, environmental degradation, or some combination of these. Eliminating US trade deficits would require changes – with all the associated political implications – in the way income is distributed in these countries.

The irony is that the main beneficiary of the end of US-dollar dominance would be the US, and among the main losers China, along with other countries with large, persistent trade surpluses. In fact, more generally a world without US-dollar dominance would probably spell the end of the success of the Asian development model, even though it would be positive for the global economy overall.[1] This is because it would spell the end of a global trading system in which countries compete internationally mainly by directly or indirectly reducing the share their households retain of domestic GDP, and, with that, reducing their contribution to global consumption. Eliminating the global dominance of the US dollar, in other words, would eliminate a mechanism by which trade competition can systematically depress aggregate global demand.

But with so many major economies locked into structural domestic demand deficiencies, any policy that forces an elimination or sharp reduction of global trade imbalances would in the short term also force deep institutional changes on the global economy. These changes would likely be economically and even politically disruptive for many countries, especially those, like China, whose economies have become structured

---

1.   In the two to three decades after 1945, in a world of capital controls and limited trade imbalances, capital-importing Latin American economies were generally considered to be the most successful developing economies, and the ones most likely to converge to Western levels of income, while the East Asian economies struggled to achieve growth. By the 1970s and 1980s, the tables had turned completely and it was the high-savings capital-exporting East Asian economies that had vastly outperformed, while Latin America became bogged down in surging debt and unsustainable trade deficits. While the possible reasons for this are beyond the scope of this essay, it may have to do with important monetary and financial shifts in the 1970s and 1980s that saw huge increases in global trade imbalances and in the global export and import of capital.

                                    Journal compilation © 2022 Edward Elgar Publishing Ltd

around persistent trade surpluses and who have tried for many years, with almost no success, to rebalance domestic demand.

2 CAN THE RENMINBI BECOME AN ALTERNATIVE TO THE US DOLLAR?

The dollar is the most widely used currency in international trade not just because of network effects but for reasons that are even harder for other countries to replicate. The world uses the dollar because the United States has the deepest and most flexible financial markets, the clearest and most transparent corporate governance, and (in spite of recent sanctions on countries like Iran and Russia) the lowest amount of discrimination between domestic residents and foreigners.

These qualities attract the savings of foreigners, whether these are rich oligarchs who need to store money abroad, investment funds managing the savings of the wealthy and middle classes, central banks who want liquid, high-quality reserves, or even businesses and banks looking to diversify their operations by acquiring operations abroad. For another currency to compete with the US dollar, its home economy would have to provide similar conditions.

This further implies another, more important reason for the widespread use of the dollar. The global trading system is unbalanced, with several large economies – including those of China, Germany, Japan, Russia, and South Korea – locked into income distributions that reduce domestic consumption and force up savings rates. Weak consumption leads to weak investment from private businesses that depend mainly on local consumers to buy the goods they produce. These together lead to weak domestic demand. Because these economies suffer from deficient domestic demand, they must run large, persistent trade surpluses to absorb the production that drives their economies.

And this is where the US dollar matters. Surplus economies require deficit economies, which also means that surplus economies must acquire foreign assets in exchange for their surpluses. The United States – and to a lesser extent other Anglophone economies with similar markets and governance, like the United Kingdom – play their most important global trade role in providing these assets. The deficits that balance the surpluses of the surplus economies must automatically accrue in those countries in which the surplus economies acquire ownership of assets. It is in the US and the other Anglophone economies that they mostly choose to do so.[2]

3 CAN CENTRAL BANKS ACQUIRE OTHER ASSETS BESIDES US DOLLARS?

It helps in this context to consider the alternative assets surplus countries can accumulate. In principle, surplus-running economies can accumulate assets in other advanced

2. See Klein and Pettis (2020). For this reason, the US has no control at all over its capital account. This lack of control explains a phenomenon that many economists find puzzling. If foreign capital is 'pulled' into the US economy for domestic reasons, as many assume, the size of the US trade or current-account deficits should be positively correlated with US interest rates. The fact that they are either uncorrelated or, in certain periods, negatively correlated suggests that foreign capital isn't pulled into the US to respond to the needs of domestic American users of capital. Instead, it is 'pushed' into the US in response to the needs of foreign savers. But whether it is pulled or pushed, it must be balanced by a trade deficit.

economies besides the US, but with the exception of the European Union and perhaps Japan, none is big enough to balance more than a small share of the world's accumulated trade surpluses.

More importantly, Japan and the European Union (EU), along with most advanced, non-Anglophone economies, run persistent surpluses themselves, so they must be net acquirers of assets abroad. If foreigners were to acquire large amounts of assets in either of these two countries, in other words, Japan and the EU would either have to allow the undermining of their powerful export sectors, or they would have to recycle the foreign inflows with even greater outflows and reserve accumulation, with all of the damaging monetary consequences this would imply.

If China, for example, were to accumulate large Japanese yen reserves instead of US dollar reserves, the Bank of Japan would either have to tolerate enough of a rise in the international value of the yen to undermine its export sector and force the country into running deficits, or it would have to accumulate an equal amount of foreign reserves to neutralize the net impact of Chinese inflows. In the latter case, higher Chinese purchases of Japanese reserves would be matched by higher Japanese purchases of foreign-currency reserves, which would almost inevitably mean buying dollars. It would also mean uncontrolled expansion in the domestic Japanese money supply.

That's why, even as countries like China propose diversifying their reserves away from the USA, the most likely alternatives, the EU and Japan, will likely resist.[3] Some analysts argue that surplus-running countries can instead invest excess savings in the developing world, and while much of the developing world would welcome small persistent capital inflows, there are limits on their abilities to balance excess global savings. Developing economies currently absorb roughly a quarter to a fifth of global excess savings.[4] They would not be able to increase their shares meaningfully without causing significant domestic dislocations to their financial markets, and these, in turn, would make repayment very difficult. In fact, China has in the past several years reduced its already limited exports of capital to developing countries as the risks have become evident (see Horn et al. 2022).

Some analysts have also recently argued that, as a consequence of the sanctions imposed on Russia, the world is likely to see a shift in global reserve accumulation toward commodities (see Pozsar 2022). This, too, is unlikely. Countries like Russia, Iran, and Venezuela are all primarily commodity exporters, and because commodity prices tend to be positively correlated, these countries would have to accumulate reserves most aggressively when prices are high and their surpluses are large, and they would most likely have to monetize their reserves when prices are low and their economies are struggling. Not only would their reserve accumulation thus exacerbate the volatility of commodity prices, which would be damaging for their economies, but, more worryingly, their reserves would be most valuable when they needed them

3.   In the past few years, the Chinese press has made a great deal of noise about reductions in the portion of PBoC reserves held in US dollars, but there is much less here than meets the eye. First, the recorded decline is less than a few percentage points. Second, and more importantly, since 2017 the PBoC has largely stopped intervening in the currency. Instead, state-owned banks have acquired roughly $1 trillion in net foreign-exchange (FX) purchases on behalf of the PBoC. Without a breakdown in the composition of these 'hidden' reserves, we have no idea whether or not the PBoC has reduced or actually increased its direct and indirect exposure to US-dollar reserves but, given large surpluses in recent years and rising net financial inflows, it is almost certainly the case that its total exposure has increased.
4.   Benn Steil and Benjamin Della Rocca, Global Imbalances Tracker, Greenberg Center for Geoeconomic Studies, Council on Foreign Relations.

                          Journal compilation © 2022 Edward Elgar Publishing Ltd

least and least valuable when they needed them most. This is the opposite of what countries want from reserves.

China, of course, is the world's largest commodity importer, so at first it might seem to be in the opposite position of commodity-exporting countries like Russia, in which case accumulating commodity reserves instead of foreign assets might seem to make a lot of sense for its central bank. However, as the world's largest importer of commodities by far, especially industrial commodities, it turns out that China's economic performance is correlated with commodity prices in the same way as that of commodity exporters, only with the direction of causality reversed.

Whereas high commodity prices allow commodity exporters to grow more rapidly, when the Chinese economy is growing rapidly, its commodity consumption is likely to rise sharply, and given its disproportionate role in commodity markets, rising Chinese consumption will drive up the prices of commodities. When the Chinese economy is growing slowly, on the other hand, commodity prices are likely to drop. Commodity acquisition as a reserve strategy would exacerbate economic volatility and leave China, like commodity exporters, with reserves that are most valuable when it least needs them and least valuable when it presumably most needs them.

For many of the countries most determined to escape from the US dollar's dominance, in other words, investing in commodity reserves is likely to lock them into acquiring assets when prices are high and selling them when prices are low. Only smaller economies that are net importers of commodities are likely to benefit from investing a significant portion of their reserves in commodities, and even these have to worry about the positive correlation between global growth and commodity prices. The value of reserves should be either stable or inversely correlated with the performance of the underlying economy, and most global commodities are unlikely to satisfy this condition.[5]

4   FOREIGN DOLLAR ACCUMULATION DISTORTS THE US ECONOMY

As long as the global economy tolerates and encourages large, persistent imbalances, it is stuck, at least for now, with recycling a small share of excess global savings to developing countries and the rest to the US and other Anglophone economies.[6] And because of their open capital accounts and status as safe-haven investment destinations, the US and other Anglophone economies are stuck with persistent capital-account surpluses and the accommodating trade and current-account deficits, and must pay for the deficits with the export of ownership of domestic assets. They are the only stable, mature economies that are both willing and able to allow foreigners unfettered access to the acquisition of local assets or, which is the same thing, the only major economies willing and able to run the permanent trade deficits that accommodate the needs of foreign-surplus-running countries to acquire foreign assets.

This suggests something that many economists may find counter-intuitive. They assume that the US imports foreign capital because it needs foreign savings to bridge the gap between its own domestic savings and domestic investment, but this has the causality backwards. For years American businesses have had access to enormous amounts of cheap liquidity, with little desire to convert their easy access to global savings into productive investment. The investment constraint for American businesses

5.   The US dollar of course behaves in the opposite way. Its value tends to rise when global conditions are at their most unsettled, as we saw in the first half of 2022.
6.   Benn Steil and Benjamin Della Rocca, ibid. footnote 4.

                              Journal compilation © 2022 Edward Elgar Publishing Ltd

does not seem to be scarce, expensive savings but rather weak expected demand, as I will explain later in this article.

This matters a great deal. For economies whose domestic investment needs are not constrained by scarce savings and the high cost of capital, there is a cost to exporting ownership of domestic assets. This cost, as I will discuss below, effectively requires that the deficit economies must either allow unemployment to rise as net imports undermine local manufacturers, or, which is far more likely, they must create assets by encouraging a rise in household debt or in the fiscal deficit to counteract the domestic impact of their persistent deficits.

Before explaining the consequences, a brief digression. Some analysts have suggested that the issuer of a major reserve currency does not need to run persistent deficits, and in support they point to the current-account surpluses that the UK ran for much of the period when sterling was the world's leading currency (see, for example, Jones 2022). But, aside from the fact that a major currency under the gold standard exists under completely different circumstances than does the US dollar today (its main virtue being the credibility of its commitment to gold), the world didn't need sterling to be used to absorb excess savings at the time.

On the contrary, because investment in most countries at the time was constrained by scarce domestic savings, during much of the nineteenth century developing economies like the US, Canada, and Australia needed foreign savings to boost domestic investment. Rather than import savings, they wanted other economies to export them, which the UK duly did. In fact, the United States too was a net exporter of savings (it ran persistent surpluses) in the five decades ending in the 1970s, during a time when the world was rebuilding itself from two world wars and urgently needed to import savings.

The relevant point is not that the issuer of the global currency must run permanent deficits, but rather that it must run surpluses when the world wants to import scarce savings and must run deficits when the world wants to export excess savings. This is what it means to say that the issuer of the global currency must effectively give up control of its capital account to balance whatever the rest of the world requires.

5   WILL CHINA ABANDON CAPITAL CONTROLS?

Because the widespread global use of a currency is determined by the benefits that global households, businesses, and governments can obtain from the use of that currency, for the renminbi to replace the US dollar, a number of conditions have to be met that accommodate the needs of the global economy. The first and most obvious is that China would have to give up control of its capital account, allowing foreigners unfettered entry or exit into the Chinese financial markets as their own domestic needs dictated.

For example the Chinese financial system would have to accommodate a substantial reduction in net capital inflows during times of global confidence and growth, as capital flows into risky foreign ventures and economies. It would have to accommodate a substantial increase in net capital inflows during times of global economic or political uncertainty, when capital is looking for a safe haven.

What is more, whether or not the investment needs of Chinese businesses matched the change in inflows would be irrelevant. With an open capital account, the inflows would be driven by foreign considerations, not domestic; and without one, renminbi assets could not fulfill one of the fundamental roles of a dominant global currency, which is to allow non-residents to store excess savings as a form of insurance that is freely available to the investor in times of need.

But unfettered entry and exit of foreign capital requires that China's financial system accommodate these flows – which means absorbing the consequent currency volatility, the changes in interest rates, and the domestic money supply, or all three – regardless of whether or not Beijing's financial and monetary authorities approve of these changes. This is just a restatement of the *impossible trinity*, also called the Mundell–Fleming model, which posits that if an economy allows the free inflow and outflow of capital, it cannot simultaneously maintain a fixed exchange rate and independent monetary policy (Mundell 1963).

Can China accommodate the unfettered entry and exit of foreign capital in the same way as the US does? Almost certainly not, and this has to do with the very different structures of their respective economies and financial systems. There are at least three important such differences. First, the export and tradable goods sectors represent a greater share of the Chinese economy than they do of the American economy. According to the World Bank, exports comprise 19 percent of the Chinese economy, versus 10 percent of the US. This means, among other things, that the Chinese economy is more vulnerable to currency volatility than is the US economy. A period of rapid strengthening of the renminbi would consequently be more damaging to the Chinese economy than an equivalent strengthening of the US dollar would be to the US economy, especially given that Chinese growth is dependent on its trade imbalance in a way in which the US isn't.

If the PBoC wanted to control currency volatility, it could only do so while giving up control of domestic monetary policy, and the greater the extent and volatility of capital inflows, the harder it would be for Beijing to manage domestic monetary conditions.[7] That's where we see the second major difference between the two economies. The Chinese financial system is dominated by commercial banks, unlike in the US and the other Anglophone economies where stock and bond markets play a much larger role in financing businesses, households, and governments. More importantly, Chinese financial and monetary authorities exercise control of the banks administratively – similar to Japan's 'window guidance' in the 1980s – and not through traditional monetary policy.

The result is that China has a more rigid financial sector than the US, with bank credit serving policy objectives directly, and credit allocation determined from the top. An administrative system of this nature also requires that the financial system be underpinned by widespread moral hazard. None of this is consistent with the flexibility needed to accommodate large and unplanned changes in net capital inflows. An administratively controlled banking system is one that cannot simply expand and contract according to external conditions.

Finally, and this is perhaps the least appreciated of the major differences, Chinese households retain the lowest share of their country's GDP of any major economy in history. This is the reason that the consumption share of China's GDP is also among the lowest in history, and, what is the same thing, the savings share is the highest.[8] It is the low household share of GDP that locks countries like China into structural trade

---

7.   As the PBoC buys (sells) foreign currency to manage the foreign-currency value on the renminbi, it would have to create (destroy) renminbi, or money equivalents, whether or not domestic monetary management called for an expansion or contraction of the money supply.
8.   Because most consumption is household consumption (businesses don't consume any of their profits and governments consume a very low share of their revenues), the lower the household

                    Journal compilation © 2022 Edward Elgar Publishing Ltd

surpluses and, as I will explain later in this article, it is difficult for such countries to reverse the high savings rates that drive their trade surpluses.

6   BEIJING IS NOT MOVING IN THE RIGHT DIRECTION

What may surprise observers is that, for all their talk of a rising global role for the renminbi, it is clear that the PBoC understands the risks associated with an open capital account and has done the necessary to protect the domestic Chinese economy from potential consequences. In spite of nearly two decades of claiming to want to boost the renminbi's international role, the PBoC and China's State Council have never been willing to allow unfettered inflows or outflows. This is mainly because these might disrupt domestic financial markets and undermine the ability of regulators to control the financial system administratively.

This has been especially true in recent years, as China's financial system has become increasingly fragile, its debt burden has soared, and the banking system's dependence on moral hazard to maintain stability has increased. In fact it is worth noting that during much of 2021 and early 2022, as China saw an acceleration of foreign financial inflows – albeit to levels in which the share of domestic bonds and equity owned by foreigners was still a fraction of what is typical for other large developing economies – the central bank several times expressed its concern about the risks these foreign inflows posed to the financial system (see, for example, Horta e Costa and Curran 2021; Tang 2021). PBoC officials warned repeatedly against the risks associated with a sharp rise in foreign inflows and outflows – an inexorable consequence of greater capital-account openness and wider global use of the renminbi.

What is more, as the Beijing monetary authorities also recognize, it's not just the capital account that matters. Giving up control of the country's capital account also effectively means giving up control of the country's trade account. As I discussed earlier, for the renminbi to become a major global currency, China, like the United States, would have to accommodate the desire of other countries to run trade surpluses and to balance these with the acquisition of renminbi assets. The Chinese financial system would have to absorb an increasing share of the rest of the world's excess savings as these countries acquire Chinese assets in exchange for their trade surpluses.

But China's trade surplus is structural, and based on a highly unbalanced distribution of income between households and local governments. For its economy to shift towards deficits requires very substantial changes in the structure of the domestic economy, and this in turn would require, as I explain later in this article, either a surge in unemployment, rising household debt, an increase in (unwanted) infrastructure and property investment, or a major – and politically difficult – redistribution of wealth.

Aside from giving up control of its capital account and its trade account, there is at least one other major change Beijing would have to make before the renminbi could become a major global currency. For the renminbi assets to be widely held and traded by foreign investors and central banks, Beijing would have to implement significant governance reforms.

In order to encourage foreigners to acquire Chinese assets, in other words, either to pay for their trade surpluses or as financial insurance, Beijing would have to allow

(footnote 8 continued)

share of GDP, the lower the consumption share tends to be, and, by definition, the higher the savings share. It is not just coincidence that in high-savings countries like China, Germany, and Japan, households retain a lower share of GDP than among their trading partners.

foreign investors access to a wide variety of domestic assets, foreigners would have to be able easily to accumulate or liquidate these assets in a transparent and rules-based process, and there would have to be minimum discrimination between assets held by Chinese residents and assets held by foreigners. Among other things, this would require an independent judiciary and a transparent legal system that takes precedence over all other agents, including local and central-government entities.

To date China has not moved to fulfill any of the required conditions listed above: an open capital account and the associated financial reforms, an open trade account and the elimination of structural surpluses, and a radical reform in governance. There is, furthermore, little evidence that Beijing even wants to move in any of these directions, especially as the economy slows and the country's debt burden becomes increasingly hard to manage.

7   WILL THE UNITED STATES FORCE OTHERS TO STOP USING THE DOLLAR?

Much of the discussion about whether or not the US dollar can maintain its global dominance assumes as a matter of course that it is non-Americans who want to constrain the global use of the dollar, and it is Americans who will fiercely resist this process. This only indicates how confused much of this discussion has been. As Matthew Klein and I discussed in our 2020 book, the structure of international trade and capital flows does not pit the interests of nation against nation so much as it pits the interests of certain economic sectors against other economic sectors (Klein and Pettis 2020).

Among other things, this means that it is not the United States as a whole that benefits from the global dominance of the US dollar but rather certain constituencies within the United States (and similar constituencies in the rest of the world), in contrast to other constituencies in the US that pay the price for the dominance of the US dollar. The beneficiaries of US-dollar dominance include two major, and politically powerful, groups: Wall Street and the Washington foreign affairs and defense establishments. Other beneficiaries are global banks linked to the dollar system, large global businesses, and wealthy owners of movable capital, both American and non-American.

By contrast, it is American workers, farmers, producers, and small businesses that pay what amounts to a significant economic cost, along with workers in the rest of the world. The reason is because as long as other countries can easily accumulate US assets to balance their structural trade surpluses, the US must be a net importer of foreign savings – that is, it must have a capital-account surplus – whether or not it needs foreign savings for its own domestic investment.

If the US runs a capital-account surplus, however, this necessarily creates a gap between domestic investment and domestic savings – which is just another name for a current-account deficit. This has at least one obvious, but little noticed, implication. As long as the US maintains an open capital account and does not control the net inflow of capital, by definition it cannot control the gap between investment and savings. This means that either investment levels or savings levels are at least partly determined by external conditions that drive net capital inflows.

So which is it? It turns out that the answer depends on the underlying conditions at the time. When the US was a developing nation whose high investment needs were constrained by low domestic savings, as it was during much of the nineteenth century, the country's capital-account surplus was balanced by higher investment. In that case, the US economy benefitted from trade deficits and the associated capital

                    Journal compilation © 2022 Edward Elgar Publishing Ltd

inflows because these led to or accommodated higher investment and, consequently, higher growth.

In the past several decades, however, in a world of weak demand and excess savings, there has been no savings constraint on US investment. In fact, for years US companies have sat on enormous cash hoards for which they have found few productive investment opportunities at home. Much of these cash hoards have been used to pay dividends, buy back stocks, and acquire other companies, but not to increase investment in domestic production facilities.

In that case, increasing the amount of savings available to US businesses – by increasing the amount of savings foreigners export to the US – will not cause an increase in the amount of American business investment. But whether or not net capital inflows cause investment to increase, they nonetheless require domestic investment to exceed domestic savings, and so if they do not cause investment to rise, they must cause savings to fall.

This is perhaps the implication of US-dollar supremacy that is least understood by most economists, who tend automatically to assume that US savings are an independent variable that affect, but aren't affected by, the current-account deficit. As Klein and I show, however, foreign inflows can force down US savings in a number of ways, the net result of which is either higher unemployment, higher household debt, or higher fiscal deficits.

What is more, there is evidence that surplus-running countries benefit from their net absorption of foreign demand with a rising share of global manufacturing and the accumulation of foreign assets (Atkinson et al. 2012). This rising share comes at the expense of the declining share of global manufacturing retained by deficit-running countries like the United States.

This is why the global dominance of the US dollar imposes an exorbitant burden on the US economy, rather than the exorbitant privilege of French nightmares. It forces the US to balance net capital inflows either with higher unemployment or – more likely – with higher household debt and/or higher fiscal deficits; it reduces the US share of global manufacturing; and it puts downward pressure on wages if US-based manufacturers are to remain competitive.

8   WILL WASHINGTON IMPLEMENT CAPITAL CONTROLS?

As global trade imbalances rise and the American share of global GDP declines, the United States will eventually have to reject this exorbitant burden. For all the geopolitical power that control of the global currency system confers on Washington and Wall Street, it comes at a substantial economic cost to American producers, workers, farmers, and businesses, and as the rest of the world grows relative to the United States, this cost can only rise.

If the United States at some point refuses to run the permanently rising deficits that are needed to accommodate weak demand and excess savings in the rest of the world, in what form might that 'refusal' take? Tariffs and other forms of direct trade intervention cannot work because they are largely ineffective in shifting the global savings imbalances that drive the US trade deficit. The Trump administration's tariffs on Chinese goods, for example, may have shifted bilateral trade, but they did not reduce China's overall surplus, which is a function of its domestic savings imbalance, and they did not reduce the overall American deficit, which is a function of the US role in absorbing excess savings in the rest of the world.

                    Journal compilation © 2022 Edward Elgar Publishing Ltd

This suggests that the only way for the United States to be relieved of trade deficits is for measures that interrupt the unfettered global flow of international capital into the US financial system. There are basically three ways in which this is most likely to happen. One way would be for the current system to be maintained until the United States is no longer able to carry the economic burden. In that case, amid a collapse in the credibility of the US dollar, the world would abandon the currency. This would force the United States and other economies to adjust in chaotic and disorderly ways.

A second way would be for the United States unilaterally to opt out of the current system by constraining foreigners' ability to dump excess savings into the US economy. One means of doing this would be to tax all financial inflows that do not lead directly to productive investment in the US economy. There have already been such proposals in the US Congress, and while as of yet they have been rejected, there are likely to be many more (Baldwin 2019).

This would of course entail a substantial reduction in US financial power abroad and in the power of Wall Street, and it would be painful and in some cases even destabilizing for countries – such as China, Germany, Japan, Russia, and Saudi Arabia – that would likely prove unable to resolve domestic demand and savings imbalances quickly enough. It would, however, boost US manufacturing, raise domestic wages, and force US businesses once again to rely on raising productivity rather than lowering wages to achieve international competitiveness.

A third and final way would be for the United States and the world's other major economies to organize a new global trade and capital regime, based perhaps on ideas similar to those originally proposed by John Maynard Keynes at Bretton Woods, which, among other things, relied on a global synthetic currency (which he called the bancor) designed to absorb temporary global imbalances and spread out their consequences across the major economies. Washington and its allies could do this by negotiating a new set of trade agreements that would force members to resolve their domestic demand imbalances at home, rather than force their trade partners to absorb them. By requiring countries with temporary surpluses to exchange these surpluses for bonds denominated in the new synthetic currency, it would also spread more widely the adverse consequences of those surpluses.

While either of the last two options would ultimately benefit the US economy, the second of the two would be the least disruptive for the global economy and the one most likely to allow the United States and its allies to continue maintaining some degree of control over global trade and capital flows. But one way or another, Washington should take the lead in steering the global trade and capital regime away from its excessive reliance on the US dollar. For all the excited discussions about foreign antagonists forcing the US dollar to lose its global dominance, this will never happen because no other country is willing to take on the exorbitant burden that the US dollar places on the US economy. Washington itself must end the age of the US dollar's dominance for the benefit of the American economy.

9 HOW WOULD CHINA BE AFFECTED BY A REDUCED ROLE FOR THE DOLLAR?

If the United States – and presumably the other Anglophone economies – were to take steps that eliminated the role of their domestic financial markets as the net absorbers of foreign savings, by definition they would also no longer run large and persistent current-account and trade deficits. But because these countries account for 75–85 percent of the

   Journal compilation © 2022 Edward Elgar Publishing Ltd

world's current-account deficits (with the developing world accounting for most of the rest), this would also mean that, unless some other large economy were willing to convert its surpluses into massive deficits, the world would have to reduce its collective trade surpluses by 75–85 percent.[9]

For countries that are structurally reliant on trade surpluses, this could be extremely painful. To understand the implications, assume a country that runs persistent trade surpluses, like China, is forced to adapt to a world of much lower trade deficits, and hence of much lower trade surpluses. Domestic savings exceed domestic investment in countries that run persistent surpluses, and domestic savings are high in these countries mainly because ordinary households, who consume most of their income, receive a very low share of the GDP they produce – compared to the shares of businesses, the government, and the very rich.

The problem is that if some external event were to force a sharp contraction in the country's trade and current-account surpluses, like constraints on its ability to acquire US assets to balance its surpluses, and if it were not able to acquire an equivalent amount of assets in some other country, by definition the gap between its savings and its investments would shrink. There are broadly speaking five ways (or some combination thereof) by which an economy locked into structural trade surpluses can adjust to bring savings and investment back in line.

The first way is a surge in unemployment. Without an appropriate policy response the collapse in its trade surplus would most likely come about through a collapse in exports, and this would cause manufacturing unemployment to surge. Unemployed workers, of course, have negative savings, and a surge in unemployment would be one means, albeit an extremely painful means, of closing the gap between savings and investment. If a brutal enough export shock also caused domestic business investment to contract, as is likely, the rise in unemployment would have to be much greater since the decline in savings would have to accelerate to catch up to a decline in investment. This downward spiral is what happened in the US in the early 1930s, and this is obviously something Beijing would want very much to avoid.

The second way is a boost in consumer lending to spur domestic demand. China's savings would also decline, but much less disruptively, if the central bank, in response to a collapse in exports, quickly forced banks to increase consumer lending dramatically so as to replace foreign demand with domestic demand. Even if it were possible to do this efficiently, rising household debt would eventually be unsustainable. Consumer debt in China has already risen very rapidly in recent years, and as a share of household income it already exceeds that of the US and most other major economies. Not surprisingly Beijing has recently been trying to implement policies to bring household debt levels down.

The third way is a jump in government deficit spending to spur demand. Savings would decline if Beijing, in response to a collapse in exports, quickly expanded the fiscal deficit so as to replace foreign demand with domestic demand. Higher fiscal spending, for example, could be aimed at boosting indirect consumption. With a trade surplus of currently around 5 percent of GDP and growing, this would require a substantial increase every year in the fiscal deficit. Again, even if it were possible to do this efficiently and productively, rising fiscal deficits would eventually be unsustainable, especially given China's already dangerously high debt levels.

The fourth way is a surge in government and state-owned-enterprise investment. The most obvious form in which Beijing could engineer a sufficiently rapid expansion

9.   Benn Steil and Benjamin Della Rocca, ibid. footnote 4.

    Journal compilation © 2022 Edward Elgar Publishing Ltd

in fiscal spending – as it did, for example, in 2009–2010 – is with a massive increase in investment. The private sector is unlikely to respond to a collapse in exports by increasing investment, and indeed private firms would probably reduce investment, which means that more than 100 percent of the increase in investment would have to occur in the form of government and government-backed expansion. Normally Beijing would rely on a rapid expansion in property development and in infrastructure spending to balance any sharp contraction in the trade surplus, but as we saw with the clamping-down on the property sector in 2021, there is a growing sense that much if not most property development and infrastructure spending has become non-productive and leads only to a surge in the country's debt burden. Large and sustained increases in infrastructure investment from levels that are already too high, in other words, are unsustainable and would only worsen the overall adjustment cost, albeit by spreading it out over a longer period.

The fifth way is income redistribution. China's savings would decline in a healthy manner if the government were able to engineer a substantial redistribution of income from governments, who consume a very small share of their income, to ordinary households, who consume most of it. This would be sustainable and by far the best long-term outcome for both China and the world, but any substantial redistribution of income would be a slow and difficult process, and it would almost certainly be politically disruptive. China has been trying to engineer an increase in the household income and consumption shares of GDP since at least 2007, with very little success (IMF 2007).

The point is that there are only a limited number of ways in which a country that runs large, persistent surpluses, like China, can adjust to a global contraction in aggregate trade deficits. All of these adjustments except the last one – a major redistribution of domestic income – are unsustainable and can only be temporary. But this last is an extremely difficult adjustment that no country has been able to make successfully except over the very long term, perhaps because it implies politically disruptive changes in a number of domestic institutions.

This just reinforces how it is the willingness and ability of the United States to run large, persistent deficits that underpins the role of the US dollar as the world's dominant currency, and how these deficits benefit, directly or indirectly, the countries that claim to be most eager to dethrone the US dollar. Ironically these are also the countries – especially China – whose domestic economic policies make this all but impossible.

10   WHAT NEXT?

The world is stuck with the US dollar, not because it creates an exorbitant privilege for the US economy over which Washington will fight. It uses the dollar because this allows many of the world's largest economies to use a portion of American demand to resolve deficient domestic demand and fuel domestic growth, for which the US economy must then make up by increasing its household or fiscal debt.

These economies, in other words, can increase their international competitiveness by lowering the relative share households retain of what they produce, and can then run the large surpluses needed to balance their domestic demand deficiencies while keeping growth high. This is the form of beggar-thy-neighbor trade policy that Keynes most urgently warned against. Global dollar dominance accommodates this process by allowing surplus countries to exchange excess production for ownership of real assets – American real estate, factories, stocks, bonds, farmland, mines, and real businesses – that other countries would be unwilling (and largely unable) to give up.

                    Journal compilation © 2022 Edward Elgar Publishing Ltd

The point is that while the US dollar may create an exorbitant privilege for certain American constituencies, this status creates an exorbitant burden for the US economy overall, especially for the vast majority of Americans who must pay for the corresponding trade deficits either with higher unemployment, more household debt, or greater fiscal deficits. This is also why the end of the US dollar's dominance has little to do with the political desires of countries like Russia, China, Venezuela, and Iran, and everything to do with the political decisions of Americans.

Once Washington understands the cost of this exorbitant privilege – although this may unfortunately take many more years – US leaders will take steps, either unilaterally or collectively, that force the world off its dependence on the US dollar. But that will have an enormous side effect. It will force the rest of the world, and especially countries like China with low domestic demand and structural surpluses, into a very difficult adjustment as global imbalances shrink sharply. Without the widespread use of the US dollar as the mechanism that allows global imbalances to be absorbed by the US economy, these imbalances cannot exist.

REFERENCES

Atkinson, R.D., L.A. Stewart, S.M. Andes, and S. Ezell (2012), 'Worse than the great depression: what the experts are missing about American manufacturing decline,' *ITIF*, 19 March.

Baldwin, T. (2019), 'US Senators Tammy Baldwin and Josh Hawley lead bipartisan effort to restore competitiveness to US exports, boost American manufacturers and farmers,' Senator Tammy Baldwin Press Release, 31 July.

Horn, S., C. Reinhart, and C. Trebesch (2022), 'China's overseas lending and the war in Ukraine,' *Vox-EU*, 8 April.

Horta e Costa, C. and E. Curran (2021), 'China's epic battle with capital flows is more intense than ever,' *Bloomberg*, 7 April.

IMF (2007), 'IMF Survey: China's difficult rebalancing act,' 12 September.

Jones, C. (2022), 'Does sterling's slide into obscurity foreshadow the US dollar's fate?,' *Financial Times*, 7 April.

Klein, M. and M. Pettis (2020), *Trade Wars are Class Wars*, New Haven, CT: Yale University Press.

Mundell, R. (1963), 'Capital mobility and stabilization policy under fixed and flexible exchange rates,' *Canadian Journal of Economics and Political Science*, 29(4), 475–485.

Pozsar, Z. (2022), 'We are witnessing the birth of a new world monetary order,' *Credit Suisse Research*, 21 March.

Tang, F. (2021), 'China "must prevent reversal" of hot money flows as US kicks off monetary tapering, former official warns,' *South China Morning Post*, 3 November.

Review of Keynesian Economics, Vol. 10 No. 4, Winter 2022, pp. 71–90

The peso problem and dollar hegemony under inflation targeting

Juan Alberto Vázquez-Muñoz*
Benemérita Universidad Autónoma de Puebla, Mexico

Ignacio Perrotini-Hernández**
Universidad Nacional Autónoma de México, Mexico City, Mexico

This article examines the influence of US monetary policy on Mexico's exchange rate (peso/dollar) and monetary policy. It shows that the recent reduced volatility of Mexico's exchange rate is a consequence of defensive policies undertaken by Mexico's central bank to avoid sudden capital reversals and speculative attacks, usually associated with destabilizing speculative behavior. To test that hypothesis, the paper examines the effect of the accumulation of international reserves and exchange-rate variations on the Mexico–US interest-rate gap. The authors' findings confirm that international reserves permit the central bank to maneuver the exchange rate and its inflation target. Furthermore, the paper provides an estimated Taylor rule for Mexico, including the US interest rate. The estimation reveals that Mexico's monetary policy is not independent of US monetary policy. Mexico faces a liquidity trap at a higher interest rate than the United States. Whereas the United States faces a trap at the zero lower bound, Mexico encounters monetary policy ineffectiveness at an interest rate of 3.5 percent.

Keywords: *exchange rates, interest rates, Mexico, monetary policy, central banks*

JEL codes: *E420, E430, E52, E580*

1 INTRODUCTION

This article analyses the influence of the Mexico–US interest-rate gap and the accumulation of international reserves on the exchange rate (peso/dollar) and the Bank of Mexico's inflation-targeting monetary policy framework. We argue that the interest rate of the Federal Reserve of the United States exerts a strong influence on the monetary policy of the Bank of Mexico.

We also claim that the relative stability of the exchange rate of the Mexican peso derives from the rapid accumulation of international reserves the Bank of Mexico has undertaken with the aim of avoiding sudden capital stops and confronting destabilizing speculative attacks. We test our hypothesis using empirical evidence from Mexico and the United States to gauge the effect of the accumulation of international reserves and exchange-rate variations on the interest-rate gap. Our results show that those precautionary accumulations of international reserves operate as an additional regular monetary policy instrument that allows the central bank certain degrees of freedom to control the exchange rate and the inflation rate.

*   Email: juan.vazquez@correo.buap.mx.
**   *Corresponding author*: Email: iph@unam.mx.

We estimate an alternative Taylor rule for Mexico including the US rate of interest, which delivers important clues. First, Mexico's monetary policy depends on the US monetary policy. Second, Mexico faces a liquidity-trap level of the interest rate much higher than the United States. Whereas the United States faces a zero lower bound level, Mexico encounters ineffectiveness of its monetary policy at a positive interest rate of 3.5 percent. The results derived from our empirical studies lead us to conclude that the Bank of Mexico's monetary policy position is pro-cyclical. Those asymmetries speak to the hegemonic role of the dollar and the subordinate position of the peso.

The main contribution of the present article to the literature is twofold. First, it analyses the influence of the accumulation of international reserves on the interest-rate gap and the dynamics of the exchange rate. Second, it provides an estimation of an alternative Taylor rule showing the influence of the US interest rate on Mexico's monetary policy and the pro-cyclical character of the Bank of Mexico's monetary policy. Those issues are frequently overlooked in the literature. For instance, Galindo and Ros (2008) and Ros (2015) are concerned with the central-bank propensity to appreciate the exchange rate with the aim of achieving an inflation target, a policy which is viewed as the cause of slow growth and stagnation in Mexico and other emerging economies; Médici et al. (2021) criticize that view, arguing that there is no reason to believe that a competitive exchange rate can accelerate the growth rate of an economy facing structural constraints.

The paper is structured as follows: the Section 2 briefly discusses Milton Friedman's and John M. Keynes's ideas regarding the relative merits of fixed versus flexible exchange-rate regimes and the best way to attain internal and external stabilization. Section 3 presents an empirical analysis of current-account disequilibrium, currency fluctuations, and the net financial position of the Mexican economy. Section 4 explains the accumulation of international reserves, the interest-rate gap, and exchange-rate expectations. Sections 5 and 6 contain econometric estimations of the effects of the international reserves on the interest-rate gap and the alternative Taylor rule, respectively. Section 7 concludes, with some reflections on the main contributions of the article and a brief reference to the future of the dollar hegemony.

2   FRIEDMAN AND KEYNES ON EXCHANGE-RATE DYNAMICS

Friedman (1953, pp. 182–186) made 'the case for flexible exchange rates' along with free currency convertibility and perfect capital mobility in open markets on the presumption that this setting is economic-welfare-enhancing. He criticized Bretton Woods' fixed exchange-rates arrangement, arguing that it is inconsistent with multilateral trade and internal monetary stability. He maintained that rigid exchange rates and capital controls neither ensure balance-of-payments equilibrium nor boost stabilization of expectations, whereas agents under floating exchange rates can 'protect themselves hedging in a futures market' (ibid., p. 174).

Friedman wholeheartedly believed that a system of unfettered floating exchange rates harmonizes monetary and fiscal policy and dispenses with the inflation/deflation bias resulting from central-bank discretionary management. Since both the exchange rate and the balance of payments are monetary phenomena,[1] if 'any one country

---

1.   In his view, exchange rates and current-account disequilibria are just symptoms of monetary disequilibria.

inflates' (deflates), its exchange rate will depreciate (appreciate), hurting its own real income in the first place (ibid., p. 199). Thus, government interventions are ineffective.

Friedman also claimed that, contrary to hard and/or crawling pegs, a flexible exchange-rate regime allows a central bank the maximum degree of freedom to pursue an independent monetary policy consistent with both internal stability and balance-of-payments equilibrium (ibid., p. 200). Hence his contention that exchange-rate speculation is always stabilizing. Friedman's tenets rely on the assumptions that the real interest parity condition,[2] the neutrality of money hypothesis, and, therefore, the purchasing power parity (PPP) hypothesis hold. His paradigm describes an ergodic economy where domestic saving and foreign exchange are certainly substitutable; prices, interest rates, and exchange rates tend to converge to equilibrium values determined by 'fundamentals.' In sum, a freely floating exchange-rate regime accompanied by perfect capital mobility is the best antidote to sudden stops of capital flows, a phenomenon that has plagued Mexico's and other Latin American countries' recent financial history (Calvo 1998; Calvo and Mendoza 2000).

In this connection, it is safe to say that the Bank of Mexico's current monetary policy framework of inflation targeting includes most (if not all) of the essential ingredients of Friedman's case for flexible exchange rates.[3] Similarly, and paradoxically, nowadays many heterodox economists (Frenkel and Ros 2006; Galindo and Ros 2008; Wray 2015; Bresser-Pereira 2016) share Friedman's belief that a floating exchange-rate regime is the key to solving the pressing problem of economic stagnation. Unfortunately, as Palley (2020, p. 481) contends, a flexible regime 'has its own adverse financial and inflation complications,' for 'if the balance of payments constraint is structural' it is ineffective (see also Vernengo 2006).

Keynes (1936 [1964], pp. 262 and 266), in turn, maintained that it is fallacious to think of the capitalist economy as a self-adjusting system, for a belief that flexible wages and prices and competitive exchange rates epitomize a 'method of securing full employment' is groundless. Such policies are likely to impart deleterious effects, for instance a redistribution of real income against wage-earners (real devaluations depress real wages), financial fragility,[4] reduced effective demand, output contraction, and higher unemployment rates (Keynes 1936 [1964], p. 264; Palley 2018).

In the 1920s, amidst the crisis of the pound sterling and the initial ascent of the dollar to the status of the world economy's new hegemonic currency, Keynes (1923) was concerned with the trade-off between the stability of internal prices and that of the exchange rate. Whilst Keynes did not abandon the quantity theory of money altogether, he challenged it, contending that money is not neutral (at least) in the short term so that inflation and deflation tend to impinge on production, employment, saving and investment levels, economic growth, and wages (Vicarelli 1984). The PPP doctrine is also valid only under extremely unrealistic conditions, and hence it is not a sound theory of the determinants of the exchange rate (Keynes 1923 [2013], p. 71 labeled it 'jejune' doctrine). Debunking of the PPP hypothesis also led Keynes to reject

---

2.   Capital flows are said to be infinitely elastic vis-à-vis interest-rate differentials; Friedman's rendition of exchange-rate behavior relies on a basic confusion between the stabilizing properties of arbitrage and those (not necessarily stabilizing) of speculation (Davidson 1999, p. 15; Lavoie 2014, pp. 478–480).
3.   The *Annual Report on Exchange Arrangements and Exchange Restrictions 2021* of the International Monetary Fund (IMF 2022) classified Mexico as a free-floating country.
4.   A higher national debt burden and, given elastic exchange rate expectations, increasing monetary, nominal exchange rate and financial instability (Serrano et al. 2021).

the uncovered interest parity (UIP) as an appropriate explanation of exchange-rate dynamics. He was probably the first to discover what are now known as UIP and PPP 'failures' (Sarno 2005; Serrano et al. 2021).

Keynes (1923 [2013], p. 103) claimed that the interest-rate differential (covered interest arbitrage) paid on financial assets 'lent or deposited for short periods of time in the money markets of the two centres under comparison' is 'the most fundamental cause' of the difference between the spot and the forward rates in financial markets. Keynes (1930) further elaborated his analysis of exchange- and interest-rate dynamics by highlighting the role of financial asset markets and later, in *The General Theory* (1936), enriched it with a framework including a theory of liquidity preference, the principle of effective demand, and the determination of output to explain the causes of unemployment and stagnating slow growth.

Most instructive for this paper's purpose, and for studying the riddles of today's international monetary hegemony, is a prescient remark Keynes (1923) made while examining the implications, for the majority of nations, of a few central banks – most importantly the United States' Federal Reserve – controlling the world's gold reserves in the 1920s. He foresaw the emergence of a new asymmetric monetary and financial arrangement with key currencies – the dollar, primarily – at the apex and peripheral currencies with lower liquidity and dependent monetary policies at the subservient bottom of the system.

Keynes's conception of money as chiefly a unit of account and a store of value, in contrast to Friedman's medium of exchange definition, is relevant *a propos* understanding today's international asymmetric monetary 'nonsystem' (Williamson 1976), the unraveling effects of dollar hegemony on peripheral countries' monetary policy capability, and for dealing with the uneven cost distribution of balance-of-payments adjustments between debtors and creditors.

3   CURRENT ACCOUNT, NOMINAL EXCHANGE RATE, AND EXTERNAL NET FINANCIAL POSITION

The main sources of accumulation of international reserves are the current account (CA), foreign capital inflows, and foreign debt. A current-account surplus (deficit) tends to increase (decrease) the demand for international reserves. The exchange-rate regime may be significant; a flexible (fixed) exchange-rate setting should reduce (expand) the demand for international reserves.

Mexico presents an apparently curious situation. During the period 1960–1994, a fixed exchange-rate regime prevailed and Mexico alternated with CA equilibrium during 1960–1973, a deficit in 1974–1981 (financed through increasing foreign debt leading to the debt crisis of 1982), a surplus in 1982–1988 obtained by means of a drastic recession, and a sizable deficit in 1989–1994 triggered by trade and financial liberalization.

A flexible exchange-rate arrangement replaced the old regime after the Tequila crisis of 1995 and an inflation-targeting monetary policy framework was adopted in 2001. The new macroeconomic policy has delivered poor results (see Figure 1). The cumulative CA deficit of the fixed regime was equal to –$39.1 billion, whereas that of the flexible regime plus inflation-targeting period (1996–2021) was –$64 billion. Irrespective of the exchange-rate scheme, the declining trend of the CA does not account for the accumulation of international reserves over the whole period. Furthermore, it takes a severe crisis to correct increasing CA imbalances. That speaks to the structural constraints of the balance of payments and to the so-called 'peso problem' being not exclusively

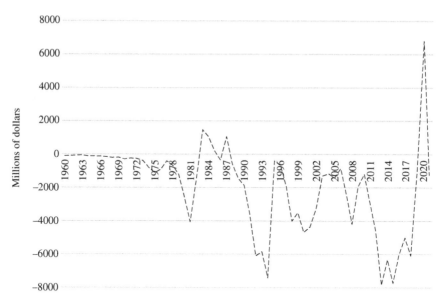

Source: Authors' elaboration with data from the Sistema de Información Económica database (SIE) of the Bank of Mexico (BM).

Figure 1   Current-account balance (annual data), 1960–2021

related to a fixed exchange rate, and it can very well arise in a flexible exchange-rate setting. The peso problem is best understood as the combination of dollar hegemony and the structural constraints plaguing the Mexican economy.

It is noteworthy that during the period of the fixed exchange-rate regime there was a strong positive correlation between the annual rate of depreciation of the nominal exchange and the CA balance: nominal and real devaluations caused CA surpluses in crisis times (see Figure 2, left panel). However, the same is not true of the era of inflation targeting, when annual nominal and real currency depreciations have not brought about CA surpluses (see Figure 2, right panel), except for the remarkable 2020 pandemic-related crisis. The deindustrialization of the Mexican economy induced by the export-led growth *cum* inflation-targeting model is to blame for this deteriorated behavior of the CA.

Figure 3 shows the significant reduction of volatility of the peso/dollar exchange rate as the Mexican economy shifted from a fixed exchange-rate regime to an inflation-targeting monetary policy *cum* flexible exchange rate. During 1970–1994 the cumulative depreciation of the nominal exchange rate was 26 901 percent compared to 501 percent over the period 1995–2021.[5] Speculative attacks against the Mexican peso continued over the latter period, but at a much lower pace. Is this a sign of fading of the peso problem? What accounts for the reduced volatility of the Mexican currency? For that, we must turn to the role of accumulation of international reserves, but beforehand let us briefly look at Mexico's external net financial position shown in Figure 4.

5.   The annual average rate of depreciation for those years with devaluations higher than 10 percent within the period 1970–1994 was 74.77 percent, compared to 25.70 percent for years with similar devaluation rates in the period 1995–2021.

                                    Journal compilation © 2022 Edward Elgar Publishing Ltd

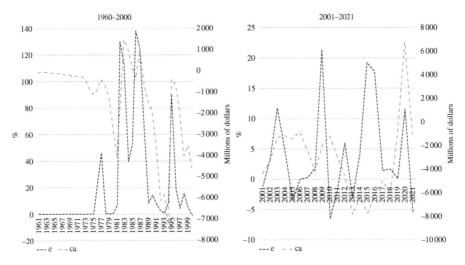

Source: Authors' elaboration with data from the SIE database of the BM.

Figure 2 Annual nominal exchange-rate depreciation and current-account balance (annual data)

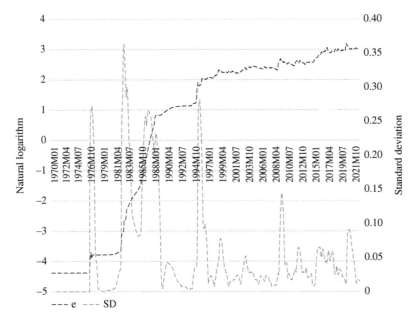

Note: The volatility of the nominal exchange rate was calculated as the standard deviation of the nominal exchange rate measured in natural logarithms during the period considered between the relevant month indicated in the figure and the previous 11 months.
Source: Authors' elaboration with data from the Banco de Información Económica (BIE) database of Mexico's National Institute of Statistics and Geography (INEGI).

Figure 3 Nominal exchange rate, level, and volatility (monthly data), 1970M1–2022M5

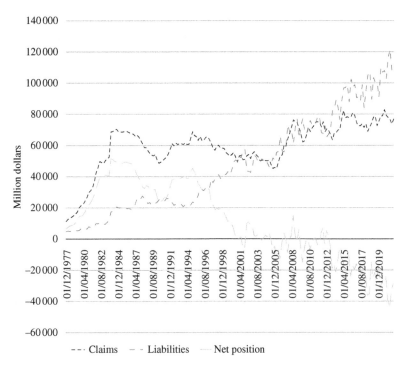

Source: Authors' elaboration with data from the debt securities statistics database of the Bank of International Settlements.

Figure 4   Local positions in current dollars (outstanding at the end of each quarter), 1977Q4–2021Q4

The concomitant result of Mexico's continued CA deficits, resulting from increasing financial openness and greater flexibility of the exchange rate, has been a significant worsening of its international net financial position. The dollar-denominated claims of all the sectors of the Mexican economy grew faster than their liabilities during 1977–1999; claims and liabilities converged thereafter, reaching an equilibrium during 2001–2013. The position turned negative after that and has worsened with each crisis throughout the inflation-targeting period. Mexico's current net financial position is negative.[6]

4   ACCUMULATION OF INTERNATIONAL RESERVES, THE INTEREST-RATE GAP, AND EXPECTED DEPRECIATION

Mexico has experienced several episodes of sudden reversals of capital involving liquidity, banking and exchange-rate crises, costly output contractions, high unemployment,

6.   It is worth noting that the banking sector is the main contributor to Mexico's negative net local position, its liabilities having increased after the 1995 financial crisis, while its claims exhibited a cyclical behavior around a stable mean between the last quarter of 1983 and 2021.

and welfare loss. The 1995 financial crisis is perhaps the most important experience of recent times because it produced a structural change in the government's policy towards foreign debt, inflation, exchange rate, and international-reserve management.

We have seen that volatility of the peso/dollar exchange rate greatly diminished in the aftermath of the 1995 financial crisis. However, the abandonment of the fixed exchange-rate regime as an anchor for inflation and the transition to a floating exchange rate did not provide a sufficiently effective cushion against speculative currency attacks and sudden stops of capital inflows. Given the relative weakness of the domestic financial system, the government engaged in an accelerated accumulation of precautionary international reserves as an additional barrier to rein in exchange-rate instability arising from the asymmetric relationship between a peripheral currency and a key currency, the true source of the peso problem. Figure 5 illustrates the rising trend of international reserves as a percentage of gross national income (GNI). It suggests that precautionary international reserves play a much greater stabilizing role in today's environment of inflation targeting *cum* floating exchange rate than in the context of the fixed exchange rate of the 1970s and 1980s.

The fact that an emerging-market economy is subject to exogenous monetary and financial hegemony strengthens the need for short-term means to cope with financial fragility entrenched in the structure of the balance of payments. Consequently, the monetary authorities are compelled to accumulate precautionary international reserves

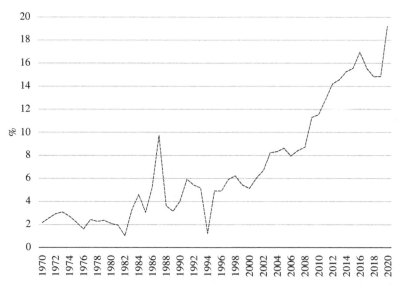

Note: Total reserves comprise holdings of monetary gold, special drawing rights, reserves of IMF members held by the IMF, and holdings of foreign exchange under the control of monetary authorities. The gold component of these reserves is valued at year-end (31 December) London prices. GNI is the sum of value added by all resident producers plus any product taxes (less subsidies) not included in the valuation of output plus net receipts of primary income (compensation of employees and property income) from abroad.
Source: Authors' elaboration with data from the International Debt Statistics database of the World Bank.

Figure 5   International reserves as a percentage of gross national income (annual data), 1970–2020

   Journal compilation © 2022 Edward Elgar Publishing Ltd

to cover unexpected risks of speculative attacks and sudden capital stops, absent addressing the deep origins of the problem rooted in the asymmetric nature of the international monetary system. In this connection, Figure 6 shows Mexico's increasing accumulation of international reserves as a ratio of total long-run and short-run external debt during 1970–2020. First, the fastest rate of international-reserve accumulation occurred during the period of inflation targeting *cum* flexible exchange rate. Second, the case of short-run external debt calls for special attention as it jumps in times of turbulence and crisis. Third, this pattern exposes *de facto* what Keynes (1923; 1936) criticized, namely the detrimental effect of an asymmetric international monetary system.

Accumulating international reserves requires an attractive (higher) rate of return to draw in capital. Consequently, the Bank of Mexico must set an interest rate higher than that of the United States if it is to capture portfolio capital inflows. That bilateral interest-rate gap is affected by the potential speculative attacks against the peso. Balanced against that, international-reserve accumulation as a percentage of total external debt prevents such speculative attacks. Therefore, an increase in the domestic interest rate allows the Bank of Mexico to reduce the gap. On the other hand, if the nominal exchange rate increases, the Bank of Mexico must increase the interest-rate gap.

Figure 7 shows that the expected variation of the nominal exchange rate follows the Mexico–US interest-rate gap, with expected variations of the nominal exchange rate being higher than the interest-rate gap. Absent accumulation of international reserves, the volatility of the exchange rate would be larger.

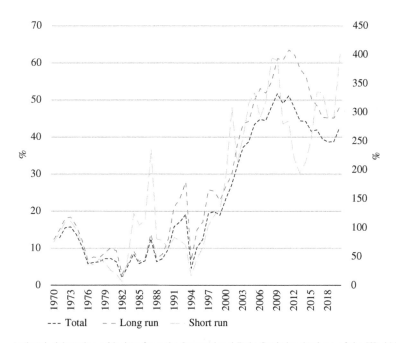

Source: Authors' elaboration with data from the International Debt Statistics database of the World Bank.

Figure 6   International reserves as a percentage of total, long-run, and short-run external debt (annual data), 1970–2020

                                    Journal compilation © 2022 Edward Elgar Publishing Ltd

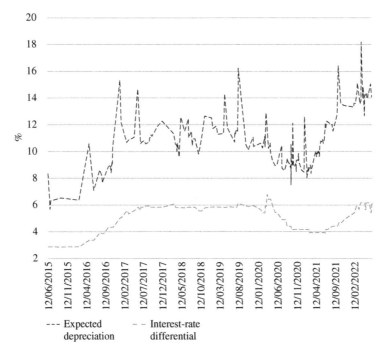

--- Expected   - - Interest-rate
    depreciation   differential

Note: Expected depreciation was calculated as the percentage difference between the spot value of the exchange rate and its future value for a two-to-three-year range.
Source: Authors' elaboration with data from the SIE database of the BM, the BIE of the INEGI, and the Federal Reserve Economic Data (FRED) database of the Federal Reserve of St. Louis.

Figure 7   Uncovered interest parity hypothesis (daily data), June 2015–July 2022

5   ESTIMATING THE INFLUENCE OF INTERNATIONAL RESERVES ON THE INTEREST-RATE GAP

It can be argued that Mexico's monetary policy is not autonomous from the United States' monetary policy. Not merely because we assume that there must be a positive Mexico–US interest-rate gap, but because this gap depends on Mexico's financial fragility measured as the international reserves as a percentage of external debt.

To test for the existence of the relations stipulated in the previous paragraph, the following equation is estimated:

$$gi_t = \beta_0 + \beta_1 RD_t + \beta_2 e_t + u_{1t}, \tag{1}$$

where β_i are the parameters to be estimated, gi is the Mexico–US interest-rate gap, RD is Mexico's international reserves as a percentage of total external debt, e is the nominal exchange rate, u_1 is an error term, and t is a time index. All variables are expressed in natural logarithms terms.

Sources and data are as follows: the Mexican interest rate is the annual average of (i) the monthly interest rate of the Treasury Certificates at 91 days (CETES) from January 1978 to August 1982 and from August 1983 to January 1985; (ii) the monthly interest rate of the Treasury Certificates at 28 days from September 1982 to July

1983 and from February 1985 to January 2008; and (iii) the daily Bank of Mexico's target interest rate from February 2008 to December 2020. The data are provided by the Sistema de Información Económica database of the Bank of Mexico. The United States interest rate is the annual average of the monthly federal funds effective rate, obtained from the Federal Reserve Economic Data database of the Federal Reserve of St. Louis. International reserves as a percentage of total external debt were taken from the International Debt Statistics database of the World Bank. Lastly, the nominal exchange rate is the annual average of: (i) the monthly average of the settlement-date exchange rate from January 1978 to October 1991; and (ii) the determination-date exchange rate from November 1991 to December 2020, obtained from the Sistema de Información Económica database of the Bank of Mexico.

As a first step, we examine for a unit root in the series to be used in the estimation of equation (1). Table 1 reports our results. It shows gi and RD are stationary series while e is an integrated series of order one. So, we can use the bounds-testing approach cointegration methodology (Pesaran et al. 2001) to estimate equation (1).[7]

According to our results shown in Table 2, the estimated elasticity of gi with respect to RD is equal to -1; it shows the major importance of the accumulation of international reserves for Mexican monetary policy relative to United States monetary policy. On the other hand, the elasticity of gi with respect to e is equal to 0.21. Therefore, when e tends to depreciate, gi increases; and when e appreciates, gi decreases. As can be seen in Figure 8, although our fitted gi tends to be lower than the actual one, its general behavior is very consistent with the latter. Moreover, our results show that a higher gi prevailed during the period 1978–1999 compared to the period 2000–2020. That is explained by the lower international reserves accumulated as a percentage of total external debt (see Figure 6), the fixed exchange regime and the monetary policy framework in operation at the time, and the relatively low significance of financial liberalization during the former period.

Table 1   Unit-root test for the series used in the estimation of equation (1)

Series	Period	Augmented Dickey–Fuller test (*t*-statistics)	Phillips–Perron test (adj. *t*-statistics)
gi	1979–2020	−3.50***	−3.49***
RD	1979–2020	−3.65**	−3.65**
e	1979–2020	−1.40	−1.40
$d(e)$	1979–2020	−3.86*	−3.32**

Notes: *, **, and *** are statistically significant at 1 percent, 5 percent, and 10 percent levels. All variables are measured in natural logarithm terms. $d(\cdot)$ stands for the first difference operator. All level tests were done assuming the existence of intercept and trend, while the first difference test was done assuming only the existence of intercept. The number of lags used for the ADF tests were chosen in accordance with the Schwarz information criterion, whilst the number of bandwidths used for the PP tests were chosen according to the Newey–West criterion.
Source: Authors' elaboration with data from the SIE database of the BM and the FRED database of the Federal Reserve of St. Louis.

7.   This approach is applicable regardless of whether the underlying regressors are purely I(0), purely I(1), mutually cointegrated, or any combination of these characteristics. This is, indubitably, a considerable advantage given the low power of the unit-root test and the relatively small size of our data.

Table 2   Estimation of the Mexico–US interest-rate gap (equation (1))

Period	1978–2020
Dependent variable	*gi*
RD	−1.06*
	(0.13)
e	0.21*
	(0.07)
Constant	4.76*
	(0.38)
Model type	Restricted constant, no trend
ARDL model	(2, 4, 3)
F-bounds test	
F-statistic	8.80*
Adjustment coefficient	
u_{1t-1}	−0.97*
	(0.15)
Jarque–Bera test	3.01
LM test (*F*-statistic, 1 lag)	0.36
White test (*F*-statistic)	0.41
Ramsey RESET (*t*-statistic, one fitted term)	0.46

Notes: * is statistically significant at the 1 percent level (standard errors in parentheses). All variables are measured in natural logarithm terms. White test does not include cross terms. ARDL model indicates the number of lags of the dependent and independent variables. A complete report of the estimation is available on request from the authors.
Source: Authors' elaboration using data from the SIE database of the BM and the FRED database of the Federal Reserve of St. Louis.

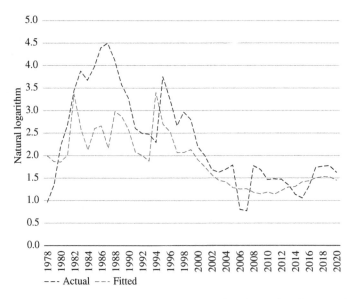

Source: Authors' elaboration with data from the SIE database of the BM and the FRED database of the Federal Reserve of St. Louis.

Figure 8   Actual and fitted Mexico–US interest-rate gap (annual data), 1978–2020

6   ESTIMATING AN ALTERNATIVE TAYLOR RULE

The significant accumulation of international reserves as a percentage of total external debt and the influence of the nominal exchange rate on the Mexico–US interest-rate gap also reflect the strong dependency of Mexico's monetary policy on the United States' monetary policy. Regarding this dependency, we are only interested in the flexible exchange-rate period (that is, from the first quarter of 1995 to the first quarter of 2022). According to economic theory, a flexible exchange rate neutralizes changes in the foreign interest rate but in the case of Mexico this cannot be accepted, as admitted by the Bank of Mexico (see Banco de México 2020).

While it is true that gi has diminished due to the accumulation of international reserves as a percentage of total external debt, the Mexican interest rate has still been affected by the Federal Reserve's monetary policy decisions. The Taylor rule followed by the Bank of Mexico is commonly estimated without including the US interest rate. We believe the Bank of Mexico is concerned about both its own domestic inflation and the United States' interest rate, and we postulate that the actual Taylor rule implicitly followed by the Bank of Mexico is as follows:

$$i_{Mt} = \alpha_0 + \alpha_1 (\pi_t - \pi^\circ_t) + \alpha_2 i_{USt} + \alpha_3 i_{US}^2{}_t + u_{2t}, \tag{2}$$

where α_i are the parameters to be estimated, i_M is Mexico's interest rate, π is the annual inflation rate, π° is the Bank of Mexico's annual inflation rate target, i_{US} is the United States interest rate, u_2 is an error term, and t is a time index.

We assume a quadratic relation between Mexico's interest rate and the United States interest rate. Moreover, considering the reduction of the Mexico–United States interest-rate gap since 1999, we assume a structural break at the third quarter of 2001. We also assume that from the first quarter of 1995 to the second quarter of 2001 the quadratic term of equation (2) was positive, whilst from the third quarter of 2001 to the first quarter of 2022 it was negative.

Sources and data are as follows: the Mexican interest rate is the quarterly average of (i) the monthly interest rate of the Treasury Certificates at 28 days from the first quarter of 1995 to the first quarter of 2008; and (ii) the daily Bank of Mexico's target interest rate from the second quarter of 2008 to the first quarter of 2022. The source of all the information is the Sistema de Información Económica database of the Bank of Mexico. The rate of inflation was elaborated as the annual growth rate of the quarterly average of the monthly Consumer Price Index reported by INEGI in its Banco de Información Económica database. The United States interest rate is the quarterly average of the monthly federal funds effective rate, given by the Federal Reserve Economic Data database of the Federal Reserve of St. Louis.

As a first step, we examine for a unit root in the series to be used in the estimation of equation (2). Table 3 reports our results. As can be seen, $(\pi - \pi^\circ)$ is a stationary series and the rest are integrated series of order one. Therefore, we can use the bounds-testing approach cointegration methodology to estimate equation (2).[8]

According to the results shown in Table 4, the Bank of Mexico increases (decreases) the interest rate when the inflation rate is higher (lower) than its target; however, it is also found that from the first quarter of 1995 to the second quarter of 2001, the Bank of Mexico augmented its interest rate in an increasingly quadratic way with respect to that of the United States, while from the third quarter of 2001

---

8.   See footnote 7.

Table 3   Unit-root test for the series used in the estimation of equation (2)

Series	Period	Augmented Dickey–Fuller test (t-statistics)	Period	Phillips–Perron test (adj. t-statistics)
i_M	1998Q2–2022Q1	−2.44	1995Q2–2022Q1	−3.72**
$d(i_M)$	1998Q3–2022Q1	−2.07**	1995Q3–2022Q1	−13.72*
$\pi - \pi°$	1995Q2–2022Q1	−2.25**	1995Q2–2022Q1	−2.58**
i_{US}	1995Q4–2022Q1	−3.67**	1995Q2–2022Q1	−2.44
$d(i_{US})$	1995Q3–2022Q1	−4.84*	1995Q3–2022Q1	−4.95*
i_{US}^2	1995Q3–2022Q1	−4.18*	1995Q2–2022Q1	−2.64
$d(i_{US}^2)$	1995Q3–2022Q1	−4.46*	1995Q3–2022Q1	−4.44*

Notes: * and ** are statistically significant at the 1 percent and 5 percent level. $d(\cdot)$ stands for the first difference operator. All level tests were done assuming the existence of intercept and trend, while the first difference test was done assuming no intercept and no trend. The number of lags used for the ADF tests were chosen in accordance with the Schwarz information criterion, whilst the number of bandwidths used for the PP tests were chosen according to the Newey–West criterion.

Source: Authors' elaboration with data from the SIE database of the BM, the BIE database of the INEGI, and the FRED database of the Federal Reserve of St. Louis.

Journal compilation © 2022 Edward Elgar Publishing Ltd

Table 4 Estimation of the alternative Mexican Taylor rule (equation (2))

Period	1995Q1–2022Q1
Dependent variable	i_M
$\pi - \pi°$	0.46*
	(0.05)
$i_{US}{}^2$	0.37*
	(0.01)
$i_{US}·D0122$	2.45*
	(0.25)
$i_{US}{}^2·D0122$	−0.70*
	(0.06)
Constant	3.51*
	(0.18)
Model type	Restricted constant, no trend
ARDL model	(2, 4, 4, 1, 4)
F-bounds test	
F-statistic	114.12*
Adjustment coefficient	
u_{1t-1}	−0.45*
	(0.02)
Jarque–Bera test	0.92
LM test (F-statistic, 1 lag)	0.88
White test (F-statistic)	0.71
Ramsey RESET (t-statistic, one fitted term)	1.03

Notes: * is statistically significant at the 1 percent level (standard errors in parentheses). *D0122* is a dummy variable with a value equal to 1 from the third quarter of 2001 to the first quarter of 2022 and 0 otherwise. White test does not include cross terms. ARDL model indicates the number of lags of the dependent and independent variables. A complete report of the estimation, including the fixed regressor, is available on request from the authors.

Source: Authors' elaboration using data from the SIE database of the BM, the BIE database of the INEGI, and the FRED database of the Federal Reserve of St. Louis.

to the first quarter of 2022 the effect was still quadratic but decreasing. As can be seen in Figure 9, from the first quarter of 1995 to the second quarter of 2001, our fitted Mexican interest rate tends to be lower than the actual interest rate, but the former converges to the latter towards the end of the sub-period; from the third quarter of 2001 to the first quarter of 2022 our fitted Mexican interest rate is very similar to the actual interest rate.

One consequence of the influence of the United States' interest rate on Mexico's interest rate is that Mexico confronts an interest-rate floor at a higher level of the interest rate. For the United States the liquidity-trap level of the interest rate is at a nominal interest rate equal to zero (the zero lower bound), but for Mexico it is at a nominal interest rate equal to 3.5 percentage points. Consequently, as can be seen in Figure 10, while the United States' real interest rate was negative for a long period, Mexico's interest rate has been higher and usually positive.

Some final implications resulting from the influence of the United States' monetary policy on Mexico's monetary policy are:

1. Although Mexican policy is widely thought to be counter-cyclical, in fact it has been pro-cyclical, which is at variance with both the intent of Taylor's rule (Taylor 1993) and the Federal Reserve's policy stance.

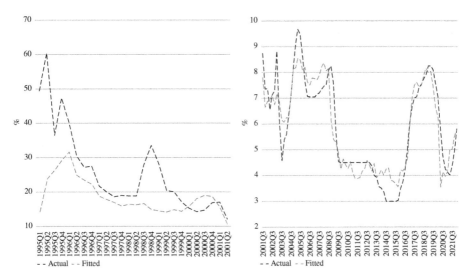

Source: Authors' elaboration with data from the SIE database of the BM, the BIE database of the INEGI, and the FRED database of the Federal Reserve of St. Louis.

Figure 9   Actual and fitted Mexican interest rates (quarterly data), 1995Q1–2022Q1

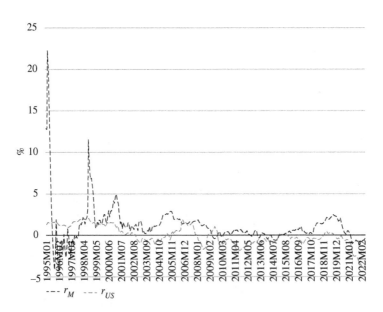

Source: Authors' elaboration with data from the SIE database of the BM, the BIE database of the INEGI, and the FRED database of the Federal Reserve of St. Louis.

Figure 10   Mexico's and the United States' real interest rates (monthly data), 1995M1–2022M5

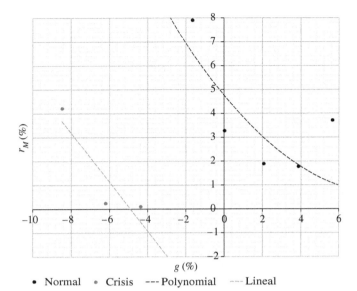

Note: Lineal and polynomial convey the ordinary least squares (OLS) estimation between r_M and g for normal and crisis periods respectively. The outlier values observed in 2020Q2 and 2021Q2 are not considered.
Source: Authors' elaboration with data from the SIE database of the BM and of the BIE database of the INEGI.

Figure 11   Annual growth rate and real interest rate (quarterly data: average for each two percentage points segments of the growth rate), 1995Q1–2022Q1

2. Mexico's interest and inflation rates increase during recession periods, and vice versa. Figure 11 shows that Mexico's economic crises are phases of stagflation.
3. Fiscal policy has been ruled out since the foreign-debt crisis of 1982, much before the advent of the inflation-targeting monetary policy framework. Such fiscal conservatism makes no economic sense: considering that the Bank of Mexico's inflation target is 3 percent and that a liquidity-trap position is reached at an interest rate equal to 3.5 percent, the corresponding liquidity-trap real interest rate is equal to 0.5 percent (a level at which monetary policy becomes ineffective). Therefore, in that scenario, the low real cost of public debt implies that there is enough fiscal policy space.

7   FINAL REMARKS

In this article, taking inspiration from Keynes (1923; 1936), we have focused on the influence of both the dollar and the US monetary policy on Mexico's exchange rate and monetary policy. It was argued that the role of the dollar as the key or hegemonic currency introduces asymmetries in the international monetary system which greatly influence the exchange-rate dynamics of peripheral currencies, and also curb the ability of emerging-market economies to independently use their monetary policy tools and set goals. Those features apply to Mexico.

We have provided evidence of some of the consequences of the dollar hegemony for the Mexican economy. The lower volatility of the exchange rate of the Mexican peso, observed in recent decades, is a consequence of defensive policies – chiefly, the accumulation of international reserves – undertaken by the central bank to discourage and address sudden capital reversals and speculative attacks arising from speculative behavior in conditions of financial fragility.

Our hypothesis was tested with statistical evidence; we conducted empirical estimations to measure the effect of the accumulation of international reserves and exchange-rate variations on the Mexico–US interest-rate gap. Our main findings confirm that those 'precautionary' acquisitions of reserves represent an additional monetary policy channel that, on the one hand, gives the central bank room to maneuver both the exchange rate and its inflation target, and, on the other, bolsters the hegemony of the dollar.

Furthermore, we estimated an alternative Taylor rule for Mexico including the US rate of interest; our estimation gave us some noteworthy clues. First and foremost, Mexico's monetary policy is not autonomous from US monetary policy; second, Mexico faces a liquidity-trap level of the interest rate much higher than the United States: while the United States faces a zero lower bound level, Mexico encounters ineffectiveness of its monetary policy at a positive interest rate of 3.5 percent.

Clearly, with hindsight, the flexible exchange-rate regime introduced in the post-Bretton Woods era and in operation up to the present time, aggravated the balance of payments disequilibria and the monetary instability it was supposed to resolve. This 'nonsystem' allowed the United States to become the only country truly free to manage (appreciate or depreciate) its exchange rate according to its own domestic macroeconomic goals. This change bolstered the dollar hegemony over international liquidity (De Paula et al. 2017; Prates 2020).

Now, as for the crucial question regarding the future of dollar hegemony, it is an open question. The ongoing conversation is that the dominant position of the dollar will decline. The IMF (Arslanalp et al. 2022) reports that central banks' portfolio diversification is the main cause for the relative decline of the dollar's share in the world's market for international reserves. What will be the evolution of the dollar? It is a moot question. There have also been calls for a new international monetary and financial order since the collapse of Bretton Woods. It would be futile to simply substitute a new key currency, be it the euro or the renminbi or whatever currency for that matter, for the current hegemonic currency, the dollar, because that dethroning of the dollar would simply mean a *gattopardo* monetary reform. In this connection, Keynes instructed, back in the 1940s, that the post-war reconstruction of the international monetary and financial system should avoid granting the international reserve right on any particular currency (Harrod 1951).

Insofar as the dollar will remain the key currency at least for the foreseeable future, problems of liquidity and assets with a differential liquidity premium will also remain with us. In this connection, it is worth wrapping up by quoting Keynes (1936 [1964], p. 155): 'Of the maxims of orthodox finance none, surely, is more anti-social than the fetish of liquidity.'

REFERENCES

Arslanalp, S., B. Eichengreen, and C. Simpson-Bell (2022), 'The stealth erosion of dollar dominance: active diversifiers and the rise of nontraditional reserve currencies,' IMF WP/22/58, Washington, DC: International Monetary Fund.

Banco de México (2020), 'Reporte de estabilidad financiera,' Banco de México, available at: {BB59C14C-03BE-58EE-6E0F-7D3EB65D52D5}.pdf (banxico.org.mx).

Bresser-Pereira, L.C. (2016), 'Reflecting on New Developmentalism and Classical Developmentalism,' *Review of Keynesian Economics*, 4(3), 331–352.

Calvo, G.A. (1998), 'Capital flows and capital-market crises: the simple economics of sudden stops,' *Journal of Applied Economics*, 1(1), 35–54.

Calvo, G. and E. Mendoza (2000), 'Contagion, globalization, and the volatility of capital flows,' in S. Edwards (ed.), *Capital Flows and the Emerging Economies: Theory, Evidence, and Controversies*, Chicago: University of Chicago Press, pp. 15–41.

Davidson, P. (1999), 'Global employment and open economy macroeconomics,' in J. Deprez and J.T. Harvey (eds), *Foundations of International Economics*, London and New York: Routledge, pp. 9–34.

De Paula, L.F., B. Fritz, and D.M. Prates (2017), 'Keynes at the periphery: currency hierarchy and challenges for economic policy in emerging economies,' *Journal of Post Keynesian Economics*, 40(2), 183–202, available at: https://doi.org/10.1080/01603477.2016.1252267.

Frenkel, R. and J. Ros (2006), 'Unemployment and the real exchange rate in Latin America,' *World Development*, 34(4), 631–646.

Friedman, M. (1953), 'The case for flexible exchange rates,' in M. Friedman, *Essays in Positive Economics*, Chicago: The University of Chicago Press, pp. 157–203.

Galindo, L.M. and J. Ros (2008), 'Alternatives to inflation targeting in Mexico,' *International Review of Applied Economics*, 22(2), 201–214.

Harrod, R.F. (1951), *The Life of John Maynard Keynes*, London: Macmillan.

IMF (International Monetary Fund) (2022), *Annual Report on Exchange Arrangements and Exchange Restrictions 2021*, Washington, DC: IMF.

Keynes, J.M. (1923 [2013]), *A Tract on Monetary Reform*, Cambridge, UK: Cambridge University Press.

Keynes, J.M. (1930), *A Treatise on Money*, vols I and II, London: Macmillan.

Keynes, J.M. (1936 [1964]), *The General Theory of Employment, Interest and Money*, New York: Harcourt Brace Jovanovich.

Lavoie, M. (2014), *Post-Keynesian Economics: New Foundations*, Cheltenham, UK and Northampton, MA: Edward Elgar Publishing.

Médici, F., A. Mario, and A. Fiorito (2021), 'Questioning the effect of the real exchange rate on growth: new evidence from Mexico,' *Review of Keynesian Economics*, 9(2), 253–269.

Palley, T. (2018), 'Recovering Keynesian Phillips curve theory: hysteresis of ideas and the natural rate of unemployment,' *Review of Keynesian Economics*, 6(4), 473–492.

Palley, T. (2020), 'What's wrong with Modern Money Theory: macro and political economic restraints on deficit-financed fiscal policy,' *Review of Keynesian Economics*, 8(4), 472–493.

Pesaran, M.H., Y. Shin, and R.J. Smith (2001), 'Bound Testing Approaches to the analysis of level relationships,' *Journal of Applied Econometrics*, 16(3), 289–326.

Prates, D. (2020), 'Beyond Modern Money Theory: a Post-Keynesian approach to the currency hierarchy, monetary sovereignty, and policy space,' *Review of Keynesian Economics*, 8(4), 494–511.

Ros, J. (2015), *¿Cómo salir de la trampa del lento crecimiento y alta desigualdad?*, El Colegio de México y Universidad Nacional Autónoma de México.

Sarno, L. (2005), 'Viewpoint: towards a solution to the puzzles in exchange rate economics: where do we stand?,' *Canadian Journal of Economics (Review Canadienne d'économique)*, 38(3), 673–708.

Serrano, F., R. Summa, and G. Aidar (2021), 'Exogenous interest rate and exchange rate dynamics under elastic expectations,' *Investigación Económica*, 80(318), 3–31.

Taylor, J.B. (1993), 'Discretion versus policy rules in practice,' *Carnegie-Rochester Conference Series on Public Policy*, 39, 195–214.

Vernengo, M. (2006), 'Technology, finance, and dependency: Latin American radical political economy in retrospect,' *Review of Radical Political Economy*, 38(4) 551–568.

Vicarelli, F. (1984), *Keynes, the Instability of Capitalism*, Philadelphia: University of Pennsylvania Press.

Williamson, J. (1976), 'The benefits and costs of an international nonsystem,' in E.M. Bernstein et al. (eds), *Reflections on Jamaica*, Essays in International Finance 115, International Finance Section, Princeton, NJ: Princeton University Press, pp. 54–59.

Wray, L.R. (2015), *Modern Money Theory: A Primer on Macroeconomics for Sovereign Monetary Systems*, 2nd edn, Basingstoke, UK: Palgrave Macmillan.

Review of Keynesian Economics, Vol. 10 No. 4, Winter 2022, pp. 91–116

Old and new proposals for global monetary reform

Jan Priewe*
Professor Emeritus of Economics, HTW Berlin – University of Applied Sciences, Germany

The post-Bretton Woods monetary system in characterised by the hegemony of the US dollar despite increasing features of a multi-currency system. There is no other currency in sight to succeed the dollar. Yet there are severe downsides that seem to increase on several fronts. The paper diagnoses five major challenges: exchange rates driven by non-fundamentals, current-account imbalances, a hierarchy of interest rates (including dependency from US monetary policy), commodity-price bonanzas, and lack of global liquidity in hard currency. Major reform proposals are reviewed, focusing on reforms of Special Drawing Rights on the one hand and on a new exchange-rate system on the other. Regarding the latter, a novel system is proposed, focused on the largest foreign-exchange market, the dollar–euro market. The proposal includes target zones, mutual interventions, and a Tobin tax on currency transactions. A precondition is strengthening the international role of the euro. The currency blocs on both sides of the North Atlantic could form a bloc of more than 80 countries. The new system of managed floating could later be extended by other reserve currencies. More exchange-rate stability around the globe would reduce the country risk premiums in the Global South and trigger other positive externalities.

Keywords: *international monetary system, dollar standard, international monetary arrangements, foreign exchange, Bretton Woods*

JEL codes: *F00, F02, F31, F32, F33, G01*

1 THE NON-SYSTEM, CAST IN STONE?

The birth of the post-Bretton Woods monetary 'system' came with the Nixon shock in 1971[1] and the rejection of the German Bundesbank to continue with the obligation to purchase US dollars in 1973 (Deutsche Bundesbank 2013), not by the deliberate design of an alternative. The old gold–dollar system was in crisis, and there were no policy-makers high in rank in the US or in Europe who were able and willing to reform it after it was clear that the Smithsonian Agreement did not hold. So it was replaced by a non-system of simple *laissez-faire*, praised by the Bundesbank as 'delinking from the dollar'. The initial interim arrangement after 1973 became permanent. The newborn pure *dollar standard*, which *de facto* did not allow detachment from the dollar, was the beginning of a new dollar and US hegemony. This hegemony (or dominance as many observers prefer to say) seems, after half a century, to be cast in stone. Despite a changeable history of crises, with extremes in its performance, the

---

* Email: jan.priewe@posteo.de.
1. The decision was made at Camp David on 13–15 August 1971. Other nations were not informed, nor was the IMF. The shock was like a coup.

Journal compilation © 2022 Edward Elgar Publishing Ltd
The Lypiatts, 15 Lansdown Road, Cheltenham, Glos GL50 2JA, UK
and The William Pratt House, 9 Dewey Court, Northampton MA 01060-3815, USA

dollar is still the only truly global currency in terms of all three functions of money, in particular the global store of value based on a large, deep, and at times very shaky financial sector including a large market of risk-free sovereign bonds. Yet all three functions are interlinked, each one only functioning if the others function, and all this is understood as relative to other countries and currencies: an uncontested monopoly for global money. Ocampo (2017, p. 211) uses this wording: the 'world economy is hostage to the monetary policy of the main reserve-issuing country …'.

The actual new dollar standard was and still is much more than just a new exchange-rate regime. It triggered much broader change. With respect to exchange rates, the dynamics led to the predominance of floating rather than intermediate regimes of exchange rates, especially in emerging-market economies (EMEs) – hence, it is an early form of financial and monetary deregulation. For central banks and for fiscal policy the emergence of the new dollar standard was a game changer. The trend in advanced countries towards full floating came alongside ever-increasing global capital-account openness and capital mobility, even though the IMF statutes allow free choice of exchange-rate arrangement as long as the current account is open and 'currency manipulation' excluded. Capital mobility promoted the predominance of short-term mobility and subsequently a high degree of exchange-rate uncertainty, a perfect precondition for a new playing field for speculation, herding, and new financial instruments, which paved the way for the derivative markets. The upscaling of multinational corporations, especially banks and non-bank financial institutions, occurred, which shattered the ownership structure of enterprises across the globe, enlarged further after the demise of the 'second world' and the rise of China. One can even say, with the wisdom of hindsight, that the end of the Bretton Woods system kickstarted economic globalisation in tandem with the gradual and pervasive turn to Neoliberalism (sometimes called hyper-globalisation or globalism) (cf. Costabile 2022). The seed was incorporated in the deregulation of foreign-exchange markets which served as a Pandora's box. Of course, there were many and diverse political and institutional counter-attempts to cope with the new reality, so that new varieties of capitalism emerged.

Virtually no observers see an alternative to the dollar, either in the yuan or the euro or a synthetic semi-currency; some hold we already have a multicurrency system with dollar dominance. Most economists believe the system may not be perfect, but it is better than all possible alternatives. The belief in its longevity is mainly based on the dollar's outstanding global credibility, the size of the foreign-exchange markets, and the unique scope of the financial sector embedded in a capitalist country with more stable institutions than elsewhere (representative for many is Prasad 2014). It seems therefore that the erstwhile claimed 'exorbitant privilege' (cf. Eichengreen 2011) of the global reserve country is deserved by merits and is therefore not really a privilege but, rather, a reward. With this judgement, any consideration of reform seems outdated or utopian and useless. A new hegemon is not in sight, and if it were, it wouldn't be better; and a multicurrency system is already on the way or coming soon, but could be competitive and therefore full of risks, unless it gives the dollar the rank of *primus-inter-pares*, hence it is only another form of hegemony.

I question this narrative, based on the following:

- The political hegemony of the US seems to be diminishing in the medium to long run and is not as stable as it seems: the break-up of the gold–dollar standard was a confidence crisis for the dollar, not least due to the loss of inflation control; the end of the gold–dollar standard was seen as the end of the dollar standard as well; later the dollar dominance was upheld with heavy currency cooperation (for example, the Plaza and Louvre accord) and also the support of the IMF in which the US is dominant due to its monopoly of a veto with > 15 per cent of total votes; this privilege will likely fade in the next few years if China's IMF quota rises due to its superseding the US in terms of GDP; the reconfirmation of dollar dominance after 2008 came with a strong revaluation of the dollar, partly due to a prior strong weakness against the euro; dollar-denominated assets are less safe if the fluctuation of the real exchange rate is considered; and finally, if deglobalisation occurs and the world economy should become divided into two large blocs, the dollar hegemony would be at risk.

- The dollar hegemony hinges on the ability to control inflation, which requires control of the oil price as the key for other commodities and a major determinant of the inflation rate; the control is critical if oil prices surge due to supply constraints. With Saudi Arabia as the main player capable of adjusting the supply, cooperation with Saudi Arabia (or other key suppliers) is a necessary buttress for the dollar, based on the political and military power of the US, having a monopoly in this respect. The Russian Federation in the meantime gained a very strong position in the global supply of both oil and gas, beyond the control of the US.

- The mirror image of the exorbitant privilege is the exorbitant disadvantages of the dollar-dependent economies, mainly in the Global South, which seem to gain weight either with more 'globalisation' or with outright de-globalisation. The hegemonic monetary policy of the US central bank, solely focused on national goals, becomes increasingly inappropriate for the rest of the world.

- The hierarchy of monies on the globe is steep, and having a national currency of low quality involves increasingly heavy burdens, also for EMEs facing monetary traps; low quality means that the functions of the local currencies can only partially be fulfilled. The quality of national currencies is eroded with pervasive dollarisation.

- The stability of the dollar standard depends on the capacity of the dollar to offer a safe parking space for international reserves, on the one hand. This requires that the dollar's real exchange rate does not devalue too much and that the US runs current-account deficits that do not go beyond a critical threshold. On the other hand, the dollar has to be able to provide the global currency to the world outside the US as a substitute for gold in the gold–dollar standard (hence coping with the Triffin dilemma; Triffin 1960), now with dollars alone, especially as the lender of last resort, together with the IMF.

- Increasing liberalisation of capital accounts in emerging countries, reinforced by financialisation, could potentialise the malfunctioning of financial markets (including foreign-exchange markets) so that the antagonism of globalising markets and stagnant or lagging adjustment of global institutions could increase. This depends to a significant extent on the institutional changeability of the IMF.

However, rising discontent with dollar dominance is a precondition for change, but not a sufficient one. There needs to be a feasible alternative. Time is on the side of change, and one can imagine and design better systems than the one from Nixon's heritage.

This paper is searching for alternatives to the present dollar standard, but not in the sense that another national currency kicks the dollar from its throne. In Section 2, I elaborate on the deficiencies of the dollar standard and the key goals where progress is needed. In Section 3, I review the most important alternatives that have been proposed, starting with the Keynes Plan from 1943. The emphasis is put on the most elaborate recent proposals, namely the ones from John Williamson (2016) and

José Ocampo (2017). In Section 4, I sketch my own idea of a currency cooperation between the US dollar and the euro, which focuses on the regulation with managed floating on the largest foreign-exchange market on the globe. This could be the nucleus for further global monetary reforms. Due to constraints of space, I deliver only a rough outline of the idea.

2   THE SHADOWS OF THE DOLLAR STANDARD AND THE CHALLENGES AHEAD

Having a national currency that fulfils a second function as a global currency generates specific contradictions. It reduces the capacity of all other currencies in fulfilling the three functions of money, and also, as a consequence, the capacity to conduct efficient national monetary policy. Only one type of money is purely sovereign; the others are dependent and incorporate less quality. It is the prerogative of the dollar to have no external value, hence its exchange rate, by definition, is 1; the global reserve country can purchase more goods and services than it produces, without a relevant external debt burden; the economy has no distinct financial budget constraint. Monetary policy is more sovereign than elsewhere, and fiscal policy has more leeway than in any other country. Official reserves from other countries pour into the reserve country, despite low interest rates; private savings from the whole world have a preference for this country and its financial habitat, which is a quasi-natural financial haven with the strongest magnetic power. So, the US financial industry has an inherent locational advantage but tends towards moral hazard. Even poor financial regulation, fraud and corruption, or a monetary policy that may ruin other countries' economies, do not deter capital inflows from all $n - 1$ countries; quite to the contrary. In the notion of the 'trilemma' (allowing only two goals out of three to be reached, namely sovereign monetary policy, stable exchange rates, and international capital mobility), all countries have the same options to choose as the US (following the Mundell–Fleming model also). However, the US sacrifices only exchange-rate stability to a certain degree; most other countries sacrifice considerable parts of all three goals – hence the options are asymmetric.

The hegemonic privilege comes with few obligations as long as no competitor currencies exist. Even inflation or deflation or high sovereign debt cannot undermine the 'number one' status. The political administration has more rule-setting capacity than any other country. There may be limits, but they are *a priori* unknown. The power of the dollar also has a firm bedrock in traditions, conventions, and the track record which corroborates trust at a large scale. Path dependency follows. The economic and financial power nourish political power and vice versa.

However, the dollar standard is not water- and shock-proof. The euro area has established its own regional universe, and the renminbi is about to do the same in other nascent forms in Asia. Smaller kings reign in niches, such as Singapore or Switzerland. Trade and currency wars occur (Bergsten 2013), but usually the global monetary hegemon has more pull. Even if the US has lost power as a global economy (regarding the share in global output and trade), the monetary hegemony seems to be maintained, at least at a rank clearly above potential competitors.

The other $n - 1$ currencies are staggered in four layers: the other four reserve currencies in the basket of the Special Drawing Rights (SDR) – euro, yuan, yen, sterling – plus the currencies from Australia, Canada and Switzerland which also host official reserves (IMF 2022); furthermore 14 currencies of the other 'advanced countries' (in the IMF classification); 34 EME currencies, classified here as having not more than 50 per cent of bank loans in dollars or euros, as an indicator of dollarisation (data from Chitu 2012, p. 42; median in the period 2000–2010); 124 currencies – that is, 69 per cent of the 180 currencies on the globe – have an inferior quality of currency, hence they are strongly dollarised (euroised) in all functions of money (see also Herr and Nettekoven 2022). Probably only the top eight currencies have the capacity to fully avoid public debt in foreign currency and to enjoy fairly low interest rates close to those in the US. Only a few countries can command foreign business partners to pay with their own currency. World market prices of goods, services and securities are denominated mostly in US dollars. Yet a closer country-by-country look at the currency hierarchy shows sharp differences within the groupings, most significantly among EMEs (see below).

What are the main challenges for the dollar standard, not only in order to survive but also to diminish the problems prevailing now and looming in the future? In more general terms, the global monetary and financial system needs to be stable, capable of avoiding crises, be they regional or global, and to support the 'real economies' regarding output growth, trade, employment, and structural change towards social and environmental goals. Supporting developing countries and EMEs will likely gain more importance than in the past, simply because of the trend to the rising share of population and GDP in the Global South. In brief, the global monetary system must become more development-friendly, which implies that the currency hierarchy has to become flatter.

More concretely, I envisage first and foremost the following four challenges for global monetary reforms. Coping with them is a precondition for managing climate change policies, which requires the modernisation of the economies of the Global South which have to shoulder the brunt of the reduction of greenhouse gases.

2.1   Reducing exchange-rate volatility and chronic exchange-rate misalignments

Freely floating exchange rates tend especially to be highly volatile and detached from fundamentals. They do not reflect deviations from purchasing power parity, inflation or interest-rate differentials; hence it is both nominal and real exchange-rate instability that aggravates monetary instability in general. This implies the risks of both high exchange-rate volatility and long-standing over- or undervaluation of exchange rates, inflation and deflation risks, currency and trade wars, and general misallocation of goods and financial assets due to mispricing. Thus, the global price system can be fundamentally flawed, temporarily or continuously. Furthermore, since exchange-rate volatility results mainly from short-term capital flows, global capital flows are tilted to short-term speculative flows. This in turn often triggers tsunami-like inflows and their sudden reversal towards safe havens in a few advanced countries. Hedging, advocated as a cure-all, is costly and limited in scope, time and efficiency. A quick look at the exchange-rate volatility among the global reserve countries and the key EMEs over the long haul provides an impression of the thrust of short-termism. The foreign-exchange markets should be seen as an asset market of its own, with an impact on all other asset markets (Priewe 2015; 2016).

Figure 1 shows the real effective exchange rate for the five global reserve currencies in the SDR basket since the late Bretton Woods years. We see strong fluctuations, with wide swings of around 20 percentage points, in the performance of dollar, DM (later euro) and sterling, an extreme upheaval of the yen until 1994 with a strong downward trend afterwards, while the renminbi devalued strongly in the first two decades after

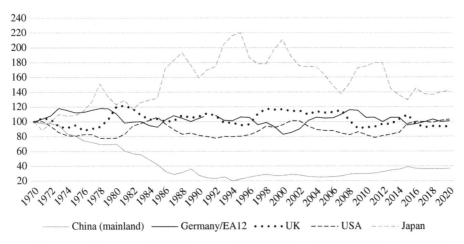

Note: Germany stands representative for the euro area (EA12) for the period 1970–1990 due to lack of data. Since 1992, data are as per EA12.
Source: Bruegel (2022); own calculation.

Figure 1   Index of annual REER against 65 countries for five international reserve currencies (index 1970 = 100)

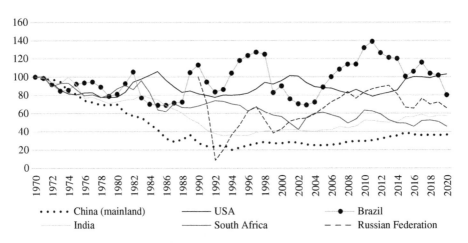

Source: Bruegel (2022); own calculation.

Figure 2   Index of annual REER against 65 countries for the BRICS group and the USA (index 1970 = 100)

the reforms had started and recovered afterwards, especially against the dollar after 2005. The dollar is clearly an unstable currency in terms of the real effective exchange rate (REER), but its international competitiveness is of less importance due to the privilege to live with a chronic current-account deficit. Financial markets care less for the REER and more for nominal exchange rates.

The REER of the leading EME, here the BRICS group (Brazil, Russia, India, China and South Africa; see Figure 2), is on average less volatile than the group of the SDR

                    Journal compilation © 2022 Edward Elgar Publishing Ltd

countries, with the exception of China and India since the mid 1990s, not least due to pegging to the dollar and later managed floating combined with capital controls. Brazil, Russia and South Africa exhibit extreme fluctuations, reflecting 'commodity currencies', which inhibits orderly development (Goda and Priewe 2020).

2.2   Preventing severe current-account imbalances

The traditional view of global imbalances was focused on the US as the biggest deficit country and China plus some others as the giant surplus countries. After China had unilaterally changed its exchange-rate misalignment in the course of the global financial crisis and the US reduced oil imports (due to fracking), this tension abated somewhat. Yet the US is still the largest deficit economy and China the mirror image in terms of *absolute numbers*. The age-old problem of imbalances has changed somewhat. A dozen or so large surplus countries (in absolute figures) face many dozens of severe chronic deficit economies mainly in the Global South (Tables 1a and 1b provide illustrative snapshots for the year 2020). Many smaller countries have huge surpluses as a share of GDP (for

Table 1   (a) Snapshot: current-account imbalances, 2020; (b) Global imbalances

(a)

Current-account balance (CAB), % of GDP	Number of countries reported	Grouping, aggregate CAB, US$ billions	
CAB > 0%	79	15 largest surplus countries	86% of global deficits
CAB > 5%	24	15 largest deficit countries	67% of global deficits
CAB > 10%	9		
CAB < 0%	124		
CAB < –5%	62		
CAB < –10%	36		
No of countries reported	203		

Source: WDI (2022).

(b)

Ten largest deficit countries 2020			Ten largest surplus countries 2020		
	US$ billions	% of GDP		US$ billions	% of GDP
US	–616.0	–2.9	China, mainland	274.0	1.9
UK	–73.7	–2.7	Germany	269.0	7.0
France	–49.1	–1.9	Japan	148.9	2.9
Turkey	–35.5	–4.9	Korea	75.9	4.6
Canada	–29.2	–1.8	Italy	72.0	3.8
Brazil	–24.5	–1.7	Netherlands	63.1	7.0
Saudi Arabia	–21.6	–3.1	Singapore	58.1	17.1
Algeria	–18.2	–12.6	Australia	36.2	2.7
Nigeria	–17.0	–3.9	Russia	36.0	2.4
Egypt	–14.2	–3.9	India	32.7	1.2

Source: WDI (2022).

example, Switzerland and Singapore), and many small countries have giant deficits relative to GDP. Hence China's surplus is still highly problematic for the global imbalances due to its sheer size, not so relative to GDP, since global surpluses equal global deficits if statistics are correct. It should be mentioned that the problem of the surpluses is not only that they exist, especially if they are persistent, but also that the recycling into long-term investments is insufficient while short-term speculative portfolio flows like carry trade, etc., prevail. It should also be mentioned that gross capital flows are a multiple of net flows and have a bearing on the latter. The group of oil-producing countries is no longer a natural surplus club. In 2020, 11 major oil producers with officially reported data had as an aggregate only a small current-account surplus, with Russia and Kuwait by far the largest of the surplus countries (data from WDI 2022).

The old confrontation of the UK and France (representative for deficit countries) versus the US (as the surplus country) during the Bretton Woods negotiations prevails on a large scale in different compositions of countries and assets. The burden still lies asymmetrically on the shoulders of the deficit countries on the verge of overindebtedness and balance-of-payments (BoP) crisis. Currency devaluation is often not a feasible remedy if debt is in foreign currency and trade is denominated predominantly in dollars which diminishes the impact of realignments (cf. Gopinath et al. 2020 and the 'dollar dominance' hypothesis). The IMF responses, with structural adjustment programmes and nine specific programmes including precautionary action, supplemented by the option of last resort with capital flow management (a form of temporary capital controls), are sometimes leading in the right direction and sometimes counter-productive, as in the case of Greece. The IMF is an insufficient lender of last resort for indebted countries, and even the large swap arrangement of the Federal Reserve, providing dollars to cope with the still continuing Triffin dilemma, may not suffice. Emergency actions prevail; preventive policies are still insufficient.

The longer countries are stuck in deficits, the worse their *net international investment position* (NIIP), since liabilities to external countries exceed their assets at a rising scale relative to GDP. This tends to lead sooner or later to a situation close to a BoP crisis. The traditional fear that the US cannot carry an ever-increasing negative NIIP is overstated as long as interest paid to external countries, especially on reserves, is small but profits earned from abroad are high. Whether this privilege will sustain is questionable if reserves from EMEs cease to arrive. Excessive reserve build-up is an expensive insurance against exchange-rate turmoil and should be rendered unnecessary.

If the traction of exchange-rate realignments is limited, though not irrelevant, other means of preventing or coping with imbalances are needed, especially on the side of surplus countries. A symmetric approach of surplus and deficit countries is needed – often said, never practised. The predominant approach with its emphasis on deficit countries is unilateral; a symmetric approach would have to be multilateral.

Persistent and large imbalances tend to impede global growth and employment as Keynes foresaw presciently in 1943 (Keynes 1943 [1969]). Deficit countries would have to depreciate, turn to fiscal and wage austerity, even deflation, and then mutate into surplus status, hence spending less than they were producing. Forcing developing and emerging economies into this dismal option supresses development.

The problem of global imbalances tends to gain relevance in the course of structural change towards phasing out the usage of fossil fuels and other contributors to greenhouse gases. Fossil-fuel-producing countries need to keep their natural capital in the ground and look for a new business model. This most likely requires massive changes in the BoP which have the potential for severe crises. The mirror image is that the group of heavy surplus countries (not necessarily as a share of GDP) will have to contribute to the abating of global imbalances.

2.3   Reducing interest rates and country risk premia in the Global South

Credit markets in developing countries and EMEs are key for private and public investment in local currency. If (real) interest rates are unaffordable, credit markets dry out, function only for the short term, or are replaced by foreign currency credits (often short-term) which bear exchange-rate risks. If credit is not sufficiently available, prior saving of profits or other incomes is necessary, or subsidised credit out of scarce public budgets. Loans in domestic currency and in foreign currency are under conditions of free capital mobility partially competing, hence both interest rates tend to converge at a level that includes a currency risk premium (assuming stable expected exchange rates, according to the interest-rate parity theory). Thus the problem of *original sin* applies, similarly to domestic currency loans. The term 'original sin' sounds as if it were a God-given curse, an immitigable fate. Evidence shows it is not.

Comparing central-bank policy rates in nominal and real terms, or the differential between real lending rates and GDP growth rates, shows unfavourable conditions for many countries, and by contrast for some countries highly positive constellations (Table 2). In the EMEs shown in Table 2, nominal policy rates were much higher than in the US, to a somewhat lesser extent the real bonds rate (ten-year loan), partly due to higher inflation than in the US. Furthermore, the differential $r - g$ was in Asian emerging economies much more favourable than in the US (partly due to 'financial repression'), while the Latin American and African economies had to bear higher interest than growth rates. The difference comes both from higher growth, lower interest rates and lower inflation in Asia, apart from using capital controls, especially in China and India. Another diverse country group for which fewer data are available (Table 2, right-hand columns) shows extremely high nominal interest rates for some countries, partly due to inflation and a high yield rate.

A $g > r$ constellation allows permanently primary budget deficits with stable debt ratios for the government budget. Something similar applies to the aggregate corporate budget, which makes incurring debt easy as well as easily growing out of debt, relative to GDP.[2] It also requires caution with foreign currency debt. Data for other developing countries are scarce, but show by and large higher nominal and real interest rates despite higher inflation.

2.4   Mitigating commodity-price boom–bust cycles

Commodity-price fluctuations are global and tend to be much stronger than GDP fluctuations or exchange-rate changes. Whatever their causes are, all of them tend to move in tandem with oil prices, whose rollercoaster is however more incisive compared to metal or agricultural commodities. Fossil energy prices have a strong influence (directly and indirectly) on inflation rates, while food prices (as well as prices for metal commodities) depend strongly on fossil energy costs. Hence excessive commodity-price hikes have a bearing on the real economy, on inflation rates (especially on cost inflation where

2.   Sovereign bond rates serve as a benchmark for low-risk private loan rates. If foreign borrowing is excluded, the sum of budget balances, household balances and corporate balances must not fall below zero.

Table 2   The global hierarchy of interest rates

Mean 2020–2022, ranking downward according to policy rate	Policy rate (nom.)	Real bonds rate 2022[a]	Real bonds rate minus real growth rate g	Eight other developing countries/EMEs with fewer data available (nominal rates)	Monetary policy rate 2022	Bond rate 2022
Brazil	12.3	5.8	3.8			
Russia	12.0	−0.3	−2.9	Argentina	47.0	49.7
South Africa	7.6	4.6	2.4	Egypt	11.3	17.2
India	6.7	0.9	−5.6	Ethiopia	7.0	n.a.
Mexico	6.6	4.3	2.8	Pakistan	9.8	13.2
Colombia	5.9	6.4	2.7	Peru	4.5	7.9
China	5.4	0.7	−7.7	Turkey	15.5	21.6
Philippines	5.2	2.7	−2.1	Uganda	6.5	14.5
Poland	4.6	3.1	−0.4	Zambia	9.0	26.0
Chile	3.6	3.2	−0.2			
Malaysia	3.3	2.3	−2.0			
Thailand	2.1	1.2	−2.1			
United States	1.6	0.3	−1.7			

Note: a. Ten-year bonds, June 2022, for Russia prior to the war with Ukraine.
Source: BIS (2022); WDI (2022); own calculations.

Journal compilation © 2022 Edward Elgar Publishing Ltd

monetary policy is stymied), and on exchange rates. Turnarounds always seem to come impetuously. No fundamental stability is visible. Dampening the fluctuations would be extremely helpful for stabilising the global economy, inflation control, development, and human needs. There have been no serious attempts to smooth the commodity prices and fight extreme speculative overreactions, despite the existence of the OPEC cartel, which is, however, fragile. Within the 13 countries comprising OPEC and the additional ten countries (called OPEC+ since 2016), Saudi Arabia and Russia are the key players. While the foundation of OPEC+ was praised as reducing dependency on Saudi Arabia, it increased dependency on Russia. Since fossil energy prices can trigger global recessions, energy price control is key for economic stabilisation and largely undervalued in most discourses. This challenge requires answers in the twenty-first century, with increasing scarcity of natural resources. Figure 3 shows the enormous thrust of the dynamics of crude oil prices over the last 60 years.

We see three phases of excessive price rises after the stability in the 1960s: the price explosions of the 1970s in two steps (1973 and 1979), then after a downward shock in 1985, a rise until 1990, leading to a trough in 1998. Afterwards prices were hiked to record levels until the global financial crisis in 2008. After a short recovery following the crisis until 2014, energy prices had started to drop sharply already before the COVID-19 pandemic, though had begun to recover by spring 2020, leading up to a price of US$120 in June 2022. Upper turning points often coincide with recessions.

Commodity-price fluctuations have a strong impact on terms of trade and on exchange rates of countries dependent on commodity production. Indirectly they influence inflation rates, monetary policy rates, and the global business cycle. Prices are fixed primarily not on spot but on forward markets, and are influenced by futures. If it were possible to smooth commodity prices at least to an extent that would diminish extreme volatility, strong distortions of exchange rates and growth dynamics could be mitigated. Last but not least, global decarbonisation requires a smooth price trend of fossil energies in a sustainable and foreseeable direction. With the turn to broad-based *laissez-faire* after the end of Bretton Woods, stabilising commodity-price dynamics

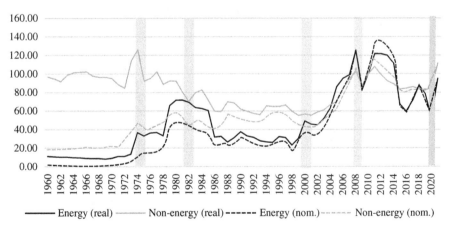

Note: In nominal US$ and in constant 2010 US$. Shaded areas are major recessions.
Source: World Bank (2022); author's calculations.

Figure 3   Commodity prices: indices for energy and non-energy commodities, 1960–2021 (index 2010 = 100)

had been ignored as a global policy goal.[3] The parallel rise of commodity prices and real exchange rates of commodity-producing countries had been named Dutch disease; long cycles of over- and undervaluation of exchange rates have highly negative consequences for the respective countries and the global economy at large.

2.5   Shortage of hard currency in emergency situations, especially in low-income countries

In specific crisis episodes, poor countries need easy access to unconditional hard-currency loans with low interest rates. A case in point was the COVID-19 crisis, which had fatal consequences for developing countries at low-income levels. Ordinary credit markets or transfers from development cooperation or charity organisations are insufficient. The provision of financial help through the global monetary system, for instance with more SDR, could be helpful (and was indeed granted to some extent).

I have touched on five areas of global monetary reforms. The first three are the core ones, centred on exchange rates, trade imbalances, and interest rates, all geared to mitigate local, regional or global crises. The privileges of the key reserve-currency country should be diminished and reallocated; the degree of dollar dominance should be reduced and the quality of currencies below the top layers improved. Looking for another hegemon currency or calling for currency competition at the top deck is looking in a false direction. Before we move forward, we review the history of key proposals for global monetary reform since 1943.

3   OLD AND CONTEMPORANEOUS PROPOSALS

3.1   Global money in a clearing union: Keynes's proposal for Bretton Woods

During the Bretton Woods negotiations, Keynes had proposed a global currency union, dubbed the International Clearing Union (ICU), with an artificial currency, the bancor, to be used only by a global central bank within the ICU in transactions with national central banks (Keynes 1943 [1969], final proposal). The bancor could only be used for payments among the member governments. It was envisaged as a basket currency, first pegged to gold in constant relation, but not redeemable in gold. All national currencies are pegged but adjustable to the bancor and thus indirectly to gold. The 'currency' is only a unit of account and a medium of intergovernmental payments; it cannot store value and is not usable for national foreign-exchange reserves. The global central bank manages the clearing union, but does not generate new money unless the quotas are raised. Each country has a quota – and finances it – with reference to its sum of exports and imports, assumed at around 75 per cent (ibid., p. 22). This quota would be very high; today the aggregate quota would be around 39 per cent of global GDP (today's quota of IMF members merely reaches only around 1 per cent of global GDP). Since the quota is set relative to trade, quotas would rise in line with the growth of trade, financed by members' governments or their central banks.

---

3.   With the fracking boom for oil and gas, the US became the world's largest oil and gas producer (Enerdata 2022 for 2021). Yet the US is so far either not able or not willing to control or smooth global fossil energy prices, despite building up national strategic gas and petroleum reserves.

                    Journal compilation © 2022 Edward Elgar Publishing Ltd

The core idea of the ICU was that both surplus and deficit countries should participate in reducing imbalances: deficit countries can overdraft their account (for a small fee) up to their quota. Beyond a threshold of a quarter of the quota, the debtor is obliged to devalue or curtail capital exports (apart from other measures); surplus countries should expand domestic demand, appreciate in terms of the bancor (or alternatively raise their money incomes), reduce import tariffs and expand international 'development loans'. Trade surpluses lead to accumulation of the bancor in the account of the surplus country within the ICU; the country is free to use the surplus in the way mentioned, instead of accumulating it. Quotas should be raised or reduced counter-cyclically, to stabilise the world economy.

Pegged exchange rates vis-à-vis the bancor could be maintained under limited and regulated cross-border capital mobility. Member governments were to decide about capital-account liberalisation, which Keynes endorsed for long-term capital transactions in contrast to speculative ones. Keynes wanted to achieve stable but adjustable exchange rates, solve problems of imbalances in the current accounts without forcing deficit-makers into deflationary policies, and delink the new global currency from a specific national currency (that is, solve the 'Triffin dilemma' by the rules of the ICU) and possibly in the long run also from gold.

Although the US government rejected Keynes's proposal, especially as the US was a surplus country at the time, a mild variant was implanted into the Bretton Woods system. The US dollar replaced the bancor, fixed but adjustable exchange rates were established, and the reserves of the IMF and the finance of the World Bank were to support deficit countries, thus assigning the residual adjustment burden solely to deficit countries.

In the ICU proposal Keynes focused mainly on trade balances. However, surplus and deficit countries, hence creditors and debtors, are normally in a net creditor or net debtor position regarding the stocks of assets and liabilities. Both may be, even initially, in a net creditor or debtor position, which is beyond the thresholds. In an earlier proposal Keynes mentioned that credit balances above the quota could be confiscated by the end of the year and then transferred to a reserve fund. This would imply that excessive debts would also be cancelled. Overall, Keynes was not very clear on the role of capital controls. What was clear to him was that capital flows needed to be regulated.

Keynes was often praised as being symmetric to debtors and creditors in the adjustment mechanism. Robert Skidelsky (2004) has commented that he was, in earnest, clearly tilted to the key role of the creditors.

An updated version of the Keynes plan was advocated by Paul Davidson (2009, pp. 134–142). He abandoned the idea of a world central bank and the bancor, but maintained the concept of an International Clearing Union in an extended version with the main responsibility on the creditor side and with no rule for the exchange-rate regime. The latter could be chosen by members freely. All financial flows would also be recorded so that the ICU became an International Monetary Clearing Union (IMCU). Surplus countries should have similar binding obligations as in the Keynes plan, including the option to buy goods from deficit countries, and the option to render transfers similar to the Marshall Plan after World War II. There seem to be no obligations for debtor countries, apart from controlling capital flows (to prevent money laundering, tax evasion, capital flight, etc.). The management of the IMCU can control cross-country capital flows with the goal either of preventing excessive deficits or financing deficits with surplus money.

The indifference towards exchange rates in Davidson's proposal implies the notion that an automatic clearing mechanism for deficits and surpluses is sufficient to cope

                    Journal compilation © 2022 Edward Elgar Publishing Ltd

with current-account imbalances and with exchange-rate volatility and misalignment. In this respect Davidson's proposal falls short of both the Keynes plan and the Bretton Woods system, but goes beyond them by including the management of all cross-border financial flows in the remit of the IMCU.

3.2   The Tobin tax

In 1972, the Nobel laureate James Tobin reinvented Keynes's idea of a tax on speculative financial transactions, now applied to foreign-exchange spot transactions. Keynes wrote in chapter 12 of *The General Theory*:

> Speculators may do no harm as bubbles on a steady stream of enterprise. But the situation is serious when enterprise becomes the bubble on a whirlpool of speculation. … The introduction of a substantial government transfer tax on all transactions might prove the most serviceable reform available, with a view to mitigating the predominance of speculation over enterprise in the United States. (Keynes 1936 [1973], pp. 159–160)

Tobin foresaw at the end of Bretton Woods a transition to strong exchange-rate volatility due to excessive inter-currency mobility; hence he proposed, as soon as 1972, a tax on financial transactions, first and foremost foreign-exchange transactions, to mitigate the strongest downsides of the post-Bretton Woods non-system (Tobin 1978). He argued that it was not a question of fixed or flexible exchange-rate regimes, but was most importantly the difference between quick adjustments of financial assets to exchange rates and sluggish responses of goods prices and wages. Tobin debunked Monetarist reasoning in favour of full floating as being elusive, especially the hope that monetary policy could gain autonomy under a flexible regime as stipulated by the Mundell–Fleming model and propagated by Friedman. Under full floating, monetary policy would become *de facto* exchange-rate policy (ibid., p. 156). Floating exchange rates would undermine the abilities of monetary and fiscal policy. Prices of goods and assets would be distorted: 'In the absence of any consensus on fundamentals, the markets are dominated by … traders in the game of guessing what other traders are going to think' (ibid., p. 158).

The Tobin tax on foreign-exchange transactions (or on all international financial transactions) could be understood as a variant of *managed floating*. In later debates the technicalities were debated: in one proposal a standard zero Tobin tax, to be activated in critical periods, or with variable tax rates (cf. Spahn 1996; Schulmeister 2012). Eichengreen (1999, p. 88) argued that the Tobin tax wouldn't work, but his argument was not fundamental but based on political feasibility. Many authors and governments have endorsed the idea but have complained about the lack of consensus among all major governments.

3.3   A global currency union: Robert Mundell

Another Nobel laureate, Robert Mundell, pleaded vocally for a world currency and fixed exchange rates:

> The flexible exchange rate experiment has been a failure. The best test of any monetary system is the degree to which it avoids unnecessary changes in real exchange rates. These changes drastically reduce the gains from trade and disqualify the arguments ordinarily made for free trade areas and the custom unions. By this criterion, the worst period in history has been the period since generalized floating that began in 1973. (Mundell 2012, p. 568)

His recommendations for foreign-exchange (forex, or FX) interventions comprise five stages: First, setting targets in line with fundamentals, with floors and ceilings, unsterilised interventions at the spot and forward markets, concerted with partners. The first step towards a global currency is setting limits to extreme exchange-rate movements. Second, a basket of the three key currencies (dollar, euro, yen) called 'DEY', should be established, with target zones and coordinated interventions as well as monetary policies, since inflation rates are low and similar in all three regions. Smoothing exchange rates could also start bilaterally, between the US and Europe, Europe and Japan, or Japan and the US. Sterling might be added, and the Chinese yuan, after having achieved convertibility. Third, the DEY should be the platform for a truly global currency, the INTOR. The transition from the DEY to the long-term goal of a global currency should be similar to the prelude of the euro, when currencies were gradually locked in at irreversible rates to the new money, which means that the euro and the yen are pegged tightly to the dollar. In contrast to the old Bretton Woods system, Mundell proposes a common inflation target related to a common price index, and establishing a joint Monetary Policy Committee, equivalent to a joint central bank.

Mundell is not very clear about the last stage, the creation of the INTOR: should it replace national currencies or just remain a basket currency as an international accounting unit (cf. Priewe 2021)? If so, then his proposal would be a G3 monetary union. Mundell ignores possible conflicts between the necessary stability of real exchange rates, emphasised by him again and again (Mundell 2001), and tight pegs or a common currency making nominal adjustments unfeasible. This poses no problem when inflation rates are equal or very similar between members, but if other countries pegged to the G3 union, inflation rates would likely differ. Furthermore, real exchange-rate adjustments might be necessary to contribute to current-account rebalancing. Even though there is fairly broad consensus that exchange-rate realignments could not be the only or even the primary mechanism for rebalancing, they might be an important supplementary price-based instrument to quantity-based adjustments.

Mundell's G3 union is more interesting than his INTOR proposal for the last stage. The latter goes far beyond Keynes's bancor-clearing-union vision. The former could also be adjusted towards a G3 monetary union with target zones, whose bandwidth could be narrowed progressively. If the monetary authority of the G3 union were somewhat tilted towards the incumbent reserve-currency country, the conception seems to be likened to the Bretton Woods system but without gold. If the three currencies have equal impact and are guided by common decision-making, the dollar standard would be replaced by a dollar–euro–yen standard with stable rates but without any adjustment mechanism.

3.4 Target zones for exchange rates

John Williamson developed the idea of target-zone exchange rates after the breakdown of Bretton Woods (Williamson 1985; 1988; 2000; Miller and Williamson 1987). The core idea is to include in this system at least the three most important currencies (at the time dollar, the yen, and the DM or euro). Target rates should have a band of +/–10 per cent to allow for flexibility and unrestricted monetary policy sovereignty. At its edges, the band should have soft buffers that allow countries to return into the band or consider a change in the target rate. In the original version, monetary policy is supposed to be the main tool to keep currencies within the band. Thus it would be an intermediate

    Journal compilation © 2022 Edward Elgar Publishing Ltd

exchange-rate regime, a compromise of fixed and flexible regimes. Williamson envisioned four main social functions of this system as being the flexibility to: reconcile differential inflation rates; provide proper incentives for trade if balance-of-payments adjustments are necessary; liberate monetary policy to allow leeway for counter-cyclical monetary policy; and absorb speculative pressure. The target should be chosen such that 'fundamental equilibrium exchange rates' (FEER), that is, target real effective rates, can be achieved (similarly to Frenkel and Rapetti 2015). Having stabilised exchange rates of leading currencies, intermediate regimes are easier to achieve for other currencies, especially from developing countries. Williamson intended to avoid misalignments under global floating, and, furthermore, forcing countries to coordinate their macro policies. Relying on full floating is a comfortable excuse for heedless policies that ignore spillovers and international repercussions. From this angle, Williamson's proposal is far superior to Mundell's extremely rigid G3 proposal, although otherwise both are similar.

Williamson revised his original proposals (2000) by denouncing the prime use of monetary policy for defending the band, and turned to advocating interventions, preferably sterilised, and (at least in developing countries) also capital inflow controls. The main reason for this revision was the widespread fear that monetary policy might be too strongly pinned to exchange-rate stabilisation, and politicians dislike the option to use fiscal policy more actively to support or replace monetary policy; besides, he found more evidence that coordinated interventions might work. Since exchange rates have an arbitrary element due to being expectations-led, he argued, publicly announced interventions could lead expectations and thus calm down volatility.

Ethier and Bloomfield (1975) proposed rule-based floating exchange rates to be enforced by the IMF in order to limit the competitive exchange-rate behaviour of central banks. A key rule should be that central-bank interventions that support deviation from the reference value should not be allowed, or should be limited to a small, predefined degree. Reference values should be adjustable in the medium term. Managed rule-based floating within a system of reference or target rates is their goal.

McKinnon (1984) called for target zones with unsterilised interventions from the viewpoint of currency substitution as a driving force for exchange-rate changes. Interventions leave global money supply unchanged. Krugman (1991) supported in a theoretical model the target-zone proposal, but relied on rational expectations and the efficient market hypothesis. Nonetheless his result, that target zones may work without interventions if the margins are perceived as credible, sounds plausible. However, speculative attacks cannot be ruled out.

Most target-zone proposals suggest forex interventions for defending the band margins, rather than monetary policy. Interventions can be conducted unilaterally either by the depreciating or the appreciating party, or bilaterally by both central banks involved. Bofinger (2000) supported the concept of sterilised interventions and added important arguments. He suggested coordinated interventions between the two parties involved. The central bank in the appreciation country should stem the appreciation by purchasing the weaker currency with its own currency. Since foreign reserves are not necessary in this case, appreciation can in principle always be prevented; interventions can be done without limitation. However, the burden of intervention should not rest on the country with devaluation pressure because it would need foreign currency reserves to buy its own currency. Hence, this bilateral rule of intervention needs to be followed. Furthermore, sterilisation can be done easily, if additional money creation for intervention against appreciation is mopped up with issuing bonds or by using the deposit facility of the European Central Bank (ECB) or similar policy tools. Central banks

                                    Journal compilation © 2022 Edward Elgar Publishing Ltd

set short-term interest rates and do not target money supply (after monetary rules are outdated); sterilisation does not change interest rates. Bofinger called for a cost-sharing scheme between the two countries involved. Williamson had argued similarly and supported Bofinger's reasoning. Empirical literature on unilateral foreign-exchange interventions by central banks against unwanted appreciation underlines the efficacy (for example, Fratzscher et al. 2017).

Questions remain regarding how much intervention, sterilised or not, is necessary to maintain the band, how to withstand speculative attacks, and whether usage of – at least partially – monetary policy tools to defend the band might be necessary or expedient. Also, how to determine the target rate is an issue. Furthermore, the control of exchange rates in the target-zone proposals does not suffice to avoid current-account imbalances.

The most prominent example of a target zone, based on a basket of currencies, was the European Exchange Rate Mechanism (ERM), the predecessor of the euro, functioning from 1979 until 1993 with a band of +/–2.25 per cent (for a few countries +/–6 per cent) and since 1993 with a broader band of +/–15 per cent (cf. Eichengreen 2008, pp. 157–164). The heart of the ERM was the European Currency Unit (ECU), a basket currency in constant composition of the participating currencies. All currencies floated against the US dollar and other external currencies, so that currencies were simultaneously in both corners of exchange-rate regimes – in full float and in pegs. The DM was seen as the nominal anchor of the ECU. The so-called ERM II provided an obligatory anchor to those countries that want to access the euro system (the 'pre-ins') – for at least two years – with a band of +/–15 per cent to demonstrate convergence. The ERM obliged members to make multilateral interventions if the band margins were reached. Countries could apply for realignment of the reference rate; decisions were made by all members and the European Commission. In ERM II the ECB could offer member states finance for intervention, but member states were seen as primarily self-responsible for interventions.

Sterilised interventions were prescribed in neither ERM nor ERM II. The ERM encountered 54 realignments during its lifespan, mainly for inflation-prone currencies. In 1992 and 1993 the ERM almost broke down, in the course of the excessively tight monetary policy of the Deutsche Bundesbank in the aftermath of the German–German currency union.

The evaluation of the ERM's performance is mixed. Certainly, the initial band was too narrow, failing to allow for the monetary policy autonomy of its members. The main goal was to enforce lower inflation with a nominal anchor. More scope for fundamentally justified realignments should have been provided. German monetary policy was imposed, more or less, on all members, in the absence of a common central bank. Compared with the exchange-rate volatility of the European currencies vis-à-vis the US dollar, volatility was much lower. Often the ERM was seen as a regional Bretton Woods and as a model for other continents. Yet Asia, Africa and Latin America were way farther from being optimal currency areas than Western Europe, not to mention the issue of what optimal currency unions really are. The ERM was a kind of target-zone implementation with a basket currency, but clearly in contrast to Williamson's proposal with a broad band and soft buffers and with mutual interventions.

3.5 John Williamson and José Ocampo: comprehensive reforms

John Williamson summarised his lifelong research on development, finance, money, and exchange rates in his book, *International Monetary Reform*, incorporating his professional experience as an insider of the Washington institutions, particularly the IMF (Williamson 2016). A year later José A. Ocampo published *Resetting the International Monetary (Non)System*, which was also a summary of his professional life as a politician and academic economist (Ocampo 2017).

In brief, Williamson proposes: (i) a thorough reform of the outdated 'Articles of Agreement' of the IMF, along the lines of thought of Keynes (1943 [1969]) and Triffin (1960; 1978; 1979); (ii) new exchange-rate arrangements, based on managed floating; (iii) the extension of the IMF as a lender of last resort based on SDR; and (iv) that the SDR should not only become the most important international reserve asset, but the only one. In principle, he follows the proposals of the *Palais-Royal Report* for the IMF authored by Camdessus et al. (2011) after the global financial crisis. What Camdessus et al. saw as a need for IMF surveillance is changed by Williamson to enforceable and sanctioned rules, but limited to a small number.

Williamson's most important criticisms of the Palais-Royal Report were the following: failing adjustment processes of imbalances in current accounts; excessive capital flows leading to bubbles; exchange rates detached from fundamentals; and excessive reserve build-up of emerging economies. His recommendations to the IMF were, among others:

- Countries should have an explicit obligation consistent with global stability.
- The IMF should adopt norms for a variety of variables, *inter alia* current-account imbalances and real effective exchange rates.
- Persistent breach of norms should trigger remedial action.
- Countries should refrain from policies that deviate further from exchange-rate norms (following the proposal of Ethier and Bloomfield 1975).
- The IMF as well as systemically relevant central banks should provide extensive international liquidity as lenders of last resort.
- Increases of SDR in emergency situations should be examined, based on norms; reconsidering 'substitution accounts' (cf. Kenen 2010).

His proposals can best be ordered under the rubrics of exchange rates and SDR. Regarding exchange rates, Williamson proposed reference rates for the FEER. These equilibrium exchange rates, defined in real and effective terms, should guarantee current-account balances between +3 per cent and –3 per cent of GDP as rough guidelines. Countries with external deficits above 3 per cent are sooner or later doomed to crisis, except in the case of reserve countries. The mirror image is an approximate maximum 3 per cent surplus, which amounts to the global aggregate of deficits (cf. Cline and Williamson 2008). Williamson argues that, by and large, there is a stable medium-term relationship between the FEER and the current account, so that no extra norms or caps for current-account balances are needed. The reference rates are to be implemented by unilateral or – better – bilateral intervention; they should also guide expectations. Deviations from the reference values should be sanctioned by the IMF. It is mentioned that penalties on non-compliant countries with regard to SDR could be instituted, but the hints are vague. He sets much hope in the Ethier and Bloomfield rule mentioned above, a minimally invasive measure that also needs penalties if member states are non-compliant.

Regarding SDR, Williamson sees with increasing globalisation under dollar hegemony an increasing need for a lender of last resort of size regarding hard currencies, just in the tradition of Triffin. This need is also shared by the IMF and many other analysts who, however, focus on the dollar, and recently lent out in upscaled size

                    Journal compilation © 2022 Edward Elgar Publishing Ltd

by the Federal Reserve. In 1969 the IMF Articles stated unambiguously that the SDR is *the* international reserve asset of the fund. The fund is built on SDR, not on dollars. Even though this sounds odd, given the indisputable dollar dominance, reforms should be built on the old idea and not bound to the money of one member. The main reasons are these: first, SDR are a compensation for member countries (ex-US) in the face of the privilege of the US to earn the full seigniorage for issuing dollars; second, with a trend to a multicurrency system, sudden switches between currencies could be destabilising and the four other reserve currencies in the basket could be strengthened; third, reserves of members, mainly from EMEs, could diversify their portfolio and reduce the need to build up reserves which serve as cheap credit for the US government; fourth, SDR could be used in a much broader way than until now, especially with a substitution account allowing members to buy SDR or – if the SDR become a commercial asset – usable by private wealth owners (or state-owned institutions). Lastly, SDR can be created *ex nihilo* by the central banks of its members without macroeconomic risks. Williamson goes farther than all others, by demanding that SDR should become the only reserve asset on the globe if all countries promise not to hold any other country's currency (Williamson 2016, p. 64). Thus, he sees the SDR as the central asset of the international monetary system of the future, so that the dollar is dethroned from the store-of-value function regarding global currency.

The allocation of SDR should be according to need, not quota – Williamson proposes 80 per cent for the nations of the South and regular allocations by a new rule, following the growth rate of world GDP. These proposals are close to revolutionary, although the ideas are old and come from within the fund (like Polak 1979), and are not totally different from those of Keynes. Similar ideas and proposals can be found in UNCTAD (2009) and in the report of the so-called Stiglitz Commission (Stiglitz et al. 2010) and in Greenwald and Stiglitz (2010) and Stiglitz and Greenwald (2010), as well as in Zattler (2010).

Ocampo (2017) is broadly on the same track as Williamson, especially regarding the extension of SDR, but is reluctant to use SDR for private assets or even as the only reserve asset. Regarding exchange rates, he also calls for reference values and managed floating, but seems to give exchange-rate reform less weight than Williamson. He does not follow the notion that target rates automatically reduce trade imbalances toward a tolerable size. Instead, he stresses an enlarged role of capital controls which the IMF has accepted, in principle, as a normal policy tool but only as a measure of last resort. He pleads for an institutional reform of the IMF that results in an international apex organisation backed by the G20 which he sees as the political backing of the reforms, to be embedded in the United Nations.

Neither author is very clear regarding a new system of managed rule-based floating, especially with the asserted capacity of target rates to correct trade imbalances. Theoretically, the envisaged role of SDR in monetary theory needs more clarification, be it indirect or eventually direct global money creation (thereby transforming SDR into global money with restricted but defined usage), or leaving SDR as a kind of voucher that allows the receiving of soft and mostly unconditional loans in hard currency. Overall, SDR seems to be a multi-purpose-tool for short-term emergency lending to members, perhaps also for long-term financing of priority spending, financing of chronic deficits in countries with limits to devaluation, or for global counter-cyclical fiscal policy, and for many other purposes. Clarification would sharpen the reasoning for more SDR. Other authors (such as Farhi et al. 2011) also stress the need for a stronger lender-of-last-resort function of the IMF but prefer to entitle the fund to issue bonds on its own.

                    Journal compilation © 2022 Edward Elgar Publishing Ltd

4   A MODEST BUT FAR-REACHING PROPOSAL

The following proposal synthesises pieces of almost all the proposals reviewed. It evolves mainly from the analysis of the dollar–euro exchange rate (Priewe 2015; 2016). The reform package related to the IMF reform, focused on SDR, is only marginally addressed. This does not mean it is less important. My idea is to re-establish a global exchange-rate system beyond *laissez-faire* on the world's largest foreign-exchange market.

In the 'Articles of Agreement' of the IMF, the rule of the present system is stated; every nation can do what it wants regarding exchange-rate arrangements except manipulating the exchange rate, a never officially defined misdemeanour.[4] A rule that there is no rule is not a rule. Such a 'rule' ends up in the full floating of some members, the pegging of smaller ones, and the muddling-through of the rest, often called managed floating without clear objectives and tools. This issue is closely connected to current-account imbalances and fully fledged capital-account liberalisation since restrictions on foreign-exchange markets can be considered as barriers to cross-border financial flows. Strong volatility of exchange rates can lead to temporary or long-standing misalignments, pro-cyclicality, and reduced monetary and fiscal policy efficacy apart from trade distortions. Unstable exchange rates obviously miss an anchor but can trigger self-made strong waves, sometimes tsunamis of short-term capital flows. Foreign-exchange markets with freely floating exchange rates obviously do not tend towards stable equilibria but towards heavy deviation from benchmarks such as purchasing power parity, inflation rate differentials, or interest-rate parity. There is a large body of theoretical and empirical research that makes the hoped-for market-driven equilibria from the early 1970s appear naïve and outdated (Priewe 2015; 2016).

Almost all the major gyrations of the nominal exchange rate – be it the dollar to DM of 1960–1998 or the dollar to euro since 1999 – stem from real, that is, inflation-adjusted, exchange rates (adjusted by the CPI differential), as shown in Figure 4. If we consider inflation-rate differentials as one fundamental determinant of exchange-rate change, then almost all fluctuations arise from non-fundamental causes. The same holds if we look at the interest-rate differential with regard to the policy rates or long-term rates; the GDP-growth differential or the current-account balances were almost irrelevant for exchange-rate changes (Priewe 2016, pp. 36–43, for the period 1999–2015). The main determinant of the enormous exchange-rate changes is due to short-term financial flows, mainly driven by changes in expectations, speculation and herding. The average inflation rate in the US, from 1960 until 1998, was 0.8 percentage points (p.p.) higher than in Germany; in the euro area during 1999–2022 it was only 0.5 p.p. (cf. also Priewe 2016). The major turbulence in this period is the excessive revaluation of the euro from US$0.90 per euro by the end of 2001 to US$1.55 in spring 2008, similar to the extreme appreciation of the DM in 1969–1980 and again in 1985–1995. Europe's problems coping with the strong euro (2005–2008) were reinforced by China's pegging of the yuan to the dollar at the time.

The changeover to managed floating backed by market-based capital controls of the Tobin-tax type should start on the biggest forex market but be extended in the course of practice and learning to the other three reserve currencies. The yuan should be fairly easily

---

4.   The US Department of the Treasury (2022) uses three self-defined criteria to identify currency manipulation or unfair currency practice (net purchases of US$ ≥ 2 per cent of GDP, current-account surplus ≥ 2 per cent of GDP, bilateral trade surplus (goods) with US ≥ US$20 billion).

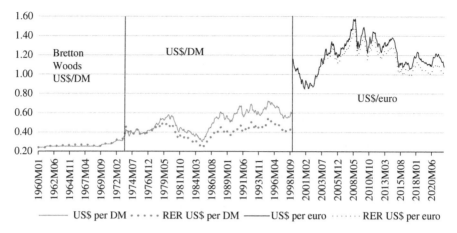

Notes: Monthly rate is the rate on the first day of the month. The real bilateral exchange rate (RER) is calculated with the bilateral CPI differential. Data until April 2022. Upward movement means appreciation of the DM or euro.
Source: FRED (2022); own calculations.

Figure 4   Nominal and real exchange rates US$/DM and US$/euro, 1960–2022 (monthly data)

includable in the new system – if purely geopolitical reasons can be disregarded – since China has practised managed floating vis-à-vis the dollar since 2005 and is challenged to adjust its traditional mode of capital controls (cf. Zhou 2009; Zhang 2014).

The largest foreign-exchange market in the world is the eurodollar market, measured by the daily turnover of 27.2 per cent of global transactions in which the dollar is involved and 24 per cent of global transactions in all currencies (BIS 2019). The yen has a share of 15.0 per cent in those transactions in which the dollar is included, sterling 10.8 per cent, and the yuan only 4.6 per cent. 88 per cent of all transactions involve the dollar, and 35 per cent involve the euro (since each transaction has two partners, 100 per cent is the maximum for one currency). The daily turnover on the US$/€ market was US$1584 billion in 2019, roughly 16.5-fold of the combined daily GDP of the US and the euro area, which is 39 per cent of the world domestic product. For most countries the dollar is a vehicle currency, which connects to other countries and currencies. A number of currencies are more or less satellites to the dollar, if they peg or somehow follow the dollar; others swing with the euro. Following both currencies is impossible if the eurodollar rate fluctuates heavily. My proposition is that a stabilisation of this hegemonic forex market would trigger vast positive externalities to both blocs and also the rest of the world.

The simple idea of stabilising this exchange rate at a sustainable level with fewer imbalances in the current accounts helps to better connect Europe and the Americas and indirectly the other continents too. The Global South, which trades with both major currencies, benefits a lot if these currencies stand in a fairly stable relation. The starting point is defining reference values – seen here as targets – with upper and lower bounds and switching from free-floating to rule-based managed floating with mutual interventions of both central banks. The interventions should be supported by the Tobin tax on all foreign-exchange transactions with all currencies in order to prevent bypassing the dollar–euro market. In a way, this is a reload of the Smithsonian

                                   Journal compilation © 2022 Edward Elgar Publishing Ltd

Agreement of 1971–1973 after the end of the gold convertibility of the dollar, but it is no longer a pure dollar standard; it should be a dollar–euro standard based on floating around target rates.

The inclusion of the Tobin tax (in a slim form, since Tobin applied it to all financial transactions) uses Tobin's answer to the failure of the post-Bretton Woods *laissez-faire* 'rule'. Interventions plus the Tobin tax might together allow less heavy use of each instrument, and better feasibility and efficacy. Both instruments – Tobin tax and interventions – complement each other perfectly. The former is an automatic stabiliser which discriminates against short-term currency transactions and makes speculative attacks more costly; the latter is a discretionary instrument involving the potential full firepower of both central banks, without using monetary policy for exchange-rate stabilisation. This increases the credibility of the target rates and stabilises expectations. Besides all this, it sets a limit to unfettered cross-border capital mobility.

Mutual interventions mean that the Federal Reserve buys euros should the euro be flagging, and the ECB buys dollars in the reverse case. The firepower of both central banks is unlimited since they use their own money for the purchases and pile up their currency reserves. The aggregate quantity of both monies in circulation would not change. Regarding sterilisation, consult Bofinger (2000). A wide band of initially +/–10 per cent might be manageable, later a bit less. The target rates should be reconsidered by both sides, say every two years to guarantee a certain degree of flexibility. The targets should be set in a way that both blocs' current accounts should drift to zero as an average in the medium term but without the intent that the dollar–euro target rate alone can achieve this. This implies that the euro appreciates, inflation adjusted, and the dollar depreciates accordingly. Since the current accounts of both sides are also influenced by the rest of the world, only bilateral trade could move toward balance. The euro area is presently the biggest surplus 'country' in the world, driven by Germany and the Netherlands, and the US the biggest deficit-maker. Global imbalances would be massively diminished if both sides achieved the goal set. Yet imbalances cannot be cured solely by real exchange-rate changes if the Marshall–Lerner conditions do not fully apply, if continuous growth differentials exist, or if real devaluations are systemically blocked due to foreign currency debt and dollar dominance due to dollarisation of global trade, among other reasons. Even though the US has currently no problem financing its current-account deficit, relying to a large extent on low-interest foreign reserves, the need of EMEs to pile up reserves should be reduced in the course of global monetary reforms. Yet it is unlikely that reserves will melt down to zero.

Since, contrary to Williamson, there is no stable relationship between real exchange rates and trade balances, because the latter are influenced by more than one variable, other measures should be used to further improve imbalances. Remember Keynes's proposal from 1943 for surplus countries. Sanctions could also be agreed upon with respect to penalties in terms of SDR or even voting rights in the IMF.

Can the US deficit be reduced as the dollar is the hegemonic currency country and lives from private and official capital inflows? Yes, and therefore the euro has to become an international currency, beyond the present predominantly regional scale (cf. ECB 2021). This requires reforms in the euro area, in particular the unification and stabilisation of the sovereign bonds markets, but also the implementation of the capital market union. More euro bonds should be issued, and a euro Treasury under deeper integration is advisable. This does not require the United States of Europe, but overcoming the present fragility and lack of capacity to act as a union (with majority voting), at least in major economic and financial issues. Complementarily, shifting international reserves from the dollar to the reformed IMF with a special SDR-based facility for reserves – along the lines of Williamson, Ocampo and Stiglitz – would be highly supportive.

The euro bloc comprises 19 members of the euro area, 9 other EU members, and also those (circa) 25–30 other countries that anchor their currencies to the euro, many small ones but also large ones like Poland and Turkey, or use the euro as legal tender (ECB 2021, statistical annex, table A3; IMF 2020, pp. 9–11). The bloc includes more than 50 countries. In the IMF statistics counted for 2020, 25 IMF member countries use the euro as a currency anchor, and 38 for the dollar, be it pegging or similar (IMF 2020, pp. 9–11 and 60). A closer look shows that from 189 IMF members, 80–90 use either the euro or the dollar, or anchor to the dollar or the euro, which is 42–47 per cent of all members. 63 members report 'floating' or 'free floating' exchange-rate arrangements (31 'free floating' countries including 19 euro area members, hence without the latter only 12 free floaters including the USA).

Most EMEs reported 'floating' (not 'full floating') or 'inflation targeting', apart from China, which is classified as 'other managed arrangement' (IMF 2020). The classification overestimates the floating group, because floaters like Brazil, India, South Africa, Indonesia and Mexico to some extent use capital controls or outright monetary policy to manage their exchange rates. The nuanced picture shows that the vast majority of countries refrain from free floating plus fully fledged capital-account openness and stick to some kind of intermediate regime or a currency union. Whatever classification is chosen, the combined dollar and euro bloc is a heavyweight in global forex markets and in the world economy.

A knee-jerk argument against my proposal comes from the fear of a reduced monetary policy space under a regime of managed floating. But: inflation targets in both blocs are the same, and the actual inflation rates differ only minimally. Also interest-rate differences with respect to policy rates had been small between the Federal Reserve and the ECB, with few exceptions and some time lags. To allow for effective monetary policy geared to manage the respective currency area, there is built-in flexibility in the exchange-rate margins. It's not a reload of Bretton Woods and it's not a mega currency union *à la* Mundell. However, a turn to managed floating requires a high degree of willingness for international cooperation. A replication of the unilateral Volcker experiment of 1979–1980 by the Federal Reserve would destroy the project, and the excessive tightening of monetary policy in 1991–1992 by the Deutsche Bundesbank would be incompatible as well. 'America first' policies (or similar for Europe) must be banned. For idiosyncratic challenges, other solutions have to be found. Mutual considerateness is indispensable but requires similar broad interests and constrained competition of the blocs, something like *cooperative competition*, similar to international trade agreements.

If the five SDR currencies would cooperate under a regime of managed floating, a common anchor would be needed to define the target rates. The SDR would then play a similar role as the ECU (the erstwhile European Currency Unit) played prior to the euro. This would incorporate a big leap towards reducing the dollar hegemony or dollar dominance (a rank as *primus inter pares*) to a cooperative multi-currency system. Due to its biggest financial sector, the dollar would likely continue to dominate as the key global store of value for private financial wealth; the other countries could offer increasingly store-of-value functions for sovereign reserves if they strive for it. The dominant dollar as a means of payment could be gradually diminished if the fluctuations among the four currencies could be constrained. Then the global-unit-of-account function could be transferred gradually to the SDR. It should be clear from the very beginning that change in the dollar–euro market is the starting point for a longer journey. It must not be misunderstood as bloc-building and further global divide.

A number of open questions remain that cannot be discussed here. The remaining imbalances in the current accounts, especially in the approximately 100 Southern countries with unsustainable deficits (Table 1), need to be addressed in the framework of the SDR reforms. The so-long neglected commodity-price bonanzas with concomitant Dutch disease cycles in real exchange rates remain unaddressed too. Again, the proposal approaches only one issue of global monetary reform, in this sense a modest proposal.

Those who reject such reform projects as highly unrealistic and therefore way beyond the curve, should compare the difficulties to accomplish a transatlantic free-trade agreement and a transatlantic monetary reform. I would not bet against one of the two being more difficult.

REFERENCES

Bergsten, C.F. (2013), 'Currency wars, the economy of the United States and reform of the International Monetary System', 16 May, available at: http://www.iie.com/publications/papers/bergsten201305.pdf.

BIS (2019), *Triennial Central Bank Survey of Foreign Exchange and Derivatives Market Activity in 2019*, Basle: BIS.

BIS (2022), *Central Bank Policy Rates Statistics*, Basle: BIS.

Bofinger, P. (2000), 'A framework for stabilising the euro/yen/dollar triplet', *The North American Journal of Economics and Finance*, 11(2), 137–151.

Bruegel (2022), 'Real effective exchange rates for 178 countries: a new database', available at: https://www.bruegel.org/publications/datasets/real-effective-exchange-rates-for-178-countries-a-new-database/ (accessed 25 June 2022).

Camdessus, M., A. Lamfalussy and T. Padoa-Schioppa (2011), 'Reform of the International Monetary System: a cooperative approach for the twenty first century (The Palais-Royal Report)', 8 February, available at: http://www.global-currencies.org/smi/gb/telcchar/news/Rapport_Camdessus-integral.pdf (accessed 30 June 2022).

Chitu, L. (2012): 'Was unofficial dollarisation/euroisation an amplifier of the "Great Recession" of 2007–09 in emerging economies?', European Central Bank, Working Paper Series, No 1473, September.

Cline, W.R. and J. Williamson (2008), 'New estimates of fundamental equilibrium exchange rates', Policy Briefs in International Economics 08-7 (July), Washington, Peterson Institute for International Economics.

Costabile, L. (2022), 'Continuity and change in the International Monetary System, the dollar standard and capital mobility', *Review of Political Economy*, doi: 10.1080/09538259.2022.2038438.

Davidson, P. (2009), *The Keynes Solution: The Path to Global Economic Prosperity*, New York: Palgrave Macmillan.

Deutsche Bundesbank (2013), 'The end of Bretton Woods: when exchange rates learnt to float', 14 October, available at: https://www.bundesbank.de/en/tasks/topics/1973-the-end-of-bretton-woods-when-exchange-rates-learned-to-float-666280.

ECB (2021), *Twentieth Annual Review of International Role of the Euro*, Frankfurt am Main: European Central Bank.

Eichengreen, B. (1999), *Toward a New International Financial Architecture: A Practical Post-Asia Agenda*, Washington, DC: Institute for International Economics.

Eichengreen, B. (2008), *Globalizing Capital: A History of the International Monetary System*, Princeton, NJ and Oxford: Princeton University Press.

Eichengreen, B. (2011), *Exorbitant Privilege: The Rise and Fall of the Dollar*, Oxford: Oxford University Press.

Enerdata (2022), *Yearbook*, available at: https://yearbook.enerdata.net/natural-gas/world-natural-gas-production-statistics.html (accessed 7 August 2022).

Ethier, W. and Ch.I. Bloomfield (1975), 'Managing the managed float', Princeton Essays in International Finance No 112, Princeton, NJ.

Farhi, E., P.O. Gourinchas and H. Rey (2011), *Reforming the International Monetary System*, London: Centre for Economic Policy Research (CEPR).

Fratzscher, M., O. Gloede, L. Menkhoff, L. Sarno and T. Stöhr (2017), 'When is foreign exchange intervention effective? Evidence from 33 countries', DIW Discussion Paper 1518 (revised), Berlin.

FRED (2022), 'Federal Reserve economic data', Federal Reserve Bank St. Louis, available at: https://fred.stlouisfed.org/ (accessed 3 August 2022).

Frenkel, R. and M. Rapetti (2015), 'The real exchange rate as a target of macroeconomic policy', in A. Calcagno, S. Dullien, A. Márquez Velázquez, N. Maystre and J. Priewe (eds), *Rethinking Development After the Financial Crisis, Volume I: Making the Case for Policy Space*, Geneva and New York: UNCTAD, pp. 81–91.

Goda, Th. and J. Priewe (2020), 'Determinants of real exchange rate movements in 15 emerging market economies', *Brazilian Journal of Political Economy*, 40(2), 214–237.

Gopinath, G., E. Boz, C. Casas, F.J. Díez, P.-O. Gourinchas and M. Plagborg-Møller (2020), 'Dominant currency paradigm', *American Economic Review*, 110(3), 677–719.

Greenwald, B. and J. Stiglitz (2010), 'A modest proposal for international monetary reform', in S. Griffith-Jones, J.A. Ocampo and J. Stiglitz (eds), *Time for a Visible Hand: Lessons from the 2008 World Financial Crisis*, Oxford: Oxford University Press, pp. 314–344.

Herr, H. and Z. Nettekoven (2022), 'International money, privileges and underdevelopment', in B. Bonizzi, A. Kaltenbrunner and R. Ramos (eds), *Emerging Economies and the Global Financial System: Post Keynesian Analysis*, London: Routledge, pp. 116–136.

IMF (2020), *Annual Report on Exchange Arrangements and Exchange Restriction*, Washington, DC: International Monetary Fund.

IMF (2022): *Currency Composition of Official Foreign Exchange Reserves (COFER)*, Washington, DC: International Monetary Fund.

Kenen, P. (2010), 'Reforming the global reserve regime: the role of a substitution account', *International Finance*, 13(1), 1–23.

Keynes, J.M. (1936 [1973]), *The General Theory of Employment, Interest and Money*, in *The Collected Writings of John Maynard Keynes*, vol. XII, Cambridge, UK: Macmillan–Cambridge University Press.

Keynes, J.M. (1943 [1969]), 'Proposals for an International Clearing Union', Version 1943, in J. K. Horsefield (ed.), *The International Monetary Fund 1945–1965, Vol. III: Documents*, Washington, DC: International Monetary Fund, pp. 19–36.

Krugman, P.R. (1991), 'Target zones and exchange rate dynamics', *Quarterly Journal of Economics*, CVI(3), 669–682.

McKinnon, R. (1984), *An International Standard for Monetary Stabilization*, Cambridge, MA: MIT Press.

Miller, M. and J. Williamson (1987), *Targets and Indicators: A Blueprint for International Coordination of Economic Policy*, Washington, DC: Institute for International Economics.

Mundell, R. (2001), 'Currency areas and international monetary reform at the dawn of a new century', *Review of International Economics*, 9(4), 595–607.

Mundell, R. (2012), 'The case for a world currency', *Journal of Policy Modelling*, 34, 568–578.

Ocampo, J.A. (2017), *Resetting the International Monetary (Non)System*, Oxford: Oxford University Press.

Polak, J. (1979), 'Thoughts on an International Monetary Fund based fully in the SDR', in *Pamphlet*, No 28, Washington, DC: International Monetary Fund.

Prasad, E.S. (2014): *The Dollar Trap: How the U.S. Dollar Tightened its Grip on Global Finance*, Princeton, NJ: Princeton University Press.

Priewe, J. (2015), 'Rätsel Wechselkurs – Krise und Neuanfang der Wechselkurstheorie', in H. Hagemann and J. Kromphardt (eds), *Für eine bessere gesamt–europäische Wirtschaftspolitik*, Marburg: Metropolis, pp. 205–248.

Priewe, J. (2016), 'The enigmatic dollar–euro exchange rate and the world's biggest forex market performance, causes, consequences', IMK Study 49, Macroeconomic Policy Institute (IMK), Düsseldorf.

Priewe, J. (2021), 'The rise and demise of Robert Mundell's theory of optimum currency areas', *The World Orders Forum*, 22 June, available at: https://www.wgresearch.org/_files/ugd/bdf8dc_e03ceefb78754828aae9d402ea00e376.pdf.

Schulmeister, St. (2012), 'A general financial transaction tax: strong pros, weak cons', *Intereconomics: Review of European Economic Policy*, 47(2), 84–89.

Skidelsky, R. (2004), *John Maynard Keynes 1883–1946: Economist, Philosopher, Statesman*, London: Pan Books, available at: www.panmacmillan.com (accessed 1 June 2022).

Spahn, P.B. (1996), 'The Tobin tax and exchange rate stability', *Finance & Development*, June, 24–27.

Stiglitz, J.E. and B. Greenwald (2010), 'Towards a new global reserve system', *Journal of Globalization and Development*, 1(2), 1–24.

Stiglitz, J.E. and Members of a UN Commission of Financial Experts (2010), *The Stiglitz Report: Reforming the International Monetary and Financial System in the Wake of the Global Crisis*, New York and London: The New Press.

Tobin, J. (1978), 'A proposal for international monetary reform', *Eastern Economic Journal*, 4(3–4), 153–159.

Triffin, R. (1960), *Gold and the Dollar Crisis: The Future of Convertibility*, New Haven, CT: Yale University Press.

Triffin, R. (1978), *Gold and the Dollar Crisis: Yesterday and Tomorrow*, Essays in International Finance, Princeton, NJ: Princeton University.

Triffin, R. (1979), 'The international role and fate of the dollar' *Foreign Affairs*, 57(1978/79), 269–286.

UNCTAD (2009), *Trade and Development Report 2009*, Geneva: United Nations Conference on Trade and Development.

US Department of the Treasury (2022), 'Press release', 10 June, available at: https://home.treasury.gov/news/press-releases/jy0813#,~,text=Treasury%20has%20placed%20twelve%20economies, Taiwan%2C%20Vietnam%2C%20and%20Mexico.

WDI (2022): *World Development Indicators*, Washington, DC: World Bank, available at: https://databank.worldbank.org/source/world-development-indicators.

Williamson, J. (1985), *The Exchange Rate System*, rev. edn, Washington, DC: Institute for International Economics.

Williamson, J. (1988), 'The target zone proposal', *Journal of Foreign Exchange and International Finance*, 11(3), 249–255.

Williamson, J. (2000), *Exchange Rate Regimes for Emerging Markets: Reviving the Intermediate Option*, Washington, DC: Institute for International Economics.

Williamson, J. (2016), *International Monetary Reform: A Specific Set of Proposals*, Abingdon, UK and New York: Routledge.

World Bank (2022), 'Commodity price data (the Pink Sheet)', 2 August, available at: https://thedocs.worldbank.org/en/doc/5d903e848db1d1b83e0ec8f744e55570-0350012021/related/CMO-Pink-Sheet-April-2022.pdf.

Zattler, J. (2010), 'A possible new role for Special Drawing Rights in and beyond the global monetary system', in S. Dullien, D. Kotte, A. Marquez Velázquez and J. Priewe (eds), *The Financial and Economic Crisis of 2008–2009 and Developing Countries*, Geneva: UNCTAD, pp. 287–305.

Zhang, L. (2014), 'Reform of the global reserve system and China's choice', in S. Dullien, E. Hein and A. Truger (eds), *Macroeconomics, Development and Economic Policies: Festschrift for Jan Priewe*, Marburg: Metropolis, pp. 425–435.

Zhou, X. (2009), 'Reform the international monetary system', Mimeo, People's Bank of China, Beijing.

Review of Keynesian Economics, Vol. 10 No. 4, Winter 2022, pp. 117–137

'King dollar' forever? Prospects for a New Bretton Woods

Jörg Bibow*
Economics Department, Skidmore College, Saratoga Springs, NY, USA

This paper investigates the evolution and future of US-dollar hegemony in the global monetary system. Financial liberalization acted as the most potent transformative force in the evolution of the dollar system, ushering in the post-Cold War era of hyper-globalization. Rising financialization and cross-border financial interconnectedness have produced the opposite of shared prosperity, yielding mounting fragilities and inequalities instead. The global financial crisis of 2008–2009 marked a turning point: the world has become ever more challenged with maneuvering the push and pull of its two primary poles, America in the money and finance sphere, China in trade and production. For America, too, the extraordinary dollar privilege comes with a growing extraordinary burden. No other currency seems likely to fill the shoes of the mighty dollar for decades to come. A multipolar world of several more evenly balanced key currencies is the more likely prospect.

Keywords: *US dollar, international monetary system, globalization, international finance, hegemony*

JEL codes: *E12, E42, E44, F33, F42, F50, F60*

1 INTRODUCTION

This paper investigates the evolution and future of US-dollar hegemony in the global monetary system. Financial liberalization – a key tenet of Neoliberalism – acted as the most potent transformative force in the evolution of the dollar system, ushering in the post-Cold War era of hyper-globalization. Rising financialization and cross-border financial interconnectedness have produced the opposite of shared prosperity, yielding mounting fragilities and inequalities instead. The global financial crisis (GFC) of 2008–2009 marked a turning point: the world has become ever more challenged with maneuvering the push and pull of its two primary poles, America in the money and finance sphere, China in trade and production. For America, too, the extraordinary dollar privilege comes with a growing extraordinary burden.

Yet no other currency seems likely to fill the shoes of the mighty dollar for decades to come. Instead, a multipolar world of several more evenly balanced key currencies is the more likely prospect. A multipolar world would require effective global cooperation and shared leadership. The climate challenge might perhaps create the environment for a 'New Bretton Woods' agreement. But the chances of such an outcome in the near term – potentially even featuring a 'bancor-style' symmetric monetary order replacing the dollar system – currently appear slim.

* Email: jbibow@skidmore.edu.

Journal compilation © 2022 Edward Elgar Publishing Ltd
The Lypiatts, 15 Lansdown Road, Cheltenham, Glos GL50 2JA, UK
and The William Pratt House, 9 Dewey Court, Northampton MA 01060-3815, USA

The analysis proceeds as follows. Sections 2 and 3 review the evolution of the dollar system, emphasizing the hegemonic dollar's critical role as a driver of fragility and inequality in the era of hyper-globalization – an era that started to unravel in the aftermath of the GFC. Section 4 zooms in on the sources of fragility in the status quo. The potential challengers of the US dollar are the subject of Section 5, highlighting that there is no other currency in sight that could replace the dollar as the solitary hegemon. Section 6 briefly reviews the rapidly changing world of payments as certain developments pertain to the future of the dollar system; or, rather, any future global monetary system. Sections 7 and 8 speculate about the future, Section 7 discussing the prospects of multipolarity in currency arrangements as the center of gravity in the global economy is shifting towards Asia, and Section 8 exploring the possibility of a New Bretton Woods. Section 9 concludes.

2   THE EVER-EVOLVING DOLLAR SYSTEM

The US dollar's global role and predominance started to develop in the aftermath of World War I, challenging the pound sterling's reign as Britain emerged weakened from the Great War. 'King dollar' became firmly established after World War II, as Europe, once again, emerged enfeebled from its new civil war and its empires were crumbling. Yet the nature of the dollar's global hegemony of 80 years has changed fundamentally in the process (Keynes 1923; Eichengreen 2008; 2012; Eichengreen et al. 2017; Cohen 2019; Costabile 2022).

The US dollar started out as the anchor, supposedly backed by gold, of a system of fixed (but adjustable) exchange rates in a world of expansive capital controls: an internationally agreed global monetary system that was by design centered on the US and the International Monetary Fund (IMF) without much of an international financial system by its side. In the 1970s, the dollar's hegemony transitioned through a phase when the 'barbaric relic,' which had been deposed of its despotic control a generation earlier, also lost its position as currency backing and 'constitutional monarch' – and America and the dollar much of their international (self-)esteem. Macroeconomic instabilities were unsettling the 'golden age' of the post-war 'Keynesian' era and global finance was gradually reinventing itself. The mighty dollar firmly re-established itself as the apex of global money in the age of Neoliberalism when America became the sole superpower pursuing hyper-globalization, with the Bretton Woods institutions as touring gospel singers of the 'Washington Consensus.'

So unfettered global finance came to rule the world again – this time with Wall Street and the US Federal Reserve in the cockpit of an ever-more financialized and hyper-globalized world, a world in which the Bretton Woods institutions turned into little more than an appendage of the Washington–Wall Street axis of global monetary–financial power.

The Neoliberal world of hyper-globalization is a world of fear and fragility – which suits the powerful, and above all those with US dollar backing. America is home to the greatest concentration of financial wealth in the world. America's political system allows concentrated wealth to play an extraordinary role in its domestic affairs and global ambitions. Under the spell of the monied interests and 'trickle down' economic fairytales, its political elite came to champion financial liberalization like nothing else.

Liberalized finance provides the conduit through which wealth exerts its power in the economy, with financialization expanding its reach economy-wide, just as hyper-globalization performs the same trick across the globe. Liberalized finance is

                    Journal compilation © 2022 Edward Elgar Publishing Ltd

organized around liquidity – the very opposite of commitment. Liquidity embodies and empowers an ever-present threat to pull out and leave – making the vulnerable fearful and obedient, including the political class. As the barriers fall, America's wealthy, with their firepower denominated in dollars, managed by Wall Street's global giants, and ultimately backed by the Federal Reserve and the US Treasury, are facing a world of opportunity for further enlarging their wealth and hegemonic powers.

Liquidity by design means fragility by design. Short-termism rules; long-term planning – 'to defeat the dark forces of time and ignorance' (Keynes 1936 [1971], p. 155) – gets impeded.

The material consequences of fragility by design first befell the developed world, both America itself and its chief rivals in Western Europe and Japan, taking the form of banking and currency crises (BIS 1993). Like America's 'savings and loan' meltdown, the first generation of banking crises in Japan and Europe (especially the Nordic countries), following liberalization in the 1980s, also remained national.

Then financial matters turned into a regional affair. As part of its 'Single Market Programme,' Western Europe was at the forefront of deepening financial market integration that was becoming the mantra of the time (Abdelal 2007). The push was initially motivated and (mis-)guided by naïve ideas about regional liberalization and integration as an efficiency booster without any associated risks or detriments. Seemingly inevitably, efficient financial integration then also became instrumentalized – under Padoa-Schioppa's 'inconsistent quartet' argument – in the next big push for Europe's single currency (Bibow 2020).

Geopolitical developments gave the euro project the regional spin that it needed for take-off and also fired up the global push for hyper-globalization. Free-market capitalism was triumphant. Following the Bundesbank's monetary overkill response to German unification (Bibow 2003), the Exchange Rate Mechanism of the European Monetary System that had been in place since the late 1970s came under attack; to be 'rescued' by a widening of its standard bands (to +/–15 percent). Looking briefly ahead here: 20 years later, under the common euro currency, Europe came to relive the experience that market integration without policy integration, especially in the domain of finance, and monetary integration without fiscal integration, are unsafe ideas (see below).

Next, fragility by design popped up, again and again, in a series of 'emerging-market' crises in Latin America and East Asia, unhinging numerous countries that had paid tribute to the Washington Consensus gospel by opening their doors to unfettered global finance. Countries got burned, countries turned cautious. In response to learned lessons from playing with foreign financial firepower, countries set out to bolster their lost policy space by exploring defensive macro policies.

So the mantra of trade and financial openness got paired up with 'self-insurance' by reserve accumulation. Disarmed to properly macro manage their national economy, obliged to always obey the powers of free capital to sustain 'market confidence' instead, developing countries are striving for both export market share and a competitive exchange rate – by buying plentiful US dollars. Amassing safety in the form of low-yielding dollar liquidity is the financial counterpart to the power of liquid and flighty financial wealth from the center, seeking rich profit on foreign shores; the infamous 'exorbitant privilege,' greatly boosted by hyper-globalization, as seen from the non-privileged peripheral side of the bargain (Bibow 2009a; 2011c; 2012; Akyüz 2018).

As both the first-generation Bretton Woods periphery, especially Japan and Germany, as well as today's developing countries, especially China, were pursuing defensive-style macro policies in a global environment made unsafe by unfettered global finance, strong global systemic disinflationary forces were the 'natural' result. With too many players aiming to sell rather than buy in global product markets, accumulating US dollar liquidity as a counterweight to flighty yield-searching financial capital, the system will succumb to deflation unless there is sufficient elasticity of reserve material and liberty of spending forthcoming somewhere in the system. Naturally, it will have to be the issuer of the international currency, 'king dollar,' that takes on that burden of responsibility (Bibow 2007; 2008; 2021b).

In the glory days of hyper-globalization, systemic disinflationary pressures kept inflation in check almost everywhere, with 'independent' central banks and their 'inflation targeting' strategies receiving much of the credit. In the world's largest consumer goods market and, by extension, in America's labor markets, disinflation automatically provoked activism on the part of the US Federal Reserve (the Fed), operating under its domestic 'dual mandate' in an increasingly hyper-globalized world.

In this way, the heightened precautionary global demand for dollar liquidity is being met by an elastic supply, provisioned both through America's sizeable and quite stable current-account deficit position, powering global spending, as well as America's rather unstable private capital outflows. Seen from a global perspective, the former – spending – channel and source of earned dollar reserves provides something of a safety valve helping to balance the instability instigated through the latter – Wall Street – channel of adventurous capital flows and driver of borrowed reserves.

Apart from any support it might receive, on occasion – that is, in emergencies – from US fiscal policy, the Fed is thereby positioned as the leading global macro policy player. Guided by its domestic dual mandate, the Fed's monetary policy not only shapes US financial conditions and, supposedly, total spending in line with full employment and price stability in the US, but it also provides the anchor and benchmark for global financial conditions as transmitted through unfettered global finance. Wall Street is in the driver's seat of dollar-based global finance – as the Fed has its back (Bibow 2021b).

3   HYPER-GLOBALIZATION UNRAVELS IN THE AFTERMATH OF THE GLOBAL FINANCIAL CRISIS

The 'Volcker shock' revived 'strong dollar' hegemony and ushered in the era of Neoliberalism (Galbraith 2022). Three Fed policy cycles denote the period until the global financial crisis of 2008–2009. The first cycle (the 1980s) captures America's revival under Reaganomics: supply-side military Keynesianism. Tax cuts and military spending produced the fiscal deficits that were the domestic counterpart to America's external deficits – primarily driving the global recovery of advanced economies. Meanwhile, many developing countries were bogged down by international debts (owing to mainly US and European banks' loans that had facilitated the so-called 'petrodollar recycling' of the 1970s). The second cycle (the 1990s) featured the 'dot-com boom,' with rising household and especially corporate debts as the domestic counterpart to America's external deficits. The briefer third cycle (the 2000s) had a fiscal component at the beginning (tax cuts for the rich and military spending), but primarily featured household mortgage debts as the counterpart to America's soaring external deficits (Bibow 2010a).

The end of the third Fed policy cycle, the bursting of the US 'subprime' mortgage and housing bubbles, saw fragility-by-design finally strike hard at the very core of unfettered global finance: America's Wall Street and its European satellites (Bibow 2009b; 2011a).

Showcasing dollar hegemony and the leading role of finance in the economy, the crisis at the heart of – supposedly very sophisticated – global finance quickly gathered global reach. For developing countries, the crisis of unfettered global finance provided a wake-up call undermining trust in 'Washington Consensus'-style Western economic ideology and liberal institutions. Especially China, becoming the foremost economic engine of global recovery from the crisis at the core, by supercharging its macro policy muscles, learned to appreciate the power of its well-safeguarded policy space even more. Europe, on the other hand, discovered the hard way that financial-market integration without proper policy integration and the dismantling of national macro policy levers through monetary union without fiscal union make for a potentially fatal vulnerability (Bibow 2020).

In the aftermath of the global financial crisis, Europe, and specifically the euro area, massively underperformed economically and became ever more divided politically – much in contrast to the vision whereby economic and monetary integration would not only deliver shared prosperity but help to unite the peoples of Europe politically, too. So much so that, in 2016, the UK voted to exit from the EU while numerous right-wing nationalists among remaining members have turned into capricious anti-EU forces inside the EU. The outcome is potentially quite explosive (Tooze 2018).

Important developing countries, too, took a turn for the worse, embracing right-wing nationalists (India, Brazil), incompetent kleptocrats (South Africa), or bolstering autocrats with dubious geopolitical ambitions (Russia, China). Economically, among the BRICS nations, China and India have continued to perform well since the global financial crisis while Brazil, Russia, and South Africa got stuck in stagnation.

Meanwhile, America missed its brilliant opportunity to reconstruct its economy and restore its global leadership by embracing large-scale infrastructure upgrading through fiscal expansion (Bibow 2010b; 2011b). Following an undersized fiscal stimulus to fight the Great Recession, America embraced fiscal austerity and protracted 'quantitative easing' instead. The consequences were long-term mass unemployment, featuring soaring inequalities and 'deaths of despair,' as well as rising political polarization and right-wing nationalism.

So it was China that used US frailty as an opening for a massive splurge on domestic infrastructure development, externally paired by the 'Belt and Road Initiative' designed to expand China's global position – by way of establishing institutions that can either be complements or alternatives to the Western Bretton Woods order.

China's big push put the country on track to match and soon exceed America's GDP weight in the global economy in US-dollar terms (when measured in purchasing power parity (PPP), the handover already happened in 2017). Its fast growth and hunger for raw materials have made it an especially important pull factor for commodity-exporting developing countries. By providing new sources of funding for infrastructure investment, China is bringing some welcome competition to global development support that can potentially also add substance to the catchwords that Western authorities have come to highlight regarding growth in the aftermath of the crisis (as exemplified by the G20 framework for 'strong, sustainable, balanced, and inclusive' growth). But there are of course also risks involved in potential new dependencies and global fragmentation.

America, on the other hand, wasted a whole decade by underinvesting in its people and economy, while engaging in warfare rather than constructive endeavors abroad. The Obama presidency got hamstrung early on by divided government and austerity. The Trump presidency then sought new American greatness in gifting a tax cut to billionaires that, together with other regressive and reactionary measures, took inequality and social polarization to new heights, while simply denying climate change and a raging pandemic that was to kill a million Americans by 2022 along the way.

All along, the Federal Reserve, forced by disinflationary pressures in a neglected and sluggishly growing US economy, was firing up asset prices by ultra-easy money policies. Rising profit margins and bulging liquidity combined to see stock prices skyrocket as corporates focused on stock buy-backs rather than productivity-enhancing investment. A new chapter of casino capitalism opened up when so-called cryptocurrencies, as the latest fad of financial innovation allegedly enhancing human welfare, incited bubble frenzy – apart from enabling illicit international payments and large-scale fraud.

America's lost decade culminated in the events of 6 January 2021, a failed coup to push America into autocracy, staged by the avowed Vladimir Putin fan and wannabe czar of America, Donald Trump. The fact that the political instigators of the attempted *coup d'état*, led by the former president himself, were not even brought to trial raises serious questions about the rule of law and judicial justice in the leading country of the West. The rest of the world could watch in sheer amazement that the former president's claim that he would get away with daylight murder on New York City's Fifth Avenue was not a joke – but a rare true statement of his about the state of America's plutocracy and its judiciary.

The Biden presidency started in the middle of a pandemic (seriously botched by the previous government) while confronting a grotesquely unequal and ferociously divided society poisoned by his predecessor. Little over a year later, the invasion of Ukraine by Vladimir Putin's Russia opened up the acute specter of potential global fragmentation, if not war, at just the time when global cooperation to meet the global challenges of climate change and the pandemic was needed more than ever.

The pandemic and the Ukraine war underscored two important facets of the dollar system in its current shape and stage of development. First, similarly to their role in the earlier global financial crisis, the pandemic triggered a revival of central-bank swap lines centered on the US dollar that brought certain important US allies under the protective umbrella of the Federal Reserve in a global emergency; though not others (Mehrling 2015). Second, the Ukraine war triggered financial sanctions by the US and its Western allies intended to financially undermine Russia's capacity to wage war, including the freezing of the Russian central bank's foreign-exchange reserves held in the West and the exclusion of some key Russian banks from the global dollar-based payment system channeled through SWIFT. Observers described these financial sanctions as the 'weaponization' of the dollar. The dollar swap lines and financial sanctions signify hegemony, privilege, and discrimination among the ins and outs of the dollar fraternity. Clearly both facets fall in the domain of US foreign policy, underscoring that dollar hegemony is about far more than seigniorage (narrowly defined as gains derived from printing greenbacks with a higher nominal value than their production cost).

4   SOURCES OF FRAGILITY IN THE STATUS QUO

The key strengths and weaknesses of the current dollar system may be succinctly described as follows. The key strengths are that the dollar system is working and that the dollar is not facing any acute competition from any alternative that could easily dethrone 'king dollar' in the foreseeable future. The dollar system is providing a good measure of stability in its working.

The current dollar system is working in the sense that payments across the globe related to trade and finance are generally quite easily effected, with global networks of regulatory and supervisory authorities spanning the systemic parts of the global financial system put in place, and global cooperation in cases of emergencies – featuring those critical dollar-swap lines backstopping the system – having proved effective in containing systemic crises and upholding the functioning of the system. The dollar's past, present, and potential future challengers will be discussed in the next section.

Before that, the weaknesses of the dollar system need to be acknowledged. They are profound and worsening. The four most important ones are: first, the lack of policy space in the periphery; second, the clashing of domestic and international responsibilities at the center; third, the amplification of inequalities both at the center and the periphery; and, fourth, the prevailing glut of fickle short-term financing conjoined by a dearth of long-term financing available to meet the climate threat and development challenges more generally. The situation is worsening as America's relative economic weight in the global economy is declining while inequalities are generally on the rise, undermining economies, democracies, and societies.

The lack of policy space in the periphery is a most direct consequence of financial liberalization and hyper-globalization. At the time of the Bretton Woods conference, war-time capital controls were in place. Keynes and White agreed that capital flows, especially short-term ('hot money') flows, had to be contained at both ends to safeguard the system's stability and countries' macro policy space in peace-time too (Bibow 2009b; 2017; Steil 2013). With the rise of Neoliberalism, these original ideas were replaced by promises that poor countries would be enabled to grow and catch up faster by freely drawing on the plentiful savings of rich countries. The best that governments could do was to leave markets alone and have an independent central bank control inflation. And mainstream macroeconomic theory à la Mundell's 'trilemma' suggested that flexible exchange rates would offer policy autonomy even under free capital mobility (Helleiner 1994; Fischer 1997; Dornbusch 1998; Chwieroth 2010).

In the aftermath of the GFC, the mainstream reconsidered these beliefs to some extent as Helene Rey's 'dilemma' critique caused quite a splash in official policy circles (Rey 2014). Suffice to mention here that Keynes and generations of Post-Keynesian economists have argued that policy autonomy under free capital mobility was a mirage, emphasizing the need for effectively protecting policy space from the whims of unfettered global capital (Eatwell and Taylor 2000; Kregel 2004; Terzi 2006; Harvey 2009; De Paula et al. 2017). Among international organizations, UNCTAD (various years) has consistently been the counter-pole to the IMF's push for financial-account liberalization.

The IMF has modified its position on financial openness and the use of financial flow management to some extent. Initially, in response to the GFC, the IMF gave its blessing to capital controls that were used exceptionally, temporarily, and when all other measures had been exhausted while a country was facing an acute inflow surge (IMF 2012). More recently, the IMF (2022) also accepted a country's *pre-emptive* use of capital controls under some circumstances and signaled its tolerance of certain capital controls introduced for national or international security reasons.

These are welcome developments. But they do not go nearly far enough (Rodrik 2011; Gallagher 2015, for instance). It is an open question whether official mainstream views and actual practices will move further in the direction of de-risking global finance by properly managing financial flows, thereby restoring peripheral countries' policy space. One dares to suspect that vested interests would put up quite a fight (Obstfeld 2021).

Turning to the center of the system, while America is indeed enjoying a good measure of policy autonomy, its unique position of privilege in the dollar system neither means absence of repercussions from the rest of the world (that are partly the result of its own making) nor absence of policy conflicts these might create on the home front. In fact, policy conflicts inevitably arise between the Fed's domestic ('dual') mandate – for full employment and price stability in the US – and global policy requirements. Universally guaranteeing sufficient policy space to best align local policies with local conditions is the answer to that problem. The reality of the dollar system is that the world must put up with whatever the Fed decides to be best for America. The reality for America includes the fact that America is subject to global repercussions arising from sub-optimal policy alignments and any policy responses to that challenge taken in the periphery. Overall, America's privilege may be quite burdensome and create vast fragilities in America itself – as developments since the 1980s have all too clearly shown.

America's burden and fragility arise from its responsibility to always stimulate US domestic demand sufficiently to both meet its domestic mandate and counter-balance any global disinflationary forces arising from within the hyper-globalized dollar system. The latter part becomes more challenging as America's weight in the global economy is declining. And it becomes all the more challenging the more the rest of the world relies on defensive macro policies to cope with their vulnerability and lack of policy space. But forces at America's domestic front also help by creating self-reinforcing processes towards ever greater fragility.

The dollar's systemic overvaluation resulting from its hegemonic position is itself one driving force behind rising inequality in America, with Wall Street, tech, and wealth benefitting at the expense of industry and the middle class at large. Rising inequality, in turn, makes stimulating sufficient domestic demand ever more challenging. In the absence of public-funded infrastructure investment, relying on easy money and liberalized finance propels tendencies of rising financialization and household leveraging. In short, rising inequality and financialization combine to create more systemic fragilities.

In principle, America has the capacity to counter these harmful trends through bigger government and sufficient redistribution. But if highly concentrated private wealth takes over politics, complicit government will only further aggravate the situation.

Similarly, in the developing world, deeper integration at earlier stages of development magnifies tendencies of rising inequality while undermining state capacity to compensate any losers (Furceri et al. 2019; Gallagher et al. 2019).

Among other things, financial organization focused on liquidity cultivates the prevailing culture of short-termism and inattention to the climate threat, perhaps best reflected in ceaseless crypto-gambling euphoria and lack of long-term financing for the real challenges facing humanity. While the challenges are rapidly becoming more acutely pressing, the situation is worsening as America's relative economic weight in the global economy is declining while global inequalities are on the rise, undermining economies, democracies, and societies.

5   MEET THE (POTENTIAL) DOLLAR CHALLENGERS

The continued 'stability' (of a sort) of the dollar system also owes critically to the absence of any alternative that could easily dethrone the dollar in the foreseeable future. This section will briefly discuss currencies that have at some time competed with the dollar for hegemony or have been perceived as potential challengers.

Looking back over the past 100 years, the first thing that stands out is that the transition from sterling to the dollar was not abrupt, but happened over a quarter of a century (Eichengreen and Flandreau 2009; Eichengreen et al. 2017). The gradual rise of the US, based on its industrial prowess and gains in power, and the decline of Britain – due to world wars – were both important, as was the fact that it took America some time to accept a global leadership role and even develop a keenness for hegemony (Wertheim 2020), just as it took Britain some time to concede its diminishing capacity for global leadership. The gradual transition ended in a more tumultuous period for Britain in the early years after WWII when the status of sizeable 'sterling balances' turned from being manifestations of privilege into burdensome ballast. Today, sterling continues to play a role as a reserve currency among other (predominantly Western) currencies featuring in diversified private and public reserve portfolios and international transactions (in particular: the Australian dollar, Canadian dollar, Chinese renminbi, Danish krone, euro, Japanese yen, Korean won, Norwegian krone, Singapore dollar, Swedish krona, and Swiss franc; Arslanalp et al. 2022).

In the 1970s and 1980s, first the German Deutsche mark (and to some extent the Swiss franc) and then the Japanese yen came to be seen as serious alternatives to the US dollar. This was related to relatively higher inflation in the US and rampant speculation for dollar depreciation at the end of the Bretton Woods era.

In (West) Germany's case, global pressures for the Deutsche mark to attain a more prominent reserve currency status were resisted from the beginning and throughout. Germany and its legendary Bundesbank like to pride themselves on the country's low inflation record. But reserve currency status stands in conflict with Germany's other pride: industrial prowess – as celebrated through notorious mercantilist economic policy traditions that favor competitiveness and currency undervaluation. Nothing much has changed in this regard ever since – even under the euro (see below).

In Japan's case, the yen's brief surge in prominence and the perception of it as a challenger to the US dollar was associated with the liberalization of Japan's tightly controlled post-war financial system. Apart from expanding at home, Japan's banks also turned aggressively adventurous in their foreign pursuits. Domestic asset-price bubbles for a while suggested unheard-of strength (Vogel 1979). WWII loser Japan and its currency then deflated as a potent dollar challenger in 1990–1991, just when long-time Cold War rival the Soviet Union collapsed as an alternative economic model as well.

These developments opened the door for America's (over-)reach for hyper-globalization – while Europe was preoccupied with binding the other key WWII loser, the newly reunified Germany, more deeply into the European Union (EU) and the euro.

The euro promptly became seen as the most viable challenger to dollar primacy (Chinn and Frankel 2008). In terms of GDP and population the EU plays in the same global league as the US. The same holds for the regulatory reach of the EU 'single market.' But its military capabilities and financial markets are far from on a par with America's; and Brexit meant relegation in the global pecking order for both the UK and the EU.

Europe's experience with the euro provides many important lessons for countries around the world, both positive and negative. On the positive side, compared to pre-euro times, regional monetary integration does seem to provide a potential strategy for greater monetary stability and autonomy at a regional level. On the negative side, the euro's deficient regime design, compared to America's monetary union, underscores that monetary policy and financial market integration are not enough. Rather, deep market integration, especially financial market integration, requires correspondingly deep policy integration to maintain control over markets, just as monetary policy integration needs to go hand-in-hand with fiscal policy integration to establish adequate centralized macro policy firepower for securing economic stability (Bibow 2020).

 Journal compilation © 2022 Edward Elgar Publishing Ltd

Due to its deficient regime design, the euro area has underperformed since the 1990s. The 'convergence process' of the 1990s had provided a harbinger of things to come. The dodged pursuit of fiscal austerity cojoined with growth-unfriendly monetary policies have produced the predictable results ever since. The absence of convergence of wage trends and their misalignment with the European Central Bank's (ECB) price stability norm resulted in the emergence of grave internal divergences and persistent imbalances (Bibow 2013). The euro area had already struggled to recover from the mild recession of the early 2000s following the 'dot-com bust.' Its incapacity to deal with the implosion of internal imbalances in the context of the GFC then threatened the euro's very survival. While the ECB turned more pragmatic, creative, and symmetric in its pursuit of price stability in due course, underperformance remained the order of the day until the COVID-19 pandemic and the Ukraine war once again threw Europe's currency union badly off course.

Despite its ongoing challenges, the euro is the number 2 currency in the world – albeit at a long distance from the US dollar. Especially within the region and its time zone the euro plays a decisive role. In recent years, the euro's 'federal voices,' the ECB and the European Commission, have touted the euro's global reach and ambition somewhat more daringly as part of Europe's 'strategic independence.'

But *de facto* the euro has transformed Germany's monetary–industrial mercantilism from a national credo into a regional force. Germany continues to run persistent current-account surpluses in the ballpark of 8 percent of GDP. In addition, almost all member states saw their current-account position swing into surplus in the aftermath of the GFC and the euro crisis, so that the euro area came to establish an external surplus position in the ballpark of 3–4 percent of GDP – until the Ukraine war and energy-price exposion hit.

This European observer has not yet given up all hope that the necessary reforms of euro institutions and policies to secure the euro's viability might still come about. But I see no chance that the euro authorities might develop the kind of 'benign neglect' mindset towards the euro's external position that has characterized the American authorities. And because of that, while the euro may be a dominant regional player, its potential as a global player and challenger to the dollar's primacy is limited.

Given China's remarkable rise over the past 40 years, with its GDP in purchasing power terms exceeding that of America since 2017, the Chinese renminbi is commonly seen today as the foremost dollar challenger going forward (Prasad 2016; Cohen 2019). Economically, China is likely to continue growing ahead of the US as its income per capita is still not even 30 percent of America's. Accordingly, its military capabilities will continue to catch up as well. The Chinese authorities are engaging in refocusing China's growth model towards domestic consumption. Large external surpluses (as a share of GDP), as seen over the past 20 years, are simply not an option for an economy of China's size by now.

But in view of China's non-democratic political system and special kind of market economy, it seems unlikely that it will aim at establishing full-blown international financial openness together with a benign-neglect approach to its external position. Like the euro, the renminbi might become more of a factor at the regional level (and in bilateral relations), but seems unlikely to be able to fill the dollar's global shoes any time soon (if ever).

The rise of China and the east, and the corresponding shift away from the US (and Europe) in terms of economic weight, has been the key shaping force in the global economy since the GFC. America continues to be the number 1 monetary and financial power in the world, but China has become the world's premier global economic growth engine. This tension will continue to grow. For a long time it was held in check by the fact that the renminbi has been tied to the US dollar, acting as both a currency anchor within Asia and as a means of establishing an East–West monetary axis. But as the global economic balance continues to shift from the West to the East, the fragilities inherent in the dollar system will only get worse. How can Asia be the economic center of the world but remain on the monetary periphery?

Complicating matters, the budding Asian economic center of the world will consist of several powerhouses: China, Japan, and India, plus South Korea and Indonesia. Perhaps, as in Europe, greater regional monetary cooperation, and even integration, will ultimately be possible. The Élysée Treaty between France and Germany proves that even arch foes can become close partners. But it took several major wars and several peaceful decades thereafter to establish Europe's (troubled) 'ever-closer union' of today. There is no clear roadmap for either Asian integration or global rebalancing within and beyond the dollar system.

Finally, there is another enormous global unknown: Africa. Demographic projections imply that Africa will be the decisive factor in shaping global population trends in this century – to ultimately almost match Asia's. With some success in economic development, Africa's economic weight in the global economy would multiply from its current low base. Plans for an African monetary union already exist today, even as parts of Africa remain tied to the euro, reflecting the continent's dreadful colonial past (Dagah et al. 2019; Bibow 2022). Section 7, further below, will attempt to sketch a possible evolutionary path for the next few decades. Before that, in Section 6, we turn to developments in payment systems since the GFC.

6   THE CHANGING WORLD OF PAYMENTS

The traditional bank-based international payment system features cross-border linkages through correspondent banks, messaging systems (SWIFT), credit-card networks, and other money transfer businesses. Foreign-exchange markets and arrangements between central banks complement today's primarily dollar-based global payment system.

There have been significant ongoing changes in payment systems around the world that bear some relevance to the international monetary system as well (Bibow 2021a; Prasad 2021). Change has been driven by technology, competition, and regulatory arbitrage – as well as ideology and the persistent low-interest-rate environment in the low-inflation post-GFC era.

Existing monetary systems – including the international dollar system – are based on bank money (or credit money). They are the product of centuries of evolution. Banks create money by making loans and/or buying assets. A central bank, operating on the same banking principle but with a public mandate rather than seeking profit, stands at the core of the monetary system as 'lender of last resort' and 'dealer in money and debts,' typically setting a very short-term rate of interest in money markets as an expression of its monetary policy stance. In earlier times, gold used to play a role as money 'backing.' Today, while bank money is convertible into central-bank money on par, the latter is not convertible into anything else. Rather, the 'backing' of modern money arises from the quality of the assets on banks' balance sheets, the regulatory regime, and the overall solidity of institutions and policies that are the foundation of the whole monetary system and economy; money as a matter of trust and expedience rather than fiat.

Probably for as long as money and banks have existed, there have been 'financial innovations' and competition between banks and 'near banks' offering near-money substitutes. The profit from money issuance (seigniorage), potentially boosted by escaping the regulation of incumbent money issuers, is the motive behind such innovations. The inherent instability of banking – providing 'liquidity par excellence' against risky and illiquid assets – is the key risk.

In the period leading up to the GFC, money-market funds, competing with banks by providing liquidity supposedly on par in excellence with banks, were a constituent part of the so-called 'shadow banking system' that offered market-based banking functions – lending long-term and borrowing short-term – in the shadow of banking regulation. As systemically important money-market funds 'broke the buck' in the GFC, they had to be bailed out and were brought under the umbrella of the public safety net. As a result, they have since faced regulation and closer oversight.

Banks and banking systems too had to be bailed out and hence banking regulation was overhauled in the aftermath of the GFC in the hope of preventing the reccurrence of grave banking crises.

The post-GFC environment of severely weakened and more tightly regulated banks created an opening for new non-bank competitors entering the money business. The new entrants have especially focused on capturing terrain within banks' traditional role in payment systems, and they are of three kinds: first, technology firms focused on financial applications (so-called 'Fin Techs'); second, technology giants with huge networks of users (so-called 'Big Techs'), reaching out into the financial sphere; and, third, issuers of so-called 'cryptocurrencies,' which are instruments with some payment functionality based on blockchain technology and cryptology (a.k.a. crypto assets).

Each of the three kinds of newcomers presents competition for the incumbent regulated banks that are the traditional providers of today's bank money. Each presents its own challenges to financial regulatory bodies and central banks. And each creates new potential threats to the stability of the financial system and the powers of the authorities to govern money and finance.

Typically, Fin Techs have a competitive advantage over banks in providing specific technology-based services. In general, these have primarily been payment services, at least at the beginning, although Fin Techs' service portfolios may become more comprehensive over time. In general, Fin Techs have been smaller firms and their individual impact on the market has been less disruptive. Overall, however, Fin Techs can still be a decisive factor in reshaping payment systems and banking.

Potentially, the giant Big Techs can be far more disruptive and immediately systemically important. Their key competitive advantage lies in their huge user networks, additionally to their specific competencies as technology firms. Whereas Fin Techs' payment products generally complement existing bank-money-based payment systems, Big Techs may potentially also establish substitutes: separate network-specific (closed) payment systems spanning the globe. The Big Techs are posing complex regulatory challenges even without entering finance. The entry of Big Techs into finance would add an altogether new dimension to the challenges facing financial regulators. No wonder Facebook's 'libra' initiative set alarm bells ringing among global financial regulators and central banks.

The crypto boom of the past ten years has produced a whole jungle of new, private 'currencies.' The pioneer, bitcoin, is held by its believers to be destined to eventually displace the dollar as the global currency of choice. Yet as a means of payment bitcoin is highly inefficient (except for money launderers and other criminals), aside from being an environmental disaster. Its volatility makes bitcoin a highly speculative asset that offers no cash flow. To describe it as 'digital gold' only underscores that

   Journal compilation © 2022 Edward Elgar Publishing Ltd

it is already a historical (and barbaric) relic when seen from the perspective of monetary theory.

There is a multitude of other crypto assets of the bitcoin type that offer some limited payment functionality that comes together with extreme volatility. These private 'currencies' differ fundamentally from so-called 'stable coins,' which are a wholly different kind of crypto product that is really the latest (digital) version of money-market funds (or near-banks). Stable coins promise convertibility at a fixed nominal value, typically held stable in terms of the US dollar, with 100 percent liquid 'reserves' (income-yielding assets) as their backing. Facebook's planned 'libra' currency was originally meant to be designed as a stable coin backed by a basket of key currencies.

Among other things, the prospect of libra – together with the declining use of banknotes observed in many countries – probably did most to draw central banks around the world into the arena of currency innovation. Today, an increasing number of central banks are exploring the possibility of issuing so-called 'central-bank digital currencies' (CBDCs), that is, official digital 'banknotes' denominated in sovereign currency. Apart from being an intended substitute for traditional paper banknotes, these official digital monetary instruments also represent potential competitors for bank deposits issued by private banks.

Some of the developments and products briefly appraised in this section have true promise for making payment systems more efficient and inclusive. In rich countries innovations are mostly a matter of convenience, of being able to instantaneously manage one's payments and finances with a smartphone or smartwatch. In poor countries products like M-PESA represent a sea-change in terms of inclusion. The horrendous fees traditionally associated with small international payments by migrants to their home countries (remittances) will hopefully come under pressure thanks to these developments, leading to a better public infrastructure for small cross-country payments.

But these changes in international payments also come with enormous risks that may undermine the functioning of the international monetary order and further shrink national policy space.

Financial instabilities due to insufficient regulation is one risk. To the extent that these developments increase global integration, with vaster interconnectedness and inclusion of international payments, global contagion of initially localized instabilities becomes more of a threat, too. That is, unless global regulatory cooperation and safeguards are adequately enhanced. Especially for poor countries, the prospect of enhanced competition for their national currency from both private (say, libra) and official digital currencies (say, US dollar CBDC) means rising risks of dollarization and correspondingly reduced policy space (Pitel and Szalay 2022). Considering the influence of social media on volatile public opinion, serious abuse of private power and heightened fragilities are easily conceivable.

But the opposite of rising global interconnectedness represents another risk and observed tendency today: fragmentation. Fragmentation may not only arise through the payments innovations discussed in this section, either Big Tech-sponsored closed systems à la libra or cryptocurrency-based networks of users à la bitcoin. Other efforts in this direction include initiatives by certain countries to bypass the dollar system and SWIFT-based banking payments, especially China (Chorzempa 2021).

The ongoing Ukraine war and the sanctions imposed on Russia in response will likely inspire more (authoritarian) countries to explore new opportunities. China and Saudi Arabia are thought to be studying the possibility of settling part of their trade in renminbi, for instance (Phillips 2022). To the extent that bilateral trade relationships are balanced, even barter-like arrangements are conceivable.

Payments in international trade constitute only a small part of the demand for US dollars as a global currency. The global demand for dollar liquidity is mainly driven by global finance and trade imbalances. But developments in global payments, as reviewed here, ultimately also concern the dollar's broader role as the pinnacle of the global dollar system. Today, global payment systems are featuring tendencies for both ever-deeper global integration and vaster interconnectedness, as well as fragmentation. Geopolitics may lead to the development of parallel, disjointed payment systems or 'payment blocs' – potentially as part of the emergence of fragmentation into 'economic blocs.'

7   MULTIPOLARITY AS PROGRESS OR AS PART OF SPREADING FRAGMENTATION?

Up to this point the analysis has focused on the evolution of the dollar system over the past 80 years up to the present day. Envisioning the future evolution of the dollar system over the next 80 years or so is inherently speculative. What seems clear today is that the center of gravity in the global economy will continue shifting from the pan-Atlantic axis of power of Western civilization, which has dominated world affairs for the past few centuries, towards Asia, with great uncertainty about the eventual weight of Africa in the global order emerging during this period.

With both dollar hegemony and hyper-globalizaiton past their zenith, the essential problem clouding the outlook for coming years and decades is that America is getting increasingly overburdened by providing the global currency of the dollar system while no other nation (or union of nations) may be ready and willing to take over America's hegemonic position in the foreseeable future either. So 'king dollar' may remain the king of currencies for quite some time, but its reign will be getting more and more disagreeable for the crown holder (Bibow 2019). Managing its decline and gradual abdication, with no successor in sight, promises to be challenging and volatile, implying a leaderless world unless new modes of global cooperation and shared leadership can be found.

For decades to come, though, even as its economic weight declines further, America will continue playing a disproportionate role in global monetary and financial affairs – given its wealth and developed financial markets. Europe, too, despite its even more pronounced relative economic decline, has the opportunity for continuing to play a disproportionate global role thanks to its wealth and regional monetary integration – especially if it were to reform its 'incomplete' EMU regime. Apart from China and India, as the two most likely single-nation powerhouses of the future, there have been numerous efforts in Latin America, Africa, and Australasia, as well as Asia, for deeper regional integration, including in monetary and financial affairs. In 1944, the world had one clear economic hegemon. Today, with or without progressing regional integration, or forms of cross-regional cooperation such as BRICS (see Liu and Papa 2022), a multipolar world of multiple great economic powers is clearly emerging.

The emerging multipolarity may be seen as progress in the sense that both the privileges enjoyed and the burden carried by the contemporary hegemon in the dollar system would be spread over several broad shoulders. But spreading of power alone does not constitute progress as far as addressing global challenges is concerned. Rather, cooperation will be necessary to effectively share leadership responsibilities in a multipolar system. Without effective cooperation, currency multipolarity may simply be one aspect of spreading fragmentation into economic blocs more broadly. Global challenges might succumb to the collective action problem. How any blocs or groupings might come to organize themselves will also be critical. Just as hegemony at the global level is likely becoming less of an issue, it may become more of an issue regionally (as previously in Europe, in the currency sphere, around the Deutsche mark and Bundesbank).

Today, retreat from hyper-globalization and gradual decline of dollar hegemony are affecting both the spheres of money and finance and of production, employment, and trade. If the GFC gave rise to serious disillusionment about global financial liberalization, the COVID-19 pandemic and the Ukraine war have provided wake-up calls regarding full-speed 'offshoring' and just-in-time production and inventory management organized in global supply chains solely focused on cost efficiency and short-term profit, but at the neglect of national security. Today, national security concerns are moving from the back-seat to a front-row position. 'Reshoring,' or at least 'friend-shoring,' for greater resilience in production, is gaining currency as a key guiding principle for a different kind of organization of global production, employment, and trade. Old dependencies may get reinforced, while new ones emerge. Fairer and more equal outcomes are not inevitable even when losses in production efficiency turn out to be smaller than feared.

In the monetary and financial sphere, the argument against global capital mobility is an argument for financial fragmentation: to safeguard national policy space. National liquidity needs can be better provided for nationally. Unfettered global liquidity does not deliver the needed access to technology and stable long-term external financing for development. In fact, it is more likely than not to stand in its way. In the new era of managed globalization, a better alignment between local conditions and local polices at least becomes possible (Rodrik 2011). But with new multiple poles of regional hegemony, many developing countries might still end up being short of sufficient policy space and stable long-term external financing for development.

In short, whether a multipolar world of regional hegemons will yield fairer development outcomes for humanity is an open question.

8   CONDITIONS FOR A NEW BRETTON WOODS

No doubt the global environment that led to the original Bretton Woods agreement in 1944 was a very special one. It marked the end of a calamitous period that featured two world wars and the Great Depression in between. The period produced one clear winner, one clear economic hegemon. Humanity was fortunate enough in that the winner and new hegemon was a democracy, while much of the rest of the world was living either under national tyranny or imperialism.

The hegemon established a 'liberal' global economic order to its liking (multilateralism with a special spot reserved for America), which the Soviet Union and the People's Republic of China chose not to join. A drawn-out Cold War between the ideological rivals followed soon enough. With little doubt, the hegemon has enjoyed important benefits and privileges stemming from its position within the liberal order it created. But it has shouldered important responsibilities and burdens in maintaining its hegemonic position as well. The first few decades featured managed globalization and gradualism, and widely shared prosperity. With the ending of the Cold War, the high-speed era of hyper-globalization then propelled the fortunes of the few at the expense of the rest.

        Journal compilation © 2022 Edward Elgar Publishing Ltd

Will the emerging multipolar constellation of great economic powers find itself in a global environment conducive to establishing a New Bretton Woods order, meaning a new global arrangement of international affairs that grants nations sufficient policy space in managing their respective national affairs to their own liking while providing a forum for international cooperation on those matters that truly concern humanity as a whole? We are speculating here about the unknowable.

If it takes another shattering global calamity to recreate the spirit necessary for working together – the spirit of 1944 – climate change comes to mind above all else. Confronting the global threat of climate change vitally depends on global cooperation, on the sharing of technology and resources. Unfettered global finance organized for global liquidity and driven by short-term greed is more likely to be a foe than a helpful partner in this endeavor. Gallagher and Kozul-Wright (2022) lay out a vision for an alternative multilateral order featuring key roles for public investment and development finance for the proposed global 'Green New Deal.' Nothing short of a complete transformation of the global energy infrastructure away from fossil fuels towards renewable energies is necessary. The challenge and magnitude of resource needs is formidable but manageable if the political will can be mustered.

In many respects, China's development model has shown what is possible within 40 years when domestic finance is made to be the servant rather than the master of domestic development, and global finance is kept effectively in check (Galbraith 2022). Externally, too, China is focusing on long-term development finance of infrastructure investment rather than liquid global capital. There is, of course, a darker political side to China's development model that few would want to follow.

I suspect that the global environment might first have to deteriorate to a point where the consequences of climate change will be much more manifest than they already are today. And when that time comes, which may be sooner than we think, humanity will need to get lucky in having responsible leaders in government at the centers of its emerging multipolar world – ready to share technology and resources without respect for the presumed needs, and under the diktat, of global finance.

Keynes's 'bancor' plan for the old Bretton Woods still offers a blueprint for a monetary order without a hegemon (Bibow 2017), which could provide the global monetary framework for balanced trade and stable long-term development finance.

9   CONCLUDING REMARKS

After overtaking the pound sterling in a quarter-century-long transitionary period, 'king dollar' has ruled the world of global money and finance for some 80 years now. The dollar system has been evolving in significant ways throughout. And it will continue to do so going forward. Financial liberalization, nationally and internationally, has provided the most transformative force, climaxing in the 1990s as the US emerged victorious from the Cold War as the world's sole superpower. At its peak of global power, America's domestic political economy was ready to crank up financial hyper-globalization. Freed global capital was supposed to accelerate catch-up and spread prosperity all round. It has not delivered (Prasad et al. 2007).

The era of hyper-globalization saw the rise of financial fragilities and inequalities instead. Unfettered global capital has boosted the powers and fortunes of wealth while undermining state capacities of control. Owing to the status of the US dollar, backed by the US Federal Reserve and the US Treasury, Wall Street and highly concentrated US wealth are positioned in the driver's seat.

The global financial Armageddon of 2008–2009 marked an important seizure: America's relative economic decline accelerated as China emerged as premier global economic growth engine. The rest of the world has struggled to maneuver the push and pull of its two primary poles ever since, America in money and finance, China in trade and production. Apart from global tensions arising within the dollar system from this peculiar constellation of global powers in finance and trade, tensions between the two nations have also seen a sharp rise since the Trump presidency.

Going forward, stress within the dollar system is set to increase as America's relative economic decline continues, making it ever harder for America to meet its responsibilities in managing both domestic and global demand. In other words, for America the extraordinary burden of its extraordinary dollar privilege is getting heavier to lift. Meanwhile, innovations in payment systems and the digitalization of finance, unless met by adequate globally coordinated regulation and oversight, risk fresh financial instabilities and disruptions. In the periphery, improvements in financial inclusion might come at the cost of further diminution of policy space. Encouragingly, the IMF is no longer relentlessly peddling its former financial liberalization mantra. But any attempts at more decisive controls of global capital are bound to face strong pushback from special interests.

As the global monetary–financial hegemon's shrinkage in economic weight gradually undermines its position of power and control, no other player is getting ready to take over America's top spot. China's renminbi may seem destined to do so as the country is expected to become the world's largest economy (in US dollar terms) within the next ten years. But state control of finance has been part of China's development model. Unless technology can straddle greater global powers with sustained domestic control, the ideology of free global capital does not sit well with China's political regime. India's turn may perhaps come a generation later.

A more likely scenario is that no single player will emerge to match America's clearly dominant global position in 1944. No single currency might come to replace king dollar. Instead, the question is how the dollar system will adapt and evolve as the world economy becomes one of multiple poles, a multipolar world. The global monetary system may become one of multiple more evenly balanced key currencies.

Developments in regional integration will likely shape the eventual number of poles. The euro exemplifies that a group of smaller countries can potentially manage to play above their weight class by joining forces. The euro also illustrates that regime design is critical; integration can backfire and turn into disintegration when done poorly.

A multipolar world may either feature effective modes of cooperation to address global challenges, or it may mean a fragmented world of (potentially hostile) economic blocs with limited interactions. How developing countries will fare under either of these scenarios is an open question.

The COVID-19 pandemic and the Ukraine war have proved highly unsettling. Disruptions in global production and trade have ignited inflation and spread discontent. A Sino-Russian alliance and global fragmentation are conceivable outcomes (Rachman 2022) – at a time when the climate challenge calls for close cooperation, effective leadership, and sharing of technology and resources.

Will it take a clearer reality of a progressing climate calamity to force humanity into effective collective action? Keynes's 'bancor plan' still provides a valuable blueprint for a symmetric monetary order (without hegemon) that might suit the emerging multipolar world. The international bancor currency was meant to be part of a broader scheme of managed globalization, with national policymakers rather than free global capital in charge of pursuing shared prosperity and properly national affairs.

REFERENCES

Abdelal, R. (2007), *Capital Rules: The Construction of Global Finance*, London, UK and Cambridge, MA: Harvard University Press.

Akyüz, Y. (2018), 'External balance sheets of emerging economies: low-yielding assets, high-yielding liabilities,' PERI Working Paper Series No 476, December.

Arslanalp, S., B.J. Eichengreen, and C. Simpson-Bell (2022), 'The stealth erosion of dollar dominance: active diversifiers and the rise of nontraditional reserve currencies,' IMF Working Paper No 2022/058m, available at: https://www.imf.org/en/Publications/WP/Issues/2022/03/24/The-Stealth-Erosion-of-Dollar-Dominance-Active-Diversifiers-and-the-Rise-of-Nontraditional-515150.

Bibow, J. (2003), 'On the "burden" of German unification,' *Banca Nazionale del Lavoro Quarterly Review*, 61(225), 137–169.

Bibow, J. (2007), 'Global imbalances, Bretton Woods II, and Euroland's role in all this,' in J. Bibow and A. Terzi (eds), *Euroland and the World Economy: Global Player or Global Drag?*, Basingstoke, UK and New York: Palgrave Macmillan, pp. 15–42.

Bibow, J. (2008), 'The international monetary (non-)order and the "global capital flows paradox",' in E. Hein, P. Spahn, T. Niechoj, and A. Truger (eds), *Finance-Led Capitalism?*, Marburg: Metropolis, pp. 219–248.

Bibow, J. (2009a), 'Insuring against private capital flows: is it worth the premium? What are the alternatives?,' *International Journal of Political Economy*, 37(4), 5–30.

Bibow, J. (2009b), *Keynes on Monetary Policy, Finance and Uncertainty: Liquidity Preference Theory and the Global Financial Crisis*, London and New York: Routledge.

Bibow, J. (2010a), 'Financialization of the U.S. household sector: the "subprime mortgage crisis" in U.S. and global perspective,' IMK Study 3/2010, Düsseldorf: Macroeconomic Policy Institute.

Bibow, J. (2010b), 'Bretton Woods 2 is dead, long live Bretton Woods 3?,' Levy Economics Institute, Working Paper No 597, Annandale-on-Hudson, NY.

Bibow, J. (2011a), 'Global imbalances, the U.S. dollar, and how the crisis at the core of global finance spread to "self-insuring" emerging market economies,' *Intervention: European Journal of Economics and Economic Policies*, 7(2), 325–359.

Bibow, J. (2011b), 'The global crisis and the future of the dollar: towards Bretton Woods 3?,' in J.J. Leclaire, T.-H. Jo, and J. Knodell (eds), *Heterodox Analysis of Financial Crisis and Reform: History, Politics and Economics*, Cheltenham, UK and Northampton, MA: Edward Elgar Publishing, pp. 137–149.

Bibow, J. (2011c), 'Of unsustainable processes and the U.S. dollar,' in D.B. Papadimitriou and G. Zezza (eds), *Contributions to Stock–Flow Modeling: Essays in Honor of Wynne Godley*, London: Palgrave Macmillan, pp. 321–348.

Bibow, J. (2012), 'The case for capital account management in emerging market economies: the experience of the BRICs,' *Intervention: European Journal of Economics and Economic Policies*, 9(1), 57–90.

Bibow, J. (2013), 'The Euroland crisis and Germany's euro trilemma,' *International Review of Applied Economics*, 27(3), 360–385.

Bibow, J. (2017), 'Symmetric global order with national self-determination and no hegemon: vision and reality,' *Annals of the Fondazione Luigi Einaudi*, Special Issue 'Keynes's Relevance to the Contemporary World,' LI(1-2017), 177–206.

Bibow, J. (2019), 'Trade and finance: the two sides of today's coin of conflict,' Bretton Woods Committee, BrettonWoods@75Blog, 22 May.

Bibow, J. (2020), 'Stuck on the wrong track: 20 years of euro disillusion, denial, and delusion,' *European Journal of Economics and Economic Policies: Intervention*, July, doi: https://doi.org/10.4337/ejeep.2020.0065.

Bibow, J. (2021a), 'Digitalisierung im Zahlungsverkehr und Geldwesen: Banken und Geld im Umbruch – steigt die Wohlfahrt oder die Stabilitätsrisiken?,' HBS Study 455, February, Düsseldorf: Hans Böckler Stiftung.

Bibow, J. (2021b), 'Evolving international monetary and financial architecture and the development challenge: a liquidity preference theoretical perspective,' in B. Bonizi, A. Kaltenbrunner, and R.A. Ramos (eds), *Emerging Economics and the Global Financial System: A Post-Keynesian Analysis*, Abingdon, UK and New York: Routledge, pp. 101–115.

Bibow, J. (2022), 'The euro experience: lessons for Africa,' in D. Barrowclough, R. Kozul-Wright, W.N. Kring, and K.P. Gallagher (eds), *South–South Regional Financial Arrangements: Collaboration Towards Resilience*, International Political Economy Series, Cham, Switzerland: Palgrave Macmillan, pp. 99–135, available at: https://doi.org/10.1007/978-3-030-64576-2_10.

BIS (Bank for International Settlements) (1993), *Annual Report*, Basel: BIS.

Chinn, M. and J. Frankel (2008), 'Why the euro will rival the dollar,' *International Finance*, 11(1), 49–73.

Chorzempa, M. (2021), Statement, Testimony before the US–China Economic and Security Review Commission, Panel 4: China's Pursuit of Leadership in Digital Currency.

Chwieroth, J.M. (2010), *Capital Ideas: The IMF and the Rise of Financial Liberalization*, Princeton, NJ: Princeton University Press.

Cohen, B.J. (2019), *Currency Statecraft: Monetary Rivalry and Geopolitical Ambition*, Chicago: University of Chicago Press.

Costabile, L. (2022), 'Continuity and change in the international monetary system: the dollar standard and capital mobility,' *Review of Political Economy*, 34(3), 585–597.

Dagah, H., W. Kring, and D. Bradow (2019), 'Jump-starting the African Monetary Fund,' GEGI Policy Brief 008, Global Development Policy Center, Boston University.

De Paula, L.F., B. Fritz, and D.M. Prates (2017), 'Keynes at the periphery: currency hierarchy and challenges for economic policy in emerging economies,' *Journal of Post Keynesian Economics*, 40(2), 183–202.

Dornbusch, R. (1998), 'Capital controls: an idea whose time is past,' Essays in International Finance No 207, Princeton, NJ: Princeton University.

Eatwell, J. and L. Taylor (2000), *Global Finance at Risk: The Case for International Regulation*, Cambridge, UK: Polity Press.

Eichengreen, B.J. (2008), *Globalizing Capital: A History of the International Monetary System*, Princeton, NJ: Princeton University Press.

Eichengreen, B.J. (2012), *Exorbitant Privilege: The Rise and Fall of the Dollar and the Future of the International Monetary System*, Oxford: Oxford University Press.

Eichengreen, B. and M. Flandreau (2009), 'The rise and fall of the dollar (or: when did the dollar replace sterling as the leading reserve currency?),' *European Review of Economic History*, 13(3), 377–411.

Eichengreen, B.J., A. Mehl, and L. Chiţu (2017), *How Global Currencies Work: Past, Present, and Future*, Princeton, NJ: Princeton University Press.

Fischer, S. (1997), 'Capital-account liberalization and the role of the IMF,' IMF Seminar 'Asia and the IMF,' 19 September, International Monetary Fund, available at: https://www.imf.org/en/News/Articles/2015/09/28/04/53/sp091997.

Furceri, D., P. Loungani, and J.D. Ostry (2019), 'The aggregate and distributional effects of financial globalization: evidence from macro and sectoral data,' *Journal of Money, Credit and Banking*, 53, 163–198.

Galbraith, J. (2022), 'The dollar system in a multi-polar world,' available at: https://www.ineteconomics.org/perspectives/blog/the-dollar-system-in-a-multi-polar-world.

Gallagher, K.P. (2015), *Ruling Capital: Emerging Markets and the Reregulation of Cross-Border Financial Flows*, Ithaca, NY: Cornell University Press.

Gallagher, K.P. and R. Kozul-Wright (2022), *The Case for a New Bretton Woods*, Cambridge, UK: Polity Press.

Gallagher, K.P., G. Lagarda, and J. Linares (2019), 'Capital openness and income inequality: smooth sailing or troubled waters?,' in J.A. Ocampo (ed.), *International Policy Rules and Inequality: Implications for Global Economic Governance*, New York: Columbia University Press.

Harvey, J.T. (2009), *Currencies, Capital Flows and Crises: A Post Keynesian Analysis of Exchange Rate Determination*, London: Routledge.

Helleiner, E. (1994), *States and the Re-emergence of Global Finance*, Ithaca, NY: Cornell University Press.

IMF (International Monetary Fund) (2012), 'The liberalization and management of capital flows: an institutional view,' IMF Policy Paper, 14 November, Washington, DC: International Monetary Fund, available at: https://www.imf.org/external/np/pp/eng/2012/111412.pdf.

IMF (International Monetary Fund) (2022), 'The IMF's updated view on capital controls welcome fixes but major rethinking is still needed,' 30 March, available at: https://www.imf.org/en/Publications/Policy-Papers/Issues/2022/03/29/Review-of-The-Institutional-View-on-The-Liberalization-and-Management-of-Capital-Flows-515883.

Keynes, J.M. (1923), *Tract on Monetary Reform*, reprinted in D.E. Moggridge (ed.), *The Collected Writings of John Maynard Keynes*, vol. 4, London: Macmillan.

Keynes, J.M. (1936 [1971]), *The General Theory of Employment, Money and Interest*, reprinted in D.E. Moggridge (ed.), *The Collected Writings of John Maynard Keynes*, vol. 7, London: Macmillan.

Kregel, J. (2004), 'External financing for development and international financial instability,' G-24 DP, Discussion Paper No 32, New York: United Nations Conference on Trade and Development.

Liu, Z.Z. and M. Papa (2022), *Can BRICS De-Dollarize the Global Financial System?*, Cambridge, UK: Cambridge University Press.

Mehrling, P. (2015), 'Elasticity and discipline in the global swap network,' *International Journal of Political Economy*, 44(4), 311–324.

Obstfeld, M. (2021), 'The global capital market reconsidered,' *Oxford Review of Economic Policy*, 37(4), 690–706, available at: https://doi.org/10.1093/oxrep/grab023.

Phillips, M. (2022), 'Saudi Arabia mull oil sales in Chinese yuan,' *Axios Markets*, 18 March, available at: https://www.axios.com/2022/03/18/saudis-oil-sales-chinese-yuan-dollar.

Pitel, L. and E. Szalay (2022), 'Turks flock to cryptocurrencies in search of stability: Erdogan plans crackdown as lira turmoil encourages speculation in digital assets,' *Financial Times*, 23 January, available at: https://www.ft.com/content/02194361-a5b9-4bf0-9147-f36ba7759cf1?desktop=true&segmentId=7c8f09b9-9b61-4fbb-9430-9208a9e233c8#myft:notification:daily-email:content.

Prasad, E. (2016), *Gaining Currency: The Rise of the Renminbi*, Oxford: Oxford University Press.

Prasad, E.S. (2021), *The Future of Money: How the Digital Revolution is Transforming Currencies and Finance*, Cambridge, MA and London: Belknap Press of Harvard University Press.

Prasad, E., R. Rajan, and A. Subramanian (2007), 'Foreign capital and economic growth,' *Brookings Papers on Economic Activity*, 1, 153–230.

Rachman, G. (2022), 'Russia and China's plans for a new world order: for Moscow and Beijing, the Ukraine crisis is part of a struggle to reduce American power and make the world safe for autocrats,' *Financial Times*, 23 January, available at: https://www.ft.com/content/d307ab6e-57b3-4007-9188-ec9717c60023?desktop=true&segmentId=7c8f09b9-9b61-4fbb-9430-9208a9e233c8#myft:notification:daily-email:content.

Rey, H. (2014), 'Dilemma not trilemma: the global financial cycle and monetary policy independence, in global dimensions of unconventional monetary policy,' Proceedings of the Federal Reserve Bank of Kansas City Jackson Hole Symposium, August.

Rodrik, D. (2011), *The Globalization Paradox: Democracy and the Future of the World Economy*, London and New York: W.W. Norton.

Steil, B. (2013), *The Battle of Bretton Woods: John Maynard Keynes, Harry Dexter White, and the Making of the New World Order*, Princeton, NJ: Princeton University Press.

Terzi, A. (2006), 'International financial instability in a world of currencies hierarchy,' in L.-P. Rochon and S. Rossi (eds), *Monetary and Exchange Rate Systems: A Global View of Financial Crises*, Cheltenham, UK and Northampton, MA: Edward Elgar Publishing, pp. 3–22.

Tooze, A. (2018), *Crashed: How a Decade of Financial Crises Changed the World*, New York: Viking.

UNCTAD (various years), *Trade and Development Report*, Geneva: United Nations Conference on Trade and Development.

Vogel, E.F. (1979), *Japan as Number One: Lessons for America*, Cambridge, MA: Harvard University Press.

Wertheim, S. (2020), *Tomorrow, the World: The Birth of U.S. Global Supremacy*, Cambridge, MA and London: Belknap Press of Harvard University Press.